BOOM TOWNS

BOOM TOWNS

RESTORING THE
URBAN AMERICAN DREAM

Stephen J.K. Walters

STANFORD ECONOMICS AND FINANCE

An Imprint of Stanford University Press

Stanford, California

Stanford University Press
Stanford, California

Special discounts for bulk quantities of titles in the Stanford Economics and
Finance imprint are available to corporations, professional associations, and
other organizations. For details and discount information, contact the special
sales department of Stanford University Press.
Tel: (650) 736-1782, Fax: (650) 736-1784

Printed in the United States of America on acid-free, archival-quality paper

Library of Congress Cataloging-in-Publication Data

Walters, Stephen John Kasabuski, 1953- author.
Boom towns : restoring the urban American dream / Stephen J.K. Walters.
pages cm
Includes bibliographical references and index.
ISBN 978-0-8047-8163-3 (cloth : alk. paper)
1. Urban policy—United States. 2. Urban renewal—United States. 3. Urban
economics. 4. Right of property—Economic aspects—United States. I. Title.
HT123.W2145 2014
307.760973--dc23

2014015436

ISBN 978-0-8047-9227-1 (electronic)

Typeset by Bruce Lundquist in 10/15 Sabon

To my wonderful wife, Melanie,
and to my sons, Matthew Henry and John Joseph,
who make me happy and proud each and every day

Contents

Preface
Even Detroit

DAN GILBERT is not just a cockeyed optimist. He's a cockeyed optimist with a mission and a wide-open checkbook.

Because he's trying to rescue his hometown of Detroit—America's poorest, most crime-ridden, depopulated big city—press accounts of Gilbert's efforts thus far have been admiring but skeptical. Adjectives such as "altruistic" or "quixotic" keep popping up in these stories. Between the lines, reporters seem to be saying, "This guy might be a hero, or he might be nuts. But at least he's risking his own dough."

Lots of it. Since 2010, Gilbert, the founder of mortgage giant Quicken Loans, has moved ten thousand of his employees from the suburbs to downtown Detroit, invested over $1 billion to buy and rehab three million square feet of city property, bankrolled dozens of tiny startups, and coaxed famous-brand retailers into long-vacant buildings with dirt-cheap rents. His "Opportunity Detroit" program may be the most ambitious privately financed urban renewal effort in U.S. history.

Gilbert was undaunted even when the city declared itself bankrupt in July 2013, with $18 billion in debt—over $25,000 for every man, woman, and child yet to pack up and leave—and little with which to pay it. "We are all in," he declared, arguing that bankruptcy, though painful for many, would enable the city to "reinvent itself" and emerge stronger, much as General Motors and Chrysler did in the aftermath of the Great Recession.

Is this a savvy bet, or the pipedream of a hometown fan destined to lose his shirt?

This question is central to the business of this book. Like Gilbert, I'm optimistic about the fate of American cities. I believe all can become boom towns; none are obsolete or beyond hope. But let's not be naive: to thrive they must get right some very basic public policies and avoid others that, as they did in Detroit, inevitably lead to disaster.

For decades, sophisticated and expensive urban revitalization programs have proven to be disappointing. Governments have spent billions of taxpayer dollars on convention centers, municipal complexes, public housing, and stadiums; they have subsidized private investment in hotels, office towers, and entertainment districts. The hope has been that upgrading a city's built environment—its inventory of structures and other physical capital—would halt the flight of employers and residents to the suburbs. All too often these efforts have utterly failed to pull troubled municipalities out of their downward spirals. Detroit is Exhibit A, but there are many others.

More recently, as the U.S. economy has become more knowledge-based and service-oriented, policymakers have focused on increasing cities' stocks of human capital. They have courted tech companies and channeled funding into facilities and programs that might appeal to "creatives"—the entrepreneurs, intellectuals, professionals, and artists thought to be catalysts of urban economic revival. Again, results are mixed at best.

The theories on which these strategies are based are not wrong—but they are incomplete. Urban renewal investments often bear little fruit because planners frequently ignore the underlying conditions necessary for them to work as intended. The devil is not in the details, but in a crucial but overlooked fundamental: property rights. In a nutshell, too many cities are in trouble because they've failed to protect the value of their residents' private property and to efficiently manage the property that their citizens own in common with each other.

Cities are not just dense concentrations of people but vast reservoirs of productive capital—from the buildings residents inhabit and the infrastructure that facilitates their work and play to the intangible, such as their skills or the networks of friends and associates they rely on to enrich their lives. And the record is clear: cities grow and prosper when they encourage the formation of capital in its many forms by securing the returns that flow from it. That is, cities thrive when their residents' property rights are well specified and enforced, and they die a little each day when these rights are attenuated.

It turns out that the nature and strength of the rights that attach to a particular place have enormous influence on people's behavior and overall social welfare. We don't like it when the value of our home falls because a property tax hike is unaccompanied by added municipal services, for example. We grumble when we can't take our kids to the park because a crack dealer is using it as his office, or when the potholes on our thoroughfares seem never to be filled.

When local policies damage our property rights—when they impair our claims to the financial benefits or services generated by our property—we tend to migrate to places where those rights are better protected. And we take our human, financial, physical, and social capital with us. This is often how a city starts to spiral downward. As you'll see, Detroit is, again, a prime example. Dan Gilbert is likely to find that unless the city pays close attention to the proper specification and efficient enforcement of property rights, even his laudable efforts will end badly.

In this book, I illustrate the power and potential of this property rights approach to urban health and offer "how to" guidance for its implementation. An introductory chapter details the approach and shows how it fills gaps in other, widely credited explanations for cities' rise or fall. Chapter 2 shows how misguided tax policy can erode cities' inventories of physical capital, repelling or impoverishing those who depend on it, while Chapter 3 offers a remedy and provides evidence of its dramatic and favorable effects. Chapter 4 describes how legal and regulatory changes affecting business practices have damaged the productive partnership between labor and capital, and Chapter 5 suggests ways to repair this relationship in order to make urban economies more robust. Chapter 6 addresses complications relating to the creation and maintenance of public property and the conduct of public business, while Chapter 7 provides some rules that can enhance the odds that these things are done efficiently. Chapters 8 and 9 show how some of our attempts to rescue cities have, by attenuating owners' rights and squandering social capital in many communities, exacerbated their decline and yielded great inequity. Chapter 10 describes the consequences of conflicts about property rights in communally owned areas, with special emphasis on street crime and homelessness.

The final chapter provides ten rights-related "commandments" to which policymakers should adhere if they want to maximize the chances that their cities will become or remain healthy. These are, in effect, principles for the successful "reinvention" of any city. And the news is good:

though some proposals will surely encounter resistance from certain interest groups, none require doing the impossible (such as immediately ending racism, changing Americans' tastes for auto travel, or reversing the tide of globalization). Nor do they suggest cities must compete for a special type of employer or class of resident to serve as catalysts for their development, or fundamentally change their nature or economic profile to survive and thrive. They need only attend to residents' and employers' deep-seated and legitimate concerns about the security of their property rights, and revisit the myriad ways they might have damaged these rights. If political leaders and private entrepreneurs do so conscientiously, in bankrupt Detroit and elsewhere, they will bestow on all urban residents the chance to prosper and enjoy lives of personal fulfillment and growth.

Stephen J.K. Walters
Baltimore, July 2014

BOOM TOWNS

CHAPTER I

What We've Lost—and Why

IN THE FIRST HALF of the twentieth century, Detroit's black ghetto was known as Paradise Valley.

Apparently, this was not meant ironically or sarcastically. In one former resident's memory, the place was "next to heaven!" It delivered "economic growth, first-class entertainment, and new opportunities for Detroit's Black community."[1]

What an odd—even outrageous—thing to say about a ghetto. For many decades, if you lived in Paradise Valley and crossed certain streets into other neighborhoods you might get a beating—or at least some hard questioning by a cop. You faced relentless discrimination in the workplace and in public accommodations, your kids went to segregated and grossly underfunded schools, you got minimal services from City Hall, and you were daily confronted with injustices and indignities that today would make any sane person boiling mad. Yet it's not uncommon to read similarly fond reminiscences about other segregated neighborhoods of that era, from New York's Harlem to San Francisco's Fillmore district.

We may be less puzzled by warmhearted portrayals of the various Chinatowns, Little Italys, Poletowns, or other ethnic enclaves that have long dotted America's urban landscape. Perhaps we delude ourselves into thinking that such segregation was more about ethnic solidarity and personal choice than it really was, or are comforted by the belief that these groups faced less overt hostility than did blacks when they arrived as immigrants. At the least, however, the bias that consigned certain racial or ethnic groups to limited areas caused them to pay higher rents for smaller quarters of lower quality and greatly handicapped them in their pursuit of employment or goods and services.

Nevertheless, these groups kept flocking to America's great old industrial cities and not only put up with the indignity, overcrowding, noise, and grime that typified urban living conditions at the time but commonly *celebrated* their quality of life. Why?

Because cities worked. Or, rather, because there was every bit as much injustice and bigotry elsewhere—*plus* grinding poverty and a reduced array of opportunities for work and play. In cities, there were not only plenty of jobs, but jobs that paid wages that were far higher than those in rural areas. In Detroit in 1930, for example, the average unskilled factory worker made $1,762 a year (almost $25,000 in today's money). That may not seem like much, but it was *triple* the amount a similar worker could earn in, say, Madison County, Alabama, or Troup County, Georgia.

And the new residents of America's booming cities of the first half of the twentieth century did not just have more money to spend, but more and better things on which to spend it. Their higher incomes and cities' dense populations could sustain markets for goods and services unimaginable down on the farm. In Paradise Valley in the 1920s, that meant a sharecropper's son could, after riding the streetcar home from a lucrative shift at the Ford plant, don a suit and take his wife to hear a top jazz band at the Music Bar at Hastings and East Adams Streets; bowl a few strings at the Paradise Bowl; or—if it was a really special occasion—see Ethel Waters, the "Charleston Dance Queen," perform at the Gotham Hotel downtown. Nothing like that could be done in rural Alabama or Georgia in the 1920s—or, perhaps, ever.

A RISING TIDE, LIFTING BOATS

Because people could get richer and have more fun in cities, America was completely rearranged during the first half of the past century. Three-quarters of the nation's population lived in rural areas as the 1900s began, but over the next few decades its industrializing cities grew rapidly outward (and upward) until, sometime between the 1940 and 1950 censuses, America became a predominantly metropolitan society. By 1950, a third of its citizens resided in central cities and another 23 percent in surrounding suburbs. Detroit was the biggest boom town of all, its population exploding over six-fold, from 286,000 in 1900 to 1.85 million by mid-century. The average population density in central cities peaked at 7,500 people per square mile, 2.5 times that which now prevails in cities and almost 40 times that in modern suburbs.[2]

Though crowded, these central cities functioned quite well. Most notably, residents of the biggest American cities in 1950 were, on average, relatively well-to-do. As Table 1.1 shows, median family incomes in the ten most populous cities exceeded the national median of $3,073 (about $30,000 in today's money), usually by a comfortable margin. In Chicago and Detroit, median family incomes exceeded the national figure by 29 percent; in Cleveland and New York, by 15 percent; in Boston and St. Louis, by 6 and 4 percent, respectively. Poverty statistics had yet to be invented, but all of America's ten largest cities had a smaller proportion of families with incomes below $2,000 than the national norm. At the other end of the spectrum, all had a larger proportion of families with incomes above $5,000 than the nation as a whole.

If you had lived in one of these cities at mid-century, your neighbors likely were a representative sample of the country as a whole: their average age, education level, labor-force participation rate, and unemployment rate differed little from national norms. And if you and your neighbors had been polled on quality-of-life issues, you probably would have said that things were relatively good—though this should *not* be taken to mean, of course, good in all ways or relative to modern standards of well-being. Only a nostalgic fool would argue that living three generations ago was better, on average, than living today. In those days America was not just

TABLE 1.1 *Incomes in the Ten Largest U.S. Cities, 1950*

Cities	Median Family Income	Families with Monthly Income < $2,000	Families with Monthly Income > $5,000
Chicago	$3,956	14.5%	33.2%
Detroit	$3,955	13.2%	33.1%
Washington, D.C.	$3,800	17.6%	34.6%
Los Angeles	$3,575	21.2%	27.7%
Cleveland	$3,531	17.4%	24.1%
New York	$3,526	19.4%	28.0%
Philadelphia	$3,322	21.6%	22.9%
Baltimore	$3,275	22.7%	23.1%
Boston	$3,249	21.0%	21.2%
St. Louis	$3,205	23.5%	19.9%
United States	$3,073	27.8%	19.1%

SOURCE: *U.S. Bureau of the Census, U.S. Census of Population, 1950, Volume II, Characteristics of the Population* (Washington, D.C.: U.S. Government Printing Office 1950), Table 92.

poorer and less technologically advanced than now, but less just; for almost everyone, life then was harder and shorter than today.

What's clear is that cities were not just livable but *superior to the alternatives of the day*. They had slums, but substandard housing was common outside central cities, too. For example, 17 percent of the homes in Baltimore in 1950 were classified as dilapidated or had no running water, private bath, or toilet, but 20 percent of those in Baltimore's surrounding suburban census tracts were similarly classified.[3] And though big-city crime rates were high, they were yet to become catastrophically so. In 1950, the murder rate in large cities (those with over 250,000 residents) was just one-third above the national average for all cities and suburbs, and the burglary rate was just 15 percent higher.[4]

Even the most deprived and racially segregated neighborhoods of large cities exhibited signs of health, as sociologist William Julius Wilson has summarized:

Blacks in Harlem and other ghetto neighborhoods did not hesitate to sleep in parks, on fire escapes, and on rooftops during hot summer nights in the 1940s and 1950s, and whites frequently visited inner-city taverns and nightclubs. There was crime, to be sure, but it had not reached the point where people were fearful of walking the streets at night. . . . There was joblessness, but nowhere near the proportions . . . that have gripped ghetto communities since 1970. . . . There were welfare recipients, but only a very small percentage of the families could be said to be welfare-dependent. In short, unlike the present period, inner-city communities prior to 1960 exhibited the features of social organization—including a sense of community, positive neighborhood identification, and explicit norms and sanctions against aberrant behavior.[5]

In sum, through most of this period American cities were magnificent engines of economic and social progress. As the great urbanologist, the late Jane Jacobs, once put it, "[A] metropolitan economy, if it is working well, is constantly transforming many poor people into middle-class people, many illiterates into skilled (or even educated) people, many greenhorns into competent citizens. . . . Cities don't lure the middle class. They create it."[6] Our cities performed this wonderful work for many decades, until something fateful—and a bit mysterious—changed.

THE TIDE GOES OUT

The most obvious sign that something had gone wrong, that many core cities had lost some vital life force, was the great post-war exodus to surrounding suburbs and exurbs. In the second half of the twentieth century, the population of St. Louis fell 60 percent; Pittsburgh, Buffalo, Detroit, and Cleveland weren't far behind, losing half their residents. Newark, Cincinnati, Rochester, and Baltimore lost a third or more, Washington, Louisville, Philadelphia, Minneapolis, Boston, Birmingham, and Chicago at least a fifth, and New Orleans, St. Paul, Milwaukee, and Kansas City slightly smaller proportions. The losses would have been greater but for the fact that those cities' buildings couldn't sprint for the exits, too. While they slowly deteriorated, they'd shelter some inhabitants and give these cities an illusion of continuing viability.

This evacuation didn't merely signal that there were problems, but made them worse. With smaller populations and shrinking tax bases, city governments would experience chronic fiscal crises that forced service cuts, tax hikes, or both. And core cities' populations didn't just fall—they changed. Those who fled tended to be better-educated and have higher incomes than those who stayed or moved in to replace them. Demand for social services grew; the wherewithal to provide them shrank.

Slowly, over a few decades, public perceptions of the American city changed. Cities had never been perfect, but had been undeniably attractive and important. By the 1960s, however, many of America's core urban areas had become desperately poor and afflicted with the kinds of problems that both result from concentrated poverty and contribute to its endurance. Crime rates soared; illicit drug markets took root and flourished; schools became dysfunctional; neighborhoods crumbled; infrastructure deteriorated; good jobs became harder to find.

By the 1970s, it was clear that America's core cities were no longer cornerstones of its citizens' social, cultural, or economic lives, no longer keys to national identity and sources of strength and pride. Rather, they were things to be pitied and propped up by taxpayers living in wealthier areas or, more often, just ignored. At some point, it became routine to define cities by their problems rather than their (apparently nonexistent) virtues. By the early 1980s, for example, *The World Book Dictionary* would define the inner city as that part of a metropolitan area "characterized by congestion, poverty, dirt, and violence," adding "especially U.S."[7] Ouch.

WHODUNNIT?

Foul play was assumed, and scholars and opinion makers rounded up the usual suspects. Racism that caused some to flee from minorities toward segregated enclaves. Corporate greed that drove employers to shutter their factories and seek cheaper labor in the Sun Belt or overseas. Our unfortunate preference for cars over mass transit (or walking), for detached homes over rowhouses, and for office parks over skyscrapers—tastes which made living and working in cities passé.

Library shelves soon groaned under the weight of volumes containing stinging indictments of these perpetrators, somber discussions of the terrible consequences of their crimes, and urgent pleas for a commitment of resources to relieve the suffering of their victims. An alphabet soup of federal, state, and local agencies began handing out billions of dollars annually in subsidies to those willing to build whatever might help revive moribund central cities, from affordable housing to luxury hotels to stadiums and convention centers.[8] Other agencies tried to cope with the fallout from deindustrialization, doling out cash to the disemployed and funding training programs so that the undereducated and unskilled might participate in America's "New Service Economy." Generous subsidies flowed to mass transit projects aimed at luring commuters out of their cars and onto buses and trains. Restrictions on land use tried to keep developers from claiming more of the open spaces on the periphery of cities, motivated partly by the belief that if the suburbs became prohibitively expensive then cities would become popular again.

It would be wrong to say that all these well-intended policies failed to contribute to the revival of core cities. But even the various policies' most ardent fans might admit that, individually and collectively, they've been less than resounding successes. While the tax dollars flowed and the recovery plans proliferated, just about all the cities on the aforementioned list continued to lose population (though perhaps at a slower rate than if we had tried to do nothing to staunch the bleeding). All have much higher crime and poverty rates than a half-century ago; many of their residents continue to suffer the ill effects of failing schools, inefficient transit systems, decaying infrastructure, and restricted economic opportunities. And though some cities (or parts of them) have made progress in recent years, no dictionary is yet defining the American inner city in glowing, positive terms.

This may just mean that the time and treasure we have devoted to urban renewal are but a portion of what is needed. That is surely what many policymakers argue as they plead for more subsidies, more land-use regulations, more power to turn back the tide of deurbanization.

On the other hand, it may mean that the theories of the case are faulty or, at least, incomplete. Perhaps efforts to breathe life back into cities have proved disappointing because policymakers have never fully identified the root causes of their demise—and, so, have been misdirecting the resources committed to this noble goal. In short, *perhaps the real perpetrators are still on the loose*, continuing to do harm and defeating our best efforts to make cities great and prosperous once again.

Which is not to say that the usual suspects aren't at least accomplices. Who can deny that racial and ethnic bias have influenced urban form throughout American history? Groups have harbored prejudices against and fears about each other for as long as there have been cities—and probably before that. Which is precisely the point: cities have demonstrated their capacity to grow and prosper in the presence of bias (and a troubling ability *not* to do so even when bigotry was, arguably, on the wane). Racism has been a reasonably constant feature of American life, but cities' fortunes have not been constant; they've risen and then fallen with little regard for this ugly aspect of our national psyche. Many immigrant groups have shown up in American cities, suffered discrimination at the hands of bigoted employers, and were consigned to segregated neighborhoods—and cities nonetheless thrived.

What about corporate greed? This is another "constant" that explains little of the variation in cities' fortunes. Automakers, for example, were just as greedy when they converged on Detroit and started hiring everyone in sight (and at relatively high wages, as we've seen) in the first half of the twentieth century as they were when they started laying people off in the second half. Ditto steelmakers in Pittsburgh, shipbuilders in Philadelphia, brewers in Milwaukee, or meatpackers in Cincinnati. The real question is what happened to make so many cities repulsive rather than attractive to consistently greedy capitalists. If high wages alone were the problem, Wall Street would be an abandoned ruin. Lots of metro areas are growing despite high average wages; on the other hand, low wages alone are not enough to make others attractive. Today there's plenty of idle, cheap labor in America's stagnant core cities—but the greedy capitalists aren't, for the most part, coming back to take advantage of it.

The argument that is most widely credited and perhaps most difficult to challenge is that people evacuated just because they always hated grimy, over-crowded central cities and eventually the development of the automobile made their exodus possible and their rising incomes made it affordable. It's undeniable that cities are not for everyone. Suburbs and exurbs have many fans who can articulate compelling reasons for choosing to live there. But here's the thing: most of these reasons boil down to the fact that a lot of cities simply stopped working very well. When a suburbanite says, "City life's okay for some people, but I could never live in town 'cause it's not safe . . . and the schools aren't good . . . and the housing is dilapidated . . . and my job is near the Beltway, anyway," we're getting closer to the crux of the problem. Maybe those who fled to the suburbs from the 1950s onward actually started cities on a downward spiral—or maybe their exit was more *symptomatic* of urban problems than it was root cause; maybe problems preceded flight at least as much as flight caused problems.

In addition, it's apparent that the "we hate density" theory of urban obsolescence has a tough time explaining the cross-sectional evidence. Not all American cities reduced their population densities during the last half of the twentieth century; they certainly did not do so at uniform rates. Even amidst the suburbanization trend, many core cities maintained some high-density neighborhoods that survived in reasonably good condition—and a few actually gained population. Clearly, *some* fraction of the American populace values urban amenity in the classic sense.

Contrast San Francisco and Baltimore, two bayside cities with comparable populations. From 1950 to 1980, both saw considerable flight, their populations falling 12 and 17 percent, respectively. Baltimore has about twice as much land area, but its lower density could not have been much of an advantage, because over the next two decades its population fell another 17 percent—while "over-crowded" San Francisco's population (and density) would *rise* 14 percent.

Obviously, one anecdote can't prove that Americans really *like* density and that our desire for open spaces and greenery is of little consequence—but that's not the claim here. It just seems that the importance—or, as San Francisco's reversal of fortune illustrates, the immutability—of this taste might have been exaggerated. Density, per se, is not necessarily repulsive. Dysfunction, however, is. Yet because so many cities have become dysfunctional, it's really hard to say what fraction of Americans might value city living; many of us simply don't know anymore what city living can be like.

BEYOND RACISM, GREED, AND "BAD" TASTE

One of the worst things about the accepted wisdom on the decline of cities is that if it's really the whole story then there's not much we can do to revive them. It would be wonderful if, in Jacobs's words, cities were again "constantly transforming many poor people into middle-class people," but if we first have to eliminate prejudice, selfishness, and disregard for the environment to restart that engine—well, good luck with that.

On the other hand, what if cities can boom *despite* all our human imperfections?

My optimistic view is that they can—much as they did in the first half of the twentieth century. In this book, I will argue that the decline of U.S. industrial cities in the post–World War II era was not inevitable and that a good deal of public policy aimed at reviving them has been (and remains) misdirected and often counterproductive. Further, if we properly diagnose and treat the real causes of urban decline, cities can, once again, become engines of prosperity and central to America's social and cultural development—and my goal throughout this book is to provide practical suggestions about how to get this done.

Along the way, it will be necessary to identify some people and policies associated with these root causes of decline and dysfunction. Clearly, it's impossible to solve problems without a good understanding of their source. One thing that will become apparent is that many of those responsible meant no real harm—and often prided themselves on their good intentions. But even the ones who knew they were doing unwholesome things never intended for cities to die—they simply had larceny in their hearts.

Many of those who caused great damage to cities were, consciously or not, emulating the legendary Robin Hood. Like the Prince of Thieves, they sought to "steal from the rich in order to give to the poor"—but via democratic processes, of course, so it was not really theft. As I will discuss in some detail, however, the goals might have been noble but the results often were not. And, clearly, not all our accused even pretended to do God's work; some subverted the democratic process or otherwise pursued their selfish ends even when they knew that the consequences, at least in the long run, would be potentially devastating for their fellow citizens.

The Capital of Cities

What is it about cities that tends to attract the larcenous and makes their behavior particularly important and problematic?

The answer to the first part of this question is simple: one key attraction of cities, for both the virtuous and venal, is their abundant, durable, and immobile capital. By *capital* I mean, in the words of Nobel laureate George Stigler, our "stock of useful things,"[9] or the ordinary tools of life that help us become more prosperous and happy. These can take tangible form, like the structures in which we live, work, and entertain ourselves, or the streets, sidewalks, or subways that enable us to move about, or the infrastructure that supplies us with water, power, and other necessities. But capital can also be intangible, like the knowledge or skills we carry with us (which economists call "human capital") or the valuable networks of friends, neighbors, and colleagues with whom we interact and trade on a daily basis (thus drawing on our stock of "social capital").

We may tend to think of cities as dense concentrations of people, but we need to start thinking of them as *accumulations of capital in all its forms that help residents to flourish materially, socially, and culturally*. There were lots of horrifying things about life in Paradise Valley in the 1920s, but its residents' access to the capital there made it far preferable to rural Alabama or Georgia. Migrants to Detroit benefited from the rich stock of capital equipment in nearby factories that made them much more productive—and, so, raised their wages—but also from infrastructure and access to talented people that enhanced the quality of life in countless other ways.

Life without abundant capital is possible—it's just vastly less efficient and more difficult. To reinforce that lesson, dig a ditch with your bare hands and then repeat the experiment with a shovel—or, better still, a diesel-powered backhoe. Try trading stocks or bonds successfully without a laptop wired to the Internet. Imagine your leisure hours without a nearby park, theatre, stadium, restaurant, pub, or the like. All of these things are examples of physical capital, all are the result of investment by capitalists (or sometimes taxpayers), and all improve the efficiency with which we live and thus the quality of our lives. In short, as we accumulate physical capital (and its less visible relatives, human and social capital) it is simply easier to produce, prosper, and have fun.

Defending the Capital: Property Rights

Suburbs and exurbs have capital too, of course, but cities are particularly capital rich—and therein lies the rub. Since some forms of capital are both fixed and durable, it will often be a tempting target for those who want to *seize* some of its value for themselves (or, if they're playing Robin Hood, for other beneficiaries).

They can do so in many ways—each of which will be the focus of a later chapter. Some have mainly to do with garden-variety public policies such as taxation or regulation. Others involve governmental corruption or cynical shortsightedness by public officials. And a few involve brutal contests between competing market interests: capitalists versus organized labor (though, of course, the outcomes of these contests will be greatly affected by the rules of engagement laid out by governments and courts).

The key point, however, is that when well-meaning tax authorities or regulators or corrupt politicians or muscular unions successfully appropriate some of the value of a city's stock of capital for themselves (or others), the effects appear benign in the short run but in the long run are invariably damaging to a city's viability. To continue the Robin Hood analogy, after Robin and his Merry Men had held up a few unsuspecting travelers in Sherwood Forest, there were consequences. Not only did the Sheriff of Nottingham get on Robin's case (which is the least interesting element of the narrative from our economic point of view), but *travelers started avoiding Sherwood Forest.*

More broadly, once the returns on capital investment are driven down within a particular jurisdiction, the propensity to create new (or replenish old) capital will be reduced. True, much of the capital that's already there can't go anywhere—human capital can relocate easily; physical and social capital not so much—but it won't last forever. And as a city repels investment and sheds capital, its health will inexorably decline. Those who own the most portable forms of capital (knowledge, skills) will exit first, but even those who own fixed capital (manufacturers who use machinery extensively, or homeowners who attach a great deal of importance to the appearance or amenity of their dwellings) will eventually find it in their best interest to depart. The speed with which they do—and with which others follow—will, of course, depend on many variables: the availability of alternative jurisdictions where capital is treated more favorably, the durability of their prior capital investments, and much else. But if a jurisdiction does not respond to an initial outflow of capital—and of those who own it or most value its services—with an appropriate remedy, then the outflow will accelerate.

Over time, this problem will be impossible to ignore, but its causes may be hard to properly diagnose. There is no guarantee that those exiting will articulate all the reasons they are seeking greener pastures. Observers may therefore concoct explanations that have little to do with the underlying issues actually influencing behavior. Indeed, since no good data exist on the extent to which capital is "fleeing" (really, *not arriving*), and since the decay rate of existing capital will be so slow, it will be easy to focus on the wrong things and confuse symptoms with the causes of the disease.

Clearly, to avoid losing essential capital, cities must pay careful attention to their treatment of its owners. In the language of economics, they must properly specify and efficiently enforce owners' property rights, ensuring that those with a stake in the locale's stock of capital—tangible and intangible, private and public—do not have an incentive to flee to jurisdictions where the returns to this capital are better protected.

Again, this won't be easy. This is not simply because it may require resisting political temptation—to solve this year's budget crunch, for example, by slapping a confiscatory tax on the income yielded by the human capital of well-to-do entrepreneurs, inviting them to exit and thus creating a future budget crisis—but because it will often be difficult to appreciate how a particular policy decision may alter property rights in unwholesome ways. As we'll see in later chapters, many well-funded and long-running programs thought necessary to rescue dying cities actually damaged residents' ownership rights and unwittingly destroyed much valuable capital—some of which just happened to be invisible.

WHY WE SHOULD CARE

The idea that the destiny of cities is, first and foremost, related to their treatment of property rights and capital is admittedly unconventional, and there's no reason why readers shouldn't be a little wary of it. But if all I've done so far is arouse your curiosity and make you want to read on to find out how defending property rights can make cities healthier, then this brief introductory chapter has served its purpose.

You may not even consider yourself a "city person," but if you care about improving the lives of millions of poor city residents then you'll want to identify the root causes of so much urban dysfunction and understand how to make cities work again. As cities declined so dramatically over the past half-century, we came to think of them as places where the poor were in effect warehoused. Many viewed the condition of the "urban underclass" as static or, at best, something to be altered mainly by infusions of aid and clever social programs. We forgot that cities had long been, and could be again, not warehouses but factories, *changing* people's lives for the better. We forgot that cities could be, as Jacobs pointed out, places where people came to prosper—and usually did.

What's more, the consequences of urban dysfunction spread well beyond core cities' borders. As they depopulated, the millions formerly housed within their borders have gone elsewhere, claiming farms and forests for tract homes; demanding costly new roads, schools, stores, power lines, and sewers; guzzling energy with ever-longer commutes. For many of these outmigrants, of course, life in suburbia is part of the American Dream and a cherished lifestyle choice. For an unmeasured fraction, however, it is simply a necessary adaptation. If only cities worked better, they would have remained—or would return. So if you care about Mother Earth and want to help mitigate problems such as global warming; air, water, or land pollution; and sprawl, improving the health of America's core cities is a crucial step in the right direction. According to estimates by economist Matthew Kahn, the average suburban household (after controlling for income and other nonspatial influences on demand) drives 31 percent more miles and consumes 58 percent more land, 49 percent more fuel oil, and 35 percent more electricity than the typical city household.[10] Making cities attractive rather than repulsive should be on every environmentalist's to-do list.

Of course, there is no shortage of good ideas about ways to make cities healthier. In our increasingly knowledge-based society, for example, in which technological innovation and creativity are seen as key drivers of regional and national economic performance, it has become common for localities to base their growth strategies on attracting firms and individuals rich in human capital.[11] The premise is that this can beget a chain reaction: that intellectuals, professionals, artists, and other "creatives" will catalyze additional investment and growth that will spread prosperity widely. What is often overlooked, however, is that secure rights to the returns on creatives' intangible capital—and on returns arising from complementary physical capital—might be a necessary condition for these strategies to work. In other words, a place without secure property rights will not see the steady flows of new capital investment on which the hoped-for chain reaction depends.

Once proper attention is directed to the specification and enforcement of their residents' property rights, I'm confident that viability can be restored to all of America's dead and near-dead core cities and that they can be centers of opportunity, innovation, social mobility, and cultural uplift once again. Moreover, this can be done without trying to make people feel guilty about living in suburbs and without using coercive, regulatory means to prevent them from doing so. There's no need to try to convince people that a fondness for two-car garages or lawns is some sort of character flaw; no need to try to "guilt" people into staying in crime-riddled neighborhoods or keeping their children in bad schools; no need, even, to zone them out of the suburbs. Cities must *compete* for residents; in what follows, we'll see how they can do so successfully.

CHAPTER 2

Fleeing Robin Hood

UPON HIS DEATH IN 1958, James Michael Curley got the biggest send-off in Boston's history. Well over a hundred thousand mourners filed past his casket in the Massachusetts State House, and after his funeral Mass in a packed Cathedral of the Holy Cross, thousands more stood along the route to his burial plot at Mount Calvary Cemetery. Many shed tears for the man who had served four terms as the city's mayor, one as Massachusetts' governor, four in Congress—and two in jail.

In fact, those stints behind bars were just the tip of the Curley corruption iceberg. It was widely known that he had used blackmail to help win his first term as mayor and solicited kickbacks to support a luxurious lifestyle, which included a mansion that he built at great expense shortly after taking over City Hall. In a turn-of-the-millennium poll of historians and social scientists, Curley was voted America's fourth-worst big-city mayor of the past two centuries.[1]

He was, nevertheless, a "lovable scoundrel"—and not just because of his considerable personal charm and oratorical gifts. He was a real-life, duly elected Robin Hood. To admirers, he was "the Mayor of the Poor," with a political base consisting of people much like himself: impoverished immigrants, mostly Irish, struggling to get onto the first rung of America's economic and social ladder. Curley made it his business to help them do so and to provide aid if they slipped off. All he asked in return was their votes.

The funds with which he bought support and affection came from Boston's propertied classes—its old Yankees, or "Brahmins," as Curley called them. They naturally despised him for it. He didn't mind—and, indeed, reveled in their enmity and considered himself to be doing God's work. When one unsympathetic reporter called him a "two-fisted thief" to his face, Curley smiled and replied, "I never took a quarter from anyone who couldn't afford it."[2] Robin of Loxley couldn't have said it better.

Of course, many politicians before and since have purchased the loyalty of favored constituents with revenue drawn from others. Few, however, have done so with Curley's remarkable energy and efficiency. He saw an average of two hundred supplicants each day. On arrival at City Hall, their requests for jobs or assistance were catalogued by a platoon of secretaries so that the mayor could quickly and personally render a judgment about their worthiness. The money and favors he doled out came from a steady stream of government-funded projects. Those vying to pave a street, extend a transit line, or install a playground knew that to win Curley's favor they should pad their bids by 5 to 10 percent for "mayoral overhead," which might take the form of cash to be contributed to his administration or a ready willingness to hire any and all he would send to them. As historian Francis Russell summarized, "[h]ere lay Curley's basic formula . . . in all his administrations: a juggler's act of public works without regard for cost. When the City treasury was empty he would borrow. The outraged Yankees could pay for it all through taxes."[3] By the time Curley's reign ended, Boston's property tax rate was five times higher than he'd found it.

Infuriating the Yankees, it turned out, was a political two-fer. At first they fought back, of course, but eventually, outnumbered, they just started to leave. The more benign tax environments of the suburbs were, after all, just a few miles away. And as Curley's enemies departed, his base—by simple arithmetic—became a larger fraction of the electorate and his hold on City Hall strengthened. Economists Edward Glaeser and Andrei Shleifer have dubbed this result "the Curley Effect" in his honor.[4]

Often, however, a brilliant political strategy can be catastrophic economically. In this chapter, we'll examine how playing Robin Hood can backfire, damaging cities and ultimately impoverishing those it is intended to help. To do so, we'll focus on the economic consequences of increases in property taxes, discuss how these effects interact with other important economic forces at work in urban environments, and then take stock of the long-term consequences of redistributive politics at the local level.

THE OTHER CAPITAL PUNISHMENT

If you are determined to take from the rich and give to the poor—and *not* go to jail in the process—raising the property tax certainly looks like the best way to go.

When income is taxed, people have an unfortunate tendency to hide their earnings via simple tax fraud or more elaborate but legal dodges devised by lawyers and accountants. Or they just move beyond reach of the taxman. Real property, however, is difficult to hide. It's standing right there for all to see and the tax assessor to appraise. Further, since property owners can't strap their homes, shops, or factories to their backs and flee, evading this form of taxation is extremely difficult. Finally, the rich often hold a significant portion of their wealth in the form of real property because they value highly the creature comforts that luxurious homes provide (and, perhaps, the signals about status they transmit) or because the source of their wealth is at least partly a business that requires considerable investment in physical capital. Thus a high property tax rate seems as progressive and efficient as tax policy can be: it hits the right targets and does so with minimal apparent downside in the form of evasion or other unwholesome consequences.

A simple example can illustrate the ingeniousness and political appeal of an aggressive property tax hike. Consider the homes on opposite sides of a street that is a boundary line between two jurisdictions that we'll call Curleyville and Safe Haven. These hypothetical homes are identical: same age, lot size, number of bedrooms and baths, and so on. So are Curleyville and Safe Haven: same tax rates and services to residents. As a result, the homes in each are likely to fetch the same price—let's say $240,000—in a well-functioning, competitive real estate market.

Now suppose Curleyville raises its property tax rate from 1 percent to 2 percent of the market value of real property, while Safe Haven leaves its rate alone. The owners of the homes on the Curleyville side of the street thus face an annual tax bill of $4,800 (or $200 monthly) while those on the Safe Haven side of the street pay $2,400 annually (or $100 monthly)—for, as far as anyone can tell, essentially the same level of amenity and public services.

Indignant, the Curleyville owners decide to sell their houses and buy on the other side of the street in order to avoid the extra $100 monthly tax. But they will find, much to their chagrin, that doing so is pointless: prospective buyers looking at houses on both sides of the street will, quite rationally, offer considerably less for the ones carrying the higher future tax liability. Ultimately, the prices of homes on the Curleyville side of the street will have to be discounted enough to offset the higher tax rate there—a phenomenon economists refer to as tax capitalization. As a result, those owning Curleyville property at the time the tax rate went up will find that they've suffered a significant capital loss. But once prices on their side of the street have adjusted downward by the amount necessary,[5] they'll find that they (and any prospective buyers) are indifferent about which side of the street to live on: Curleyville prices are low enough that the ultimate, after-tax outlays for homes there match those in Safe Haven.

So, all appears well. Sure, Curleyville residents might be a bit angry about suffering those "once and for all" capital losses, but (a) cash is flowing into the coffers of Curleyville government[6] and (b) nobody has much incentive to change their behavior—chiefly, to exit. And, of course, if the higher Curleyville taxes are used to provide services much valued by Curleyville residents, it's even possible that no decline in Curleyville property values need occur. Boston's Yankee taxpayers, for example, might have concluded that the public works projects rolled out by Mayor Curley were well worth the extra tax outlays. Indeed, in 1956 economist Charles Tiebout published an enormously influential article arguing that if there are many political jurisdictions within a metropolitan area and if individuals are mobile, communities will compete for residents by offering differing packages of services and taxes. Residents would thus sort themselves out according to their tastes, with some seeking high tax rates and high amounts of local government services, others the opposite, and many other choices in between—much like consumers in markets for differentiated private goods.[7]

Unfortunately, "Curleyism" does not aim to create public goods that will *please* the well-to-do, but rather to empty their pockets and deliver the proceeds to a favored voting bloc. In such circumstances—that is, when property tax increases are unaccompanied by commensurate improvements in government services—the evidence confirms the prediction of economic theory that such increases drive property values down.[8] But what about the Curley Effect—why would the wealthy bother to *flee* higher property taxes and thus allow the beneficiaries of the redistributive program to acquire ever-greater political muscle? Once the tax rate notches upward, the propertied incur a capital loss whether they stay or move, so why move?

First, of course, they may remember an old saying: "Fool me once, shame on you; fool me twice, shame on me." Suffering one capital loss is bad enough, but rational property owners will naturally fear that more might be coming. Mayor Curley, after all, did not quintuple Boston's property tax rate all at once, but in a series of steps, each of which took a financial bite out of the hides of those old Yankees. Over time, even the most patient (or foolish) business owners or homeowners would perceive that the value of their properties were being expropriated, bit by bit. Indeed, a program of property tax hikes aimed at redistribution is best understood as a *property rights* rather than a *tax incidence* issue, with owners making relocation decisions not simply because of the impact on their cash flow of living in a high-tax jurisdiction, but on the basis of worries about the *security* of their ownership rights and wealth over the long haul.

Second, if we relax the usual simplifying assumptions about tax capitalization, some unfortunate implications of tax rate gaps across jurisdictions emerge. Consider just the effects of ordinary inflation, which are often overlooked in debates about property taxes. Neither assessed values nor property tax rates are typically adjusted (or "indexed") for the changing purchasing power of the dollar over time. In our example, if inflation adds, say, 5 percent to the nominal value of real estate in general, that would increase an owner's tax liability significantly more in Curleyville than in Safe Haven. That would, in turn, further reduce the relative value of Curleyville property,[9] and if inflation is a more or less permanent fact of economic life it will cause a steady drip, drip of capital losses for Curleyville property owners—and another reason to exit.

What's more, assets subject to the property tax emphatically do *not* last forever. As any homeowner knows, one's castle depreciates. It needs a steady flow of investment to maintain its value and keep producing high-quality service flows. But a new roof or more energy-efficient windows that might add $10,000 to the value of a home in Safe Haven will, again, have to be discounted in Curleyville[10] to offset the higher tax bill such an improvement would call forth there. Again, those averse to suffering capital losses will tend to flee.

Finally, what is true of individual structures also holds for the wondrous accumulations of physical capital that we call cities. They are not static. They need new investment by the tens and hundreds of millions of dollars annually not only to keep pace with depreciation but to adapt to new circumstances and technologies and thus enhance their citizens' quality of life. Sadly, the relentless arithmetic of tax capitalization—the repeated capital losses arising from higher property tax rates in Curleyville than in Safe Haven—will act like investment repellant there. If it costs $10 million to build a factory or office building in either locale, Curleyville's higher property tax alone may reduce the owner's bottom line by $100,000 a year relative to Safe Haven.[11] All else the same on either side of the street, who in their right minds would choose to invest in Curleyville?

COLLATERAL DAMAGE

In sum, what we have here is a prescription for disaster. As a result of its commitment to Robin Hood politics, Curleyville is quite likely to lose residents, see its remaining ones become poorer, and experience a decline in the quality and quantity of its homes and businesses.

These trends will take place very slowly—indeed, they may be imperceptible to the naked eye unless one watches patiently for many years or decades. Even then, it will be easy to get confused about what's going on. Lots of things will be changing simultaneously: the slow, steady decay of physical capital in high-tax areas such as Curleyville will occur alongside—and be obscured by—more obvious trends: demographic shifts, technological changes, up- and down-drafts in the national economy, cultural upheaval, and political swings. It will be easier to tell a convincing story about a city's destiny that points toward these rapidly changing and visible factors than toward more fundamental but obscure forces.

But no matter what people *believe* about the causes of a high-tax jurisdiction's inevitable decline, the damage will be felt by far more than those unlucky enough to own real property when the program of redistribution begins. To see why, one must appreciate the symbiotic relationship between labor and capital. All our worldly goods are a result of this partnership between people and the tools they use to produce things. Economists often describe this relationship mathematically, with formulae called production functions, but it's really not necessary to do any math to get the gist. Think of a production function as a recipe; it lists the ingredients or inputs we need (not just labor and capital, but land, technology, entrepreneurship, energy, and so on) and tells how much output we'll enjoy after the cooking is done.

Of course, the relationship between the amount of inputs applied to any task and the resulting amount of output received will vary greatly from case to case. Sometimes adding 10 percent more of all inputs to the production process might yield more than a 10 percent gain in output; at other times, less. But there is one key generalization we can make that will apply in just about all circumstances: when one of the inputs is increased, the productivity of the others rises. Give workers more tools, and the amount of output per worker will rise; give them fewer, and their output will fall.

This basic fact of productive life has profound implications for human welfare. In competitive labor markets, workers will receive wages commensurate with the value of the output they produce. That which enables them to increase their output, therefore, will also enhance their earning power. Acquiring new skills through education or training can do this, of course, as can technological advances that enable them to do more with less. But the key point here is that simply increasing the stock of capital with which they work—even if they are no smarter and inventors serve up no clever new means of working more effectively—has the capacity to raise their standard of living. A messenger with a bicycle can deliver more packages and earn more revenue than one on foot; a seamstress with a sewing machine can produce more clothing than one with a needle and thread.

This is why immigrants have always flocked to capital-rich, high-wage America from capital-starved, low-wage countries, and why core cities' populations swelled when capital-intensive manufacturing was thriving in them during America's industrial age. What's more, the efficiency-enhancing effects of capital-richness occur *outside* the workplace as well as in it. More abundant capital in the form of theatres and museums, and the transit infrastructure to get people to them, allows city-dwellers to get more out of their leisure as well as their labor hours.

Tragically, of course, *decreasing* the stock of capital with which people may work (or play) will make them less productive and reduce their incomes (or make it harder to have a good time). The effects of capital flight on city-dwellers' standard of living will be the same as if they had chosen to ignore some technological advance or to work with one hand tied behind their backs—truly silly notions. But, remarkably, when capital investment is repelled in the name of redistributive policy, many applaud.

In addition to reducing the incentive to invest in productivity- and wage-enhancing capital, practicing Robin Hood politics at the local level will kick off an unfortunate *sorting* process with respect to population and employment. As noted earlier, because physical capital is not, in fact, infinitely durable and because investments to maintain or improve its quality in high-tax areas will subject owners to repeated capital losses, such areas will repel some people but attract others.

First consider homeowners. If, as one might expect, the amenity derived from home improvements is a "normal good" (that is, one for which demand rises with income), those repelled by high property taxes are likely to be of relatively high income and education (since these variables are positively correlated), for they are likely to suffer the ill effects of tax capitalization on their wealth more frequently and severely. On the other hand, high-tax areas will actually attract residents who demand less housing amenity, plan to make fewer investments to maintain or improve the quality of their real assets, and thus are less worried about the lower returns resulting from such investments (or from ordinary inflation). These residents are more likely to be of lower income and education. And if the utility derived from ownership of a particular property is derived in part from the condition of neighboring ones, each individual's decision not to maintain or upgrade property may be contagious, thus accelerating this sorting process.

With respect to commercial property, a high-property-tax jurisdiction will repel investment in sectors where capital intensity is high, technological advance requires frequent upgrading of physical capital, or both. Manufacturing firms, for example, might look at a relatively high property tax rate with horror. On the other hand, enterprises that rely more on *human* than physical capital (for example, finance, insurance, advertising) will be bothered by high rates far less—unless the income arising from the brain power on which they rely is also taxed more heavily than in nearby locales.

Over time, then, a high-tax jurisdiction's residents will become increasingly lower-income and relatively lower-education, while a rising proportion of its job base might require significant human capital. The sociologist William Julius Wilson has attributed a great deal of the persistence of urban poverty to this sort of "mismatch."[12] Others have observed that these economic forces can produce a "self-aggravating process" or "cumulative urban decay."[13] As the investment rate falls and the quantity and quality of an area's capital stock erodes, it may mechanically raise tax rates to offset a declining tax base—adding fuel to the fire, as it were.

THE FIRST WAVE

All of the aforementioned damaging effects of Curleyism played out in Boston and other cities governed by later imitators.[14] Curley was the most aggressive and consistent practitioner of Robin Hood politics, however: in every year of his three pre–World War II mayoral terms, Boston had the distinction of imposing the highest per-capita property tax burden in the country. But, again, the pace of its resulting economic and social decline was slow, easy to overlook, and easy to blame on other causes.

From 1914 to 1925, which spanned Curley's first two terms as mayor,[15] incomes in Boston began to grow more slowly than in other northern cities. A Census Bureau study of payrolls showed that the growth of average factory workers' earnings in Boston over this period lagged that in Baltimore by 10 percent, Cleveland by 14 percent, Philadelphia by 21 percent, and New York by 27 percent. More broadly, real per-capita income growth in Boston over 1914–23 lagged that of every other northeastern city for which data exist; the average New Yorker's standard of living, for example, grew 15 percent more than the average Bostonian's during this period.[16]

In the 1930s, by which time Curley had been elected mayor a third time, Boston's population actually declined, falling 1.3 percent by 1940. It was not the only major American city to shrink in that tumultuous decade. Newark, also known for its corrupt politics, shrank 2.7 percent, for example, but this was contrary to trends elsewhere. Even as their industrial sectors struggled through the Great Depression, northern cities such as Detroit (up 3.5 percent), Minneapolis (6.0 percent), and New York (7.6 percent) all grew, while southern and western cities such as Atlanta (up 11.9 percent), Houston (31.8 percent), and Los Angeles (21.5 percent) grew even faster. And though macro-economists still debate whether the

New Deal had stimulative effects on the national economy, it was certainly a boon to the District of Columbia: Washington's population swelled 35.6 percent in the 1930s.[17]

It's hard to ascribe this early flight from Boston to racism. Only 2.9 percent of the city's population was African-American in 1930. Certainly, it was whites who were fleeing—but they appear to have been fleeing from other whites. On the other hand, the increasing availability of the automobile and a desire to escape the congestion, noise, and grime of the central city might explain some of this trend. Remember, however, that interstate highways to shorten commutes from the suburbs were still decades away, and that Depression-era conditions made it less rather than more likely that expensive tastes for lawns and single-family detached homes would rule very many Americans' residential location decisions at this time—or why such preferences, even if strong, would find expression in only a few cities. What *was* happening was that it was simply getting harder to make economic headway in Boston and places like it. With its capital stock eroding and its investment environment inferior to that in both its own suburbs and other major cities, jobs were scarcer there and often paid lower wages than elsewhere.

People sorted themselves out accordingly. The sixteenth Census included a fascinating study of internal migration in the United States over 1935–40. The national economy was in recovery from the 1933 nadir of the Great Depression during this period (save for a recessionary blip in 1937–38), but times were far from good, and there was likely more than the normal amount of movement as Americans searched for favorable environments in which to apply their talents. Many northern industrial cities suffered net out-migration, but some far more than others. Boston had a net loss of over 17,000 employed residents, about 3,000 of which were "proprietors, managers, and officials," and another 2,800 were "professional and semi-professional workers." By contrast, Baltimore—a similarly populous port city, but one with a per-capita property tax burden that was roughly half that of Boston in the mid-1930s—saw its population increase 6.7 percent from 1930 to 1940 and suffered no net loss of employed residents during the period of the Census Bureau's migration study.[18] In other words, Boston's punishment of capital not only dampened investment in that city but repelled many of its most productive, skilled, and educated residents. Almost 5,600 of its net out-migrants in 1935–40 had attended or graduated from college, thus reducing an already-thin slice of the city's population by 28 percent—perhaps just as Mayor Curley hoped.

THE RESISTANCE

While proper Bostonians fled from Robin Hood, the response elsewhere was considerably different. In particular, residents of Chicago, "the City with Big Shoulders," took a more combative stance. The problem there wasn't so much the level of the property tax but its corrupt administration. Chicago began the 1920s with a per-capita property tax burden that was roughly half that in Boston, and increases in its property tax levies during that decade were more modest than in the Hub. In Chicago, however, a practice called "tax fixing" had flourished for many years, and popular indignation about the inequities that resulted eventually provoked a full-scale tax revolt.[19]

Property taxes, of course, can produce distress for businesses and homeowners in two ways: the tax rate can be uncomfortably high, or the assessed value to which that rate is applied might be out of sync with true market prices. In theory, the assessment process in Chicago's Cook County in the 1910s and 1920s was a model of efficiency and fairness: countywide appraisals were made at least every four years under the supervision of an elected board of assessors, and taxpayers who did not agree with the outcome could appeal to an elected board of review. In reality, a political virus infected this system from top to bottom. If you were in the good graces of the local precinct captain or party boss—easily accomplished by making adequate campaign contributions and promising to vote correctly—an unaffordable assessment could be "fixed." If you didn't fuel the political machine, your tax bill might show you the error of your ways.

This shakedown racket was hardly a secret, but discontent surrounding it was largely unfocused until 1928, when the Illinois Tax Commission validated an innocent-looking petition advanced by the Chicago Teachers' Federation and joined by Cook County's Joint Commission on Real Estate Valuation. They demanded that all property tax assessments had to be made public. The union was convinced that business property in Chicago's downtown "Loop" was grossly underassessed and undertaxed, and that teachers' wages could rise if this inequity was publicized and corrected.

Assessments were indeed outrageous—but not in the way the union supposed. On average, properties were appraised at 36 percent of true market value—but some appraisals were as low as 1 percent of market and others actually *above* full market value. And assessments of the moneyed classes' holdings in the Loop were, it turned out, more than twice as high as the countywide average; to the union's surprise, "Curleyism" was already being practiced in Chicago. As economist Herbert Simpson wrote (insensitively) at the time, Chicago's tax system "provides assessing officials with as arbitrary power over the property and fortunes of wealthy citizens as any Central American dictator could desire."[20]

Calamity ensued. Not only did the teachers fail to get the revenue boost they'd been banking on, but aroused business owners and homeowners united to sue for tax limitation and equitable reassessments. While that process dragged on, through mid-1930, Chicago levied no general property taxes. Residents enjoyed a tax holiday, but the city entered a lengthy period of financial crisis. Many employees—including police and teachers—experienced "payless paydays." When city officials tried to recover the delayed tax levies with an accelerated payment schedule in 1930 and 1931, opposition coalesced into the well-financed Association of Real Estate Taxpayers (ARET). Litigating the details of Chicago's tax policy and representing thousands in tax appeals, ARET took a hard line when those appeals failed, recommending nonpayment—a tax strike. Despite an aggressive campaign against the strikers, which alternated between pleading with them to discharge their civic duty and denouncing them as anarchists, over half of Chicago's property tax levies in 1931–32 were delinquent.[21]

The increasing severity of the Great Depression ensured that tax delinquency—if not full-throated strikes—would spread to many other cities. Rising unemployment and deflation of wages and home values made mortgages and tax bills much harder to pay. A few far-sighted urban leaders, seeking to head off Chicago-scale fiscal chaos, embarked on campaigns to notch down municipal spending and tax levies apace with wages and property values in the private sector. Others—with, unsurprisingly, Newark and Boston in the vanguard—relied instead on public relations offensives:

entreaties on billboards and in storefronts to not "let our city down" and to "pay your taxes"; visits to those behind in their tax payments by "interviewers" (often teachers who could warn of the pernicious effects of tax delinquency on school quality); and even sermons from church pulpits.

A national "Pay Your Taxes Campaign"—funded in part by banks worried that tax strikes would slash the value of their portfolios of municipal bonds—perfected these tactics and took them on the road. High-profile academics, public officials, and business professionals were enlisted to sound the theme repeatedly, in print and on radio, that tax delinquency was unpatriotic and that attempts to constitutionally limit taxes and constrain public spending were unwise. In most major American cities, their arguments would triumph completely.

CURLEYISM'S LEGACY

The circumstances of the Great Depression and the philosophy of the New Deal tipped the scales of urban political economy decisively against tax limitation. With unemployment high, the appeal of job-creating public works programs was irresistible. Indeed, during his third term as mayor (1930–34), Curley argued long and loud that his Boston program should be duplicated at the national level; later in life, he would claim that he had inspired many New Deal works projects. As "pump priming" at the national level grew in public favor, it became difficult for local governments to resist the same logic. Agencies such as the Public Works Administration made it harder, offering federal dollars to help finance myriad construction projects as long as localities ponied up 55 percent of the costs. Who could resist proposals to clear slums, create affordable (public) housing, or modernize municipal buildings if 45 cents of every dollar spent was, essentially, "free money?"

Surely such spending alleviated some of the terrible misery that the Depression had brought. And the steadily rising taxes on physical capital that accompanied it had little effect for a while. During the 1940s, for example, when wartime production pushed the official unemployment rate as low as 1.25 percent and America's urban factories were running around the clock, not a single major city lost population—not even Boston (up 3.9 percent) or Newark (up 1.6 percent). In the long run, however, the tax rate differences between many core cities and their surrounding suburbs would alter investment patterns and rearrange populations in exactly the way economic theory would predict.

During the period 1950–1980, population fell in seventeen of America's twenty largest cities (as of 1950). Only Los Angeles, Houston, and Seattle grew; St. Louis's population fell 47 percent, Buffalo's 38 percent, and Pittsburgh's 37 percent. In three decades, the tally of lost residents in America's shrinking core cities would exceed five million, a remarkable shift. Those who remained found a greatly diminished range of economic and social opportunities. As their cities' tax bases eroded, so too did the quality of municipal services they could enjoy. Again, not all of this decline can be laid at the doorstep of unfriendliness to capital investment or insecurity of property rights; the "usual suspects" described in Chapter 1 were, undoubtedly, doing their dirty work. But urban tax policy was reinforcing and accelerating these other forces of urban decay.

As the exodus from core cities accelerated, the usual remedy was more energetic application of the policies that had contributed to flight in the first place: higher taxes on physical capital, more redistributive programs, ever-more-ambitious public works to eliminate blight and "renew" downtowns. The good news, however, is that while such policies were pursued widely for many years, a few cities did change course—though unwillingly—and thrive. Their experiences provide a road map for others, as we'll see in the next chapter.

CHAPTER 3

A 1-Percent Solution

PICTURE A STEREOTYPICAL 1960s revolutionary: youthful, long hair, denims, and rose-tinted granny glasses, discussing *Das Kapital* in a coffee house in Berkeley or Greenwich Village. Now imagine the opposite of all that, and you'll have a mental image of Howard Jarvis, the leader of one of the most consequential grass-roots movements of that era. Elderly, plump, jowly, clad in a rumpled suit and peering through thick glasses with enormous frames, he looked like a suburban Babbitt—and was, until he sold his home appliance business in 1962 and decided to change the world. For sixteen years he was spectacularly unsuccessful. His goal was to reduce the size and scope of government in California, chiefly by limiting its capacity to tax. Each time he ran for office, he lost. Each time he mounted a petition drive to get a referendum on the ballot, he failed. The media portrayed him as inconsequential or a dangerous crackpot.[1]

By the mid-1970s, however, economic forces in the United States— and especially in California—had made people more receptive to Jarvis's message. In 1978 he finally got his Proposition 13, which would cap property taxes throughout the state, on the ballot. That June, California voters approved it by an overwhelming 65-35 margin. Jarvis summarized his achievement in typically blunt fashion: "We have a new revolution. We are telling the government, 'Screw you!'"

His triumph would be called a "revolt of the haves,"[2] but it was really a *counter*-revolution. The decades following World War II had seen steady increases in spending at all levels of government, often to fund income transfers. Federal outlays rose from 17 percent of gross domestic product in the mid-1950s to 23 percent by 1975; the most explosive growth in transfers occurred in the mid-1960s, with President Lyndon Johnson's War on Poverty and Great Society initiatives. But many state and local governments, taking their philosophical cues from the New Deal and their political tactics from the playbook of James Michael Curley, had already implemented various redistributive programs by that time. Robin Hood had triumphed; in California, Jarvis skillfully shaped the frustration of Robin's targets into a policy response.

That response—Prop 13—routed the opposition because it was exquisitely well-timed and focused laser-like on the grievances of a large, much-ignored, and long-oppressed constituency: property owners. In short order, similar tax-limitation initiatives would sweep to victory in other states, and the over-arching theme that government needed somehow to be reined in was a cornerstone of Ronald Reagan's successful campaign for the presidency in 1980.

The indignation of California's "haves" had begun to build in the late 1960s with revelations that the property tax system was (unsurprisingly) corrupt. As Chicagoans had learned decades earlier, "tax fixing" was extremely lucrative for local politicians and therefore common. In San Francisco, for example, the county assessor was one Russell Wolden, long known for his ability to keep assessments reasonable—as long as owners came to the tax-consulting business Wolden ran on the side. There you would learn how to cut your tax bill significantly upon payment of a consulting fee that was usually set at half your tax savings.[3] That kickback scheme was exposed and Wolden sent to prison in 1965, and the following year legislation passed that took away much of local assessors' discretion and required more uniform assessment practices. As in Chicago in the 1930s, it was expected that these reforms would lighten homeowners' tax burden and shift more of it to businesses. Just as before, the opposite happened.

By the 1970s, then, California property owners were already grumbling about their ever-growing tax bills. Double-digit inflation rates—and in some areas steeper home price increases driven by one of the state's frequent real estate bubbles—eventually made them determined to do more than complain. They had three legitimate beefs.

First, tax bills that had doubled or tripled caused major cash flow problems for owners whose incomes had not risen apace (especially the elderly). While it was true that these higher bills reflected capital gains on their real estate investments, few wanted to uproot in order to realize those gains.

Second, the home price inflation and the higher tax liability it implied dissipated some of these owners' capital gains. Especially in jurisdictions with the highest rates, like San Francisco, tax capitalization was doing its dirty work, significantly reducing the real, after-tax returns on the investments of businesses and homeowners.

Finally, as economist William Fischel has argued persuasively, a 1971 decision by the California Supreme Court played a key role in Prop 13's appeal.[4] In *Serrano v. Priest*, the court effectively broke the link between local property tax levies and local school quality. Many affluent taxpayers in districts with high property values wanted to spend more on education and taxed themselves accordingly, a la Tiebout. The plaintiff in *Serrano* argued that poorer districts couldn't afford comparable school quality except at unaffordably high property tax rates and that the California constitution required that all districts should spend similar amounts per pupil. The court agreed, and the amount that any locality could spend on schools was capped and receipts above that amount redistributed to poorer districts. In effect, Robin Hood was dictating local education policy; accordingly, there was little reason for those in high-tax jurisdictions to resist Jarvis's arguments any longer.

Californians' elected representatives could have kept Jarvis's losing streak going by cutting tax rates slightly as inflation accelerated and their coffers filled to overflowing. They declined. There were, after all, so many worthwhile uses for taxpayers' money. By 1977, Jarvis had found that voters couldn't wait to sign his petition to put Prop 13 on the ballot. It pushed all the right buttons for property owners, capping property tax rates at 1 percent of assessed value, rolling back assessments to less-inflated 1975 levels, and limiting future increases in assessments to 2 percent per year until a property was sold, at which point the assessed value would be reset at the sale price. Perhaps best of all, it required a public referendum and a two-thirds affirmative vote on any attempts to raise the property tax cap in the future.

Jarvis's opponents predicted a disaster of epic proportions—a tidal wave of crime, shuttered firehouses and libraries, doubled class sizes in schools—if voters embraced his plan. Many were stunned that so many Californians were foolish (or angry) enough to do so. What is most surprising and important, however, is that the predicted cataclysm not only did not occur, Prop 13 actually *reversed* the decline of many of California's older, core cities.

IF YOU'RE GOING TO SAN FRANCISCO

In the 1960s and 1970s, San Francisco was a countercultural Mecca, drawing beatniks, hippies, gays, starving artists, rebellious musicians, and many others with flowers in their hair. It was attractive for a lot of reasons: a tolerant culture that accepted alternative lifestyles (including aggressive experimentation with mind-altering substances), elite academic institutions that provided intellectual fuel for a growing protest movement, and a natural and built environment that was truly inspiring.

The city's economy was also an attraction—but not in the usual way. By 1967, when twenty-thousand members of the counterculture gathered in Golden Gate Park for a "Human Be-In" that kicked off what would be romanticized as "the Summer of Love," San Francisco was well down the path of urban decline. Far more unhip were leaving than hip were arriving: the city's population fell 4 percent in the 1950s and another 10 percent between 1960 and 1975. As the city emptied, average rents fell: in the 1960s, they were on par with those in Oakland, and well below those in Los Angeles and San Diego. Many of its distinctive structures had decayed: the 1960 census rated only 83 percent of its housing "sound," down from 90 percent a decade earlier, and below Oakland's 85 percent and L.A.'s and San Diego's 89 percent rates. Of course, plentiful dilapidated, cheap housing was not a problem but an *attraction* for the new arrivals. Nor did they appear to mind that the city was losing jobs at an alarming rate (with manufacturing employment falling 28 percent over 1947–72), or that crime was exploding (with both homicide and total crime rates roughly double the national average by the early 1970s).[5]

None of this was a result of malign neglect by the city's government, which—guided by the best of progressive intentions—poured awesome amounts of money into state-of-the-art social programs. Between 1955 and 1965, while San Francisco was losing over thirty-five thousand residents, city government employment increased by over fifteen hundred and inflation-adjusted, per-capita spending soared by 80 percent. By contrast, Los Angeles's city government functioned on less than two-thirds as many employees and spent less than half as much (per capita). In a Tiebout-style world, where citizens vote with their feet and locate according to their preferences for municipal services and the tax price they pay for them,

San Francisco was flunking the market test. Not only was it suffering size-able net out-migration, many of its in-migrants tended to be poor or their behavior disorderly (the impetus for the Be-In, after all, was to protest a new state law making LSD illegal). When Hollywood needed a gritty (yet scenic) backdrop for crime movies and TV shows, the City by the Bay was a nice alternative to the Big Apple (think Clint Eastwood's "Dirty Harry" franchise). Herb Caen, who loved the city as much as anyone and celebrated its unique character in a long-running daily column in the *San Francisco Chronicle*, neatly summarized its condition in the late 1970s:

These may not be the best of times, but they could be among the worst. . . . [T]here was a time when everything seemed to work. These days, nothing does, starting with the workers. How is our little world of a city-state falling apart? Let me enumerate the ways: BART and ferries and teachers on strike. Bay heavily polluted again. Golden Gate Park falling apart. Cable lines shut down for months, maybe years, maybe forever. Streets more cluttered with debris than at any time within memory. . . . Union Square, "the heart of one of the few real downtowns," strewn with flotsam here, jetsam there, here flot, there jet, everywhere flot-jet.[6]

Then came Jarvis. Between 1950 and 1970, San Francisco had financed its spending spree by more than doubling its effective property tax rate, from under 1.5 percent of market value to over 3 percent. As population and employment melted away over the years and receipts from other tax sources weakened, the city budget had become increasingly dependent on the property tax. Therefore Jarvis was seen as Public Enemy #1 by elected officials, public employees and their union bosses, and opinion makers in academe and the media who saw Robin Hood government as a sacred duty. They hit him with everything they had. "If I were a communist, I would vote for Proposition 13," said former governor Pat Brown, since it would "destroy local government." Los Angeles Mayor Tom Bradley proclaimed that the initiative would "hit the city like a neutron bomb, leaving some city facilities standing virtually empty and human services devastated." Jerry Brown, son of Pat and in his first go-around as governor, warned that 270,000 to 450,000 jobs would be lost if voters joined Jarvis's counter-revolution.[7]

But, of course, they did—and none of the apocalyptic forecasts came to pass. At first, there were indeed small reductions in local government employment. One report tallied fewer than ten thousand layoffs from a workforce that totaled over 1.1 million; many of those municipal workers were soon reinstated. Some localities suspended summer school programs for a while, but in L.A., San Diego, and San Francisco, not a single firefighter, police officer, or teacher was dismissed or given notice. Oakland was briefly cited as an example of the terrible damage that Prop 13 would inflict when the city laid off sixteen police recruits on the same day they graduated from the academy—but as it became apparent that the initiative's budget fallout was far less severe than had been predicted, those rookie cops were quietly rehired.

In the near term, the budgetary shock absorber was the state government's enormous surplus, accumulated over many years as escalating inflation in the late 1960s and the 1970s pushed taxpayers into higher income tax brackets and pumped up sales tax receipts. Elected officials had tried gamely to spend that surplus down—state government employment had grown over 500 percent in the previous two decades while the state's population had increased only 56 percent—but by 1978 were nevertheless sitting on an unspent reserve of about $6 billion (twice as much as had been admitted during the campaign). Governor Brown did a skillful 180-degree turn, observing that "the people have spoken" and vowing to "make Proposition 13 work." He tightened state government's fiscal belt by instituting a hiring freeze, rescinding a promised 7.5 percent wage hike for state employees and welfare recipients, ending state funding for abortions for poor women, and dropping plans for pet projects such as a state-owned communications satellite. And, working closely with the legislature, he channeled $4 billion of the surplus into emergency transfers to local governments that suddenly saw their property tax receipts cut in half—or, in San Francisco's case, by almost two-thirds.[8] Writing sizeable checks to bail out localities was brilliant politically, since Brown faced a tough reelection fight that November and the handouts would make local officials and select interest groups appropriately grateful and supportive. But it was also necessary economically, since most of those officials had made no plans whatever to cope with the hole Jarvis and his followers had blown in their budgets.

What is notable and instructive is that those bailouts were not necessary for very long. San Francisco, for example, needed just $100 million from the state to balance its budget in fiscal year 1979, and $1 million in 1980. The following year it was off the state dole, and by its fourth "post-Apocalypse" fiscal year actually spent *more*, in inflation-adjusted terms, than it had before Prop 13 had been approved. How on earth could that have happened?

WELCOME BACK, CAPITALISTS

When it comes to tax policy, the most common blunder made by budget analysts and policymakers is to think "statically" rather than "dynamically." Static thinking assumes that human behavior is fixed; it often leads officials to assert that, for example, "every penny we cut from the city's property tax rate costs us millions in tax revenue!"—with no benefits that might partially or fully offset such losses. So it's not hard for them to imagine rate cuts of any appreciable size leading not just to belt-tightening but to permanent layoffs of police officers, firefighters, teachers, and so on. But human behavior is not fixed; we respond to incentives and disincentives—often very quickly.

In California, Prop 13 not only increased returns on investments in homes and businesses, but, perhaps more important, *protected those investments from further raids by Robin Hood.* Any attempt to raise the tax cap required approval by two-thirds of voters, and public support of Prop 13 was so strong that it soon became known as the "electrified third rail" of California politics: touch it and you die, politically. The effects were immediate and dramatic, especially in jurisdictions previously burdened with the highest tax rates and leadership most inclined to raise those rates further.

Flight from San Francisco stopped in its tracks—and, in fact, reversed (see Figure 3.1). Between 1980 and 2000, the city's population rose 14 percent, exceeding its 1950 peak level. This dynamic response to the city's suddenly favorable investment environment should not have been the utter surprise that it was. San Francisco, after all, had always been an appealing place. Its tax policy had simply made it unwise, economically speaking, to actually live and invest there. Doubling the city's tax rate between 1950 and 1970 had not only raised property owners' annual tax outlays

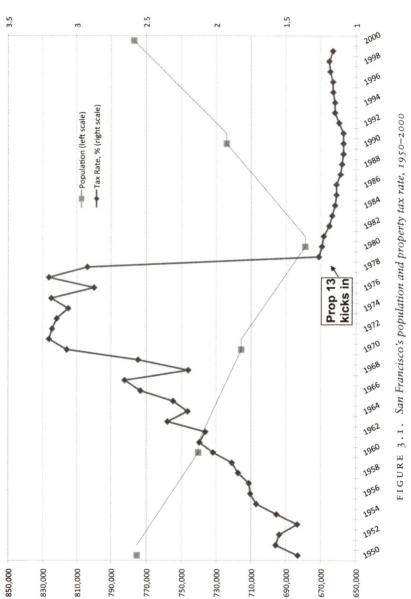

FIGURE 3.1. *San Francisco's population and property tax rate, 1950–2000*

SOURCE: U.S. Bureau of the Census, *County and City Data Book*, various editions; Office of the San Francisco Treasuer, *Annual Report*, various editions; author's calculations. Used with permission of *The Maryland Journal*.

stupendously, but—thanks to the relentless math of tax capitalization—imposed capital losses on them that, all else constant, exceeded one-fifth of a typical home's value. Fears about further losses—via additional tax rate hikes, or just ordinary inflation—had propelled many residents and entrepreneurs to the suburbs; Prop 13 welcomed them back.

As unhip capitalists joined the counterculturalists in going to San Francisco, the city's tax base expanded enormously and in a variety of ways. First, the new arrivals (and many employers) snatched up existing properties. They particularly looked in areas that had been emptying out and decaying most rapidly, for that was where the greatest bargains were to be found (in other words, where the previous high taxes and low investment rates had driven values down the most). Thus, almost immediately a surge in real estate transfer taxes started to offset the Prop 13–related decline in property tax receipts. More slowly, as in-migrants bid up prices and renovation proceeded, assessed values started to rise and those receipts began to recover as well.

In addition, despite toxic economic conditions nationwide—slow growth, high unemployment, and rapidly rising inflation, a combination that would be dubbed "stagflation" and help make Jimmy Carter a one-term president—new office towers started to sprout in downtown San Francisco. Because the city levied a payroll tax, the new jobs associated with these facilities, plus enhanced permit, license, and user fees collected thanks to a rising population and stronger local economy, all contributed to the rapid recovery and ultimate expansion of San Francisco's tax base and eventually *enhanced* the city government's capacity to spend. In effect, once "the haves" were protected from Robin Hood's excesses, they returned in sufficient numbers to provide the wherewithal to fund progressives' cherished programs more generously than when the Prince of Thieves had free reign.

Prop 13's fiscal dividend was not only sizeable but promptly delivered. San Francisco's total tax revenue (in inflation-adjusted terms) dipped for only three fiscal years after the initiative became law. By fiscal 1982, just four years after city officials had predicted Prop 13 would wreck the city, they actually collected 66 percent more inflation-adjusted dollars than they had in 1978. The investment boom and repopulation kicked off by Prop 13 rapidly replaced lost property tax receipts: between 1978 and 1982, sales and use taxes grew 39 percent, utility taxes 64 percent, parking taxes 139 percent, construction permit fees 167 percent, payroll taxes 177 percent, hotel taxes 204 percent, and business license taxes 446 percent.[9]

Most remarkably, by fiscal 1986 the assessed value of real property in the city had grown so much that, even with the property tax rate slashed to a third of its pre-revolt level, inflation-adjusted receipts from this source exceeded those realized in 1975 (the year to which Prop 13 had rolled back assessments). In 1982, a visiting correspondent from *The Economist* magazine reported, "San Francisco is embarrassed only by its riches. Its $160 million surplus is so large that a member of the Board of Supervisors has gone to court to try to make the city give some back to its taxpayers."[10] Given such resources, of course, municipal services could actually be improved, reinforcing the attractiveness of the city to new residents. Then-mayor Dianne Feinstein traveled the country and pointed to her city as a model of fiscal soundness; within a decade, its period of decline would be all but forgotten, and it would become a "superstar city."

IMITATORS AND RESISTERS

San Francisco was not the only post-industrial city that began to reverse several decades of population decline in the late 1970s. Neighboring Oakland, for example, which had lost 12 percent of its population over 1950–1980, grew 18 percent over the next two decades; again, Prop 13 deserves a healthy measure of credit for making that city's investment environment both more attractive and secure.

And California's famous tax revolution spawned imitators. The most successful was in the opposite corner of the country in Massachusetts, where property taxes had long been among the nation's highest. Once again, a court decision exposed the inequity, inefficiency, and outright corruption embedded in many localities' tax systems and animated interest in tax relief.[11]

In Boston, for example, by the late 1970s the statutory tax rate had climbed above 27 percent, to $272.70 per $1,000 of assessed value. Though homes were supposed to be assessed at about a quarter of their market value (which would have put the effective rate at a still-crushing 6.8 percent), actual assessment ratios varied greatly from neighborhood to neighborhood, and often were highest (nearing 100 percent of actual value) in poorer areas.[12] The problem was that the city's budget was chronically in crisis, and the city couldn't afford to hire adequate staff to assess property on a regular schedule. Officials just kept mailing out tax bills that were based on obsolete assessments, so effective tax rates were highest where property values had risen slowly or fallen, and lowest in more affluent areas where values had inflated. Through it all, Boston's bond rating slipped toward "junk" status and the city flirted with bankruptcy. Clearly, a high tax rate is no guarantor of solvency or high-quality municipal services when it is causing residents and employers to flee and the tax base shrinks.

Jarvis's Bay State imitators understood that property tax rates in many of the state's cities and towns were so high that a 1 percent cap might appear unreasonable to voters. They set their sights more modestly, getting a referendum on the state ballot that would limit any jurisdiction's property tax receipts to 2.5 percent of the assessed value of all property therein, and capping increases in such receipts at 2.5 percent annually (plus any amount attributable to levies on new property). "Prop 2-1/2" passed by an almost 3-to-2 margin in 1980 and became law in 1982.

As in California, there were shrill warnings from elected officials that the initiative would decimate local government. Layoffs of public workers (always those considered most crucial to voters' welfare: police, firefighters, teachers) and major service cuts were announced. Then, quietly, rehiring and restoration of services occurred as the budget implications of the proposition turned out to be far less severe than advertised. Just as in California, creating a more appealing investment environment for physical capital produced a dynamic response.

Boston had lost 30 percent of its residents over 1950–80 and 12 percent just between 1975 and 1980; in the next two decades, its population grew 5 percent. Median household income in the city grew 38 percent faster than the national average over 1979–2005. The rate of violent and property crime fell 59 percent and the murder rate fell 31 percent over that period. Despite continued public chafing at the budget constraints imposed by Prop 2-1/2, the city's fiscal condition improved rapidly; its bond rating was steadily revised upward until it received an "A" grade by the late 1980s. One 1985 report on the city's economy began with the pronouncement, "It's unanimous: Boston is a boomtown," and told how the city was enjoying "redevelopment . . . unprecedented so far this century" with over $3 billion (equivalent to $6.5 billion in today's dollars) in new, private investment planned for the following five years.[13] Like San Francisco and Oakland, Boston enjoyed a rapid turnaround once it protected property owners and investors against further raids by Robin Hood. Before very long, the city's Curley-initiated march into decline would be forgotten, and it would be celebrated as another superstar city.

What is most curious about these reversals of urban fortune, however, is that they were not widely emulated. The case of Baltimore is instructive. It had much in common with its sister bayside cities in the post–World War II era. Like them, it routinely took from the well-off propertied in order to give to those more needy. Between 1950 and 1975, the city raised its property tax rate 19 times, to double its former level. This was 19 successive expropriations of property owners' wealth. Predictably, many residents and employers fled—though by some measures, Baltimore fared less badly than Boston and San Francisco over that period. Its population had fallen less (10 percent, against San Francisco's 14 percent and Boston's 21 percent declines), and its 1975 violent and property crime rates were lower (19 percent below San Francisco's and 53 percent below Boston's)—though its homicide rate was higher.

But Baltimore declined to join any of the tax revolts underway then—or since. Part of the reason might be that opinion makers didn't help voters connect the dots: coverage of the booms in California and Massachusetts cities hewed to the story line that these happy events occurred in spite— rather than because—of those states' tax cut initiatives. Another factor was the progressive political culture that prevailed among Baltimoreans (and Marylanders), who tend to scoff at the notion that lower tax rates of any kind might have significant favorable economic effects. This too the city shared with Bostonians and San Franciscans. The difference was that voters *outside* Baltimore had no real reason to take up the tax-cutting cause and save the city from its own fiscal folly: property tax rates in every other jurisdiction in the state were (and are) less than half that in Baltimore. Nor were there any publicized inequities or inefficiencies in assessment practices to inflame voters and ignite a statewide revolt.

Baltimoreans could, however, vote with their feet—and they did. While Boston, Oakland, and San Francisco were repopulating and recapitalizing, Baltimore got smaller, poorer, and less safe. Its population fell 20 percent over 1980–2010. Its real median household income fell 6 percent over 1979–2005 (while the nation's was rising 2 percent, Boston's 26 percent, and San Francisco's 35 percent). Its homicide rate rose 38 percent over 1975–2005 (while San Francisco's fell 38 percent and Boston's 31 percent).

In effect, then, Baltimore and many cities like it—all the "Rust Belt" cities that continued to spiral downward while Boston revived were high-property-tax jurisdictions—were simply unable to break the fatal grip of the "Curley Effect." As they raised property tax rates, they repelled "tax donors" and attracted "tax consumers." The idea of nontrivial property tax cuts that could attract investment and residents in the long run faced insurmountable political obstacles in the short run: those tax consumers would fight hard against any policy proposals that seemed to require any belt-tightening, and there were simply too many of them to defy.

Which is not to say that such cities failed to see that they had a problem. But instead of attracting new investment by making their property tax rates more competitive for *all* their residents, they usually just subsidized projects by large, politically well-connected developers. Baltimore, for example, rebuilt its waterfront with an extravagant program of tax credits for new hotels, office towers, and other downtown amenities.[14] The oft-repeated rationale was that this would catalyze investments elsewhere, but as we have seen, the promised chain reaction did not eventuate. The rest of the city continued to decay and often serves as a stage set for grisly crime dramas. This should not have been a surprise: investing without the special incentives awarded by City Hall still made no economic sense. But, of course, the ability to award such subsidies enhanced public officials' power—and made fund-raising easier—so there has been little reason for them to alter their inefficient and discriminatory strategy even in the face of its evident failure.

Thus, unless a "1 (or 2 1/2) percent solution" is imposed from without, as in California or Massachusetts, there seems little hope that depopulating, investment-starved cities will adopt such a policy voluntarily. Even if, as in San Francisco, a tighter budgetary belt can be loosened in, say, the fourth budget cycle and dynamic growth enhances fiscal capacity after that, it would take a very brave politician to pursue such a radical course. In politics, four years is an eternity, and four years of budget austerity—especially when the majority of voters are tax consumers—looks like a route to political oblivion. What mayor wants to tell public employees' unions that there will be wage freezes for a few years, but after that money will roll in and all will be well? What interest groups want to hear that their pet programs will be cut in the near term, but funded more generously down the road? Little wonder, then, that the elected officials of San Francisco, Oakland, Boston, and other municipalities fought hard against the very cuts that eventually revived their cities.

How can this Gordian knot be cut? How can local leaders' focus be changed from short-run political costs to the long-run economic benefits of capital-friendliness? By, in effect, building a bridge before it's necessary to cross the financial river.[15] That is, by calling forth a fiscal dividend with a credible commitment to a future tax cut that broadens the city's tax base and makes the lower rate "affordable" and thus politically feasible in the near term.

CASH ON DELIVERY

In San Francisco and Boston, officials had to cope with a sizeable tax cut that they neither wanted nor expected. The fact that the cuts were a result of statewide referenda gave them political cover in dealing with the immediate budgetary fallout, but what really rescued them was the fact that the dynamic effects of these cuts arrived reasonably quickly and with strength, so that they could restore—and eventually increase—spending levels within a few budget cycles. In recent years, for example, San Francisco has been spending more than twice as much on city services as Baltimore, per capita, and Boston 27 percent more.

But what if the dynamic effects of a property tax rate cut could be harnessed in advance of its arrival? What if the promise of a sizeable rate cut *to be delivered at a future date certain* caused businesses and residents to start investing or relocating to the soon-to-be-more-favorable tax environment *today*? If so, the result would be an immediate in-flow of added tax receipts from various sources: higher transfer and recordation taxes as the real estate market heated up; increased property tax receipts as tax capitalization worked in reverse and as owners upgraded their property;

added local income and sales taxes (if levied in a particular locality) as population began to grow. Such receipts would then be locked up in an escrow fund that could later be tapped to offset eventual short-term reductions in receipts that occur once rates go down.

Could such a plan work, or would skeptical property owners simply stand on the sidelines and wait for that "date certain" before venturing where Robin Hood had long held sway? Clearly, a key factor here is the credibility and durability of any promise to cut taxes. The strength of the investment booms following Props 13 and 2-1/2 owed in large measure to the fact that these initiatives are very difficult to undo. Factories, shops, office towers, and homes are long-lived assets; those risking their wealth on such investments do not just want to know that their yield will be attractive, but that they will be secure from expropriation decades later. Any city that wishes to follow San Francisco or Boston along the path to superstardom must commit to a tax rate that is both competitive and essentially unchangeable. Few will invest where Robin Hood can emerge from hiding and reduce their returns to zero—or below—whenever convenient. Accordingly, it will be crucial that any promised rate cut, like those that have endured in California and Massachusetts, be secured with stipulations that it can only be undone by voters themselves—and only then with the approval of a super-majority.

With that condition met, there is strong evidence that changing an investment environment from hostile to friendly and secure does indeed cause investors to rush in. After all, "first movers" enjoy the greatest advantages and the highest yields when they target distressed markets and buy when and where prices are lowest. And given the long time horizons of investments in real property, the fact that tax rates will not fall to competitive levels for a few years after purchasing, improving, or building such property should matter little. Bostonians, for example, did not stand idly by during the nearly two years between the time Prop 2-½ was voted upon and when it was implemented as law. Nor were they much bothered by the initiative's step-by-step phase-in process, which stipulated that localities need not cut property tax receipts by any more than 15 percent in any single year on their way to compliance with the law. Nor did they worry about how bureaucrats would reform the city's previously chaotic tax assessment system. Protected by the law's virtually unalterable ceiling on their future tax liability, they made Boston a boom town immediately—even as the nation suffered a deep recession that drove unemployment to double-digit levels in late 1982.

Another key condition, of course, is fiscal discipline between the time a credible commitment to a rate cut is made and the date it is to be delivered. If the escrow fund can be raided throughout that period for any reason—from addressing cyclic shortfalls in revenue to buying the political loyalty of key interest groups—then it likely will be inadequate to the task of smoothing the fiscal bumps in the road that cities such as San Francisco and Boston had to cope with when their property tax receipts were suddenly forced downward. Accordingly, any city embarking on this strategy would need to adopt spending affordability limits that bind agencies and departments to live within their means and make the accumulating reserves in the escrow fund strictly off limits.

Creativity as well as discipline will be necessary to build the requisite financial bridge. Necessity was the mother of fiscal invention as San Francisco and Boston grappled with the near-term budgetary fallout from their states' tax revolts. Each city hunted for new revenue from sources that would be less damaging to their economies than the property tax, and they found them: new and higher user fees on some services; asset sales (including auctions of previously worthless, tax delinquent property that, at a lower tax rate, suddenly had value); cost savings from the elimination of unnecessary development subsidies and from the privatization of some services. But should all such measures fail to accumulate enough cash when the date to deliver the rate cut arrives, then debt financing similar to current "tax increment financing" commonly used by urban redevelopment authorities to stimulate investment could fill any remaining gaps.

Undeniably, there is much about this strategy that could go wrong; in any plan, the devil is often in the details. As the cities that have already delivered sizeable property tax rate cuts demonstrate, however, a growing tax base is the best and most reliable way to ensure an adequate stream of revenue to local government. Keeping Robin Hood bottled up in Sherwood Forest is a key step in making that happen.

IF YOU SECURE IT, THEY WILL COME

The experiences of Boston, Oakland, and San Francisco since their states' tax revolts are remarkable and instructive not just because of what happened in those cities, but because of what did *not* happen. Each began to reverse an outflow of population almost immediately upon adoption of a property tax system that assured homeowners and business owners that the value of their investments in fixed capital would not be—indeed, *could not be*—appropriated by local elected officials for reasons of which they did not approve. Amazingly, nothing else much changed before in-migrants began to arrive and new investments began to be made.

None of these cities experienced electoral turnover that altered their political cultures in any appreciable way. All were Democratic strongholds—indeed, liberal bastions—both before and after the tax reforms that kickstarted their revival. That didn't seem to matter to the new residents and investors. True, the political environments in which they were putting their wealth at risk had long been characterized by redistributive reflexes, ranging from corrupt Curleyism to an eager embrace of tax-and-spend renewal policies. Evidently, though, what mattered most to investors was not these cities' casts of political characters and their programmatic impulses but dependable rules and institutions that kept those impulses in check.

What's more, none of these cities "solved" what most experts and opinion makers would have identified as their most pressing problems in order to attract the in-migrants. All had experienced several decades of population loss, economic decline, demographic change, and budget crises. All had high crime rates, underachieving school systems, crumbling infrastructure, and a host of other deficiencies that popular wisdom said needed to be fixed before the cities would again appeal to new residents and investors. None of these conditions instantly disappeared, and yet people came. As they arrived, of course, they got to work improving the neighborhoods in which they lived—putting more "eyes on the street" and cutting crime, fixing up older properties, supporting and stimulating the growth of local shops and restaurants, and growing the tax base so that their local governments had greater capacity to fight crime, educate children, and make capital improvements. But all of these benefits *lagged* tax reform and repopulation rather than led it.

Of course, none of this should be taken to mean that low property tax rates are a cure-all for urban ills, or that high rates are necessarily fatal. As Tiebout taught, tastes for municipal services and the taxes that fund them can vary widely. Even people paying a low tax rate might want to flee a city that delivers negligible service flows. On the other hand, those in jurisdictions with high rates may be quite content because they are receiving fair value for their tax bills.

The property tax system can doom a city, however, when its leaders *break the link* between tax costs paid and benefits received. Obviously, corruption or inefficiency in the delivery of governmental services can do so, but so will redistributive policies that originate at the local level. Even the best-run programs that create a nontrivial gap between how much taxpayers pay for local government and how much they get back in return can tempt them to search, Tiebout-style, for a more pleasing combination of taxes and services. If nearby suburbs promise a better return on tax bills, then a city's attempt to do good by redistributing from rich to poor will, over time, likely come to naught as flight of population and wealth gradually leaves it without much of anything to redistribute.

The key lesson of Curleyism and Jarvis's counterrevolution, then, is that the cornerstone of a successful, economically vibrant city is *secure property rights*—for "the haves," the working class, entrepreneurs, and everyone. When carried out at the local level, redistributive schemes can lead to an enormously wasteful rearrangement of population. When protected against the cash flow problems and capital losses that such schemes hold for them, residents and investors seem quite willing to repopulate and recapitalize troubled cities without any other major preconditions.

Which is not to say that redistribution is a bad thing. There is a broad social consensus, in fact, that some amount of redistribution is both necessary and desirable—though, clearly, there is considerable disagreement about the *proper* amount. What is clear is that Robin Hood probably operates most efficiently (that is, with the least bad side effects) at the regional or national level rather than the local one.[16] In many countries, for example, it is a cliche to say that "the poor are the king's (or queen's, or premier's) problem" rather than the responsibility of the mayor. Since localities in such circumstances will find it easier to maintain the link between tax costs and benefits, they can generally better prevent the kind of flight many American cities suffered in the last half of the twentieth century.

As we will see in the next chapter, however, damaging redistributive schemes are not the exclusive domain of local government officials.

CHAPTER 4

The Conquest of Capital

THE "BATTLE OF THE RUNNING BULLS" was fought in freezing weather in Flint, Michigan, on the night of January 11, 1937.

No military forces were involved. Just a few hundred striking auto-workers, their supporters, and about forty-five city cops (the "bulls"). The weapons and tactics used on each side were not sophisticated. The strikers sprayed fire hoses and hurled bottles, stones, and small auto parts at the police, who had begun the skirmish with a barrage from tear-gas guns but who, by its end, were in full, panicked retreat, firing pistols wildly at their pursuers. Unlike in other legendary battles of that era between the forces of labor and capital, there was no loss of life, though thirteen strikers suffered gunshot wounds and eleven policemen were injured by assorted missiles. The confrontation nevertheless counts as one of the key turning points in labor history—and in the destiny of American industrial cities.[1]

The battleground adjoined Fisher Body Plant No. 2, a General Motors (GM) facility that normally employed a thousand workers and produced 450 auto bodies daily. On the fateful night, no more than a hundred members of the nascent United Auto Workers (UAW) occupied No. 2's second floor. They were practicing a newly popular and very bold labor strategy—the sit-down strike. Instead of protesting their wages or working conditions by setting up a picket line outside the plant on public property, on December 30, 1936, they went to their posts and simply sat. A larger plant, Fisher Body No. 1, was also held by UAW sit-downers, but No. 2 seemed the more weakly defended, and GM moved to retake that facility first.

The company knew it faced an ingenious and formidable threat. The occupation ensured that production would stop and that it could not restart with non-union "scab" workers—otherwise a virtual certainty, given that the UAW, at the time, composed a small fraction of the GM workforce. Being inside the plant gave the strikers protection not just from the harsh elements but from the company and local cops who might come to dislodge them. And though some argued that the tactic constituted illegal trespass, none of the sit-downs attempted by various unions in preceding weeks had been successfully challenged in court or opposed by public authorities.

There was, of course, considerable downside for the occupiers, even apart from their lost wages. Though food was prepared at a local restaurant and carried up to them (after inspection by plant police), they were sleeping on floors or auto seats arranged into crude beds, dealing with primitive sanitary facilities, and isolated from friends and family. As time passed, their numbers dwindled and their morale suffered.

On the sit-down's thirteenth day, GM encouraged the occupiers' departure by shutting off heat to the plant and preventing delivery of their evening meal. Far from capitulating, the union mobilized. A young organizer named Victor Reuther—later dubbed "the General" by his peers—manned a sound car to gather reinforcements outside the plant and give marching orders to those inside, who emerged to rout the company guards at the gate. The latter retreated to a ladies room and called the city police to report that they had been "captured."

That brought the bulls with the tear-gas guns. When they advanced on the plant, the occupiers rained debris down on them, while the picketers outside pressed in to join the fray. The area was soon filled with hand-to-hand combatants surrounded by a swirl of gas, smoke, water, and flying objects, until the outnumbered police were driven back, taking a position on a bridge above the Flint River. From that vantage point, they fired gas shells at long range until about midnight, but never mounted another assault on the sit-downers.

The violence and bloodshed had an electric effect. Michigan governor Frank Murphy scurried to Flint, where he mobilized the National Guard to enforce an "armistice." The whole world was soon watching. A long stalemate ensued, despite the efforts of Murphy and U.S. Secretary of Labor Frances Perkins (with behind-the-scenes help from President Franklin D. Roosevelt) to broker a deal. Murphy himself considered the sit-down illegal under then-prevailing law, but also a morally just defense of workers' rights. In effect, he felt torn between property rights and human rights, and tried to walk that fine line as he mediated the negotiations.

But the result was inevitable: victory for the union and surrender by GM. For the UAW had chosen its target incredibly well: the assets it seized in Flint were crucial to GM's viability. They included dies that fabricated key parts without which many of GM's other plants could not operate; in effect, the union controlled the company's beating heart, on which its entire health depended. As the sit-down went on, more and more of the company's assets were idled, and it fell to its financial knees.

Flint changed everything. The UAW, previously viewed skeptically by most autoworkers, was now incredibly appealing and powerful; other national unions quickly adopted its methods and became similarly muscular and effective. Over the next several decades they used that power to enormously increase the returns to their members' labors. The effects on American industry, non-union workers, and urban form, however, have been less favorable.

To see how these unions succeeded in their conquest of American industrial capital and understand the long-run consequences, it's necessary to review a bit of Detroit's history prior to the Battle of the Running Bulls.

A TARGET OF OPPORTUNITY

To call Detroit a boom town during the first third of the twentieth century would be to damn it by faint praise. It was blessed with abundant natural capital in the form of proximity to water transportation that provided easy access to nearby hardwood forests and mineral deposits that fueled the growth of carriage makers, tool works, and other manufacturers. In time, rail lines were built that carried Detroit's products to many more (and more distant) markets, so by 1900 the city was the thirteenth most populous in the United States. By 1930, however, it was home to over 1.5 million and America's fourth-largest city, its astounding 450 percent population growth rate quadruple that of New York and Chicago and nine times that of Philadelphia during the same period.[2]

It's also worth noting—so that race-based theories of urban form can be kept in perspective—that Detroit's black population increased twenty-fold, to 120,000, from 1910 to 1930 and another 150 percent (to 304,000) by 1950. That the city was attractive to both whites and blacks during this period was understandable: by 1949, the median family income of Detroiters was higher than that of any other city in America except Chicago (whose residents enjoyed a median family income just a dollar higher), and 29 percent above the national figure. In other words, while Detroit's economy functioned well, its large and rapidly growing minority population was not a destabilizing, "white flight"-inducing force but both a reason for and symptom of its success. It was only after its economy began to erode and its population began to fall that pundits assumed that racism—no doubt present, but likely showing little variation over the decades—was a major player in this drama.

The key to Detroit's success, of course, was its status as the nation's center of innovation and production in the thriving auto industry. But this was not just a happy, accidental result of the fact that many of this industry's founding figures had grown up or begun careers nearby—including Henry Ford in Dearborn, William Durant in Flint, Ransom Olds in Lansing, and the Dodge brothers and David Buick in Detroit itself. Rather, these entrepreneurs built on a foundation of industrial, intellectual, and financial capital that was well-suited to working out the engineering and production problems associated with this rapidly evolving product.

The success of the earliest automotive innovators in Detroit attracted more, in a dramatic illustration of economist Alfred Marshall's description of the economies of industrial agglomeration:

When an industry has thus chosen a locality for itself, it is likely to stay there long: so great are the advantages which people following the same skilled trade get from near neighbourhood to one another. The mysteries of the trade become no mysteries; but are as it were in the air, and children learn many of them unconsciously. Good work is rightly appreciated, inventions and improvements in machinery, in processes and the general organization of the business have their merits promptly discussed: if one man starts a new idea, it is taken up by others and combined with suggestions of their own; and thus it becomes the source of further new ideas. And presently subsidiary trades grow up in the neighbourhood, supplying it with implements and materials, organizing its traffic, and in many ways conducing to the economy of its material.[3]

So while auto production in the industry's early days was not exclusive to Detroit, it became more concentrated there because this enhanced the competitive advantages of both the firms and their host city. Firms in Detroit benefited from lower-cost links to suppliers of inputs and components, access to a larger and deeper pool of labor with specialized skills, and—perhaps most important—the technological spillovers resulting from proximity to talented minds grappling with similar problems.

One disadvantage of this co-location eventually became clear, however. The facilities necessary for the efficient design, production, and distribution of autos and related goods were installed at an incredible rate, attracting not just laborers but those who would unionize them. In effect, agglomeration economies reduced firms' production costs and accelerated innovation, but the concentration they begot also reduced the cost of organizing and maintaining cartels of labor. In concentrating their assets, automakers had made them a bit more vulnerable to those who might take them hostage, and who could focus their forces on this task rather than divide them among many targets spread more widely.

Automakers were not unaware of this vulnerability. In 1901, for example, some workers at an Olds factory in Detroit joined a national strike for higher wages and shorter workdays. When non-union workers kept the plant running, the strikers and about five hundred sympathizers tried to occupy it, and three people were injured in the brawl that ensued. Olds soon built a new facility ninety miles away in Lansing—perhaps the first example of union-related flight of capital and jobs from Detroit. As historian James Rubenstein observed, "avoiding concentrations of militant workers influenced location decisions even in the early days of the automotive industry."[4] But agglomeration economies were too important to ignore, and, overall, the labor climate in Detroit seemed benign: the city was regarded as a non-union town, and Michigan was then an "open shop" state (in which union membership was not a condition of employment, even in unionized firms). And in 1902 the city's leading industrialists had formed the Employers' Association of Detroit, which worked to eliminate any "closed shop" agreements between member employers and unions, supplied members with substitute non-union workers if and when a strike occurred, and marshaled legal resources to obtain injunctions against certain union practices and even arrest union leaders if these injunctions were ignored.

As a result, in the early decades of the twentieth century, unions usually represented less than a tenth of Detroit's labor force. And, as we have seen, the city's growth was spectacular, while its industrial base was an engine of prosperity not just for entrepreneurs, managers, engineers, and traders, but for laborers as well. In 1930, there were 275 U.S. counties with at least five thousand manufacturing workers within their borders. Those in Michigan's Wayne County (which includes Detroit and adjacent cities such as Dearborn, Hamtramck, Highland Park, and River Rouge) earned average wages higher than those in all but three other counties—which contained Youngstown and Warren, Ohio, and Gary, Indiana (where the nation's largest steelmakers had facilities). Manufacturing wages in Detroit exceeded the national average by fully 33 percent, and when compared to wages in smaller factory towns elsewhere the contrasts were even more dramatic. Factory workers in El Paso, Texas, for example, earned only 60 percent of what those in Detroit earned, while workers in York, Pennsylvania, earned 56 percent as much and those in Greenville, South Carolina, 40 percent as much.[5]

Detroit's absolute and relative prosperity is difficult to reconcile with pro-union rhetoric during this period and historic treatments since, which stress the need for countervailing power for workers in the face of employers' unfettered control of labor markets. Absent collective bargaining, the story goes, workers routinely are exploited with unjust wages and inhumane working conditions. Even if this assertion is accepted at face value, however, one would think that any battle to improve workers' welfare should start, or at least be focused, where wages were *lowest*, conditions worst, and the need for worker empowerment clearly greatest.

It did not. Instead, the efforts of America's most active labor organizations were most intense in those locales where abundant capital had already improved laborers' productivity and standards of living to levels far greater than those experienced in areas of relative capital scarcity. The bulk of labor history for this era is written about offensives against not just the owners of the burgeoning plants of Detroit, but the mills of Youngstown (average wages 37 percent higher than the national average); Gary (34 percent higher); Chicago, Cleveland, and Pittsburgh (all 19 percent higher); and Buffalo (14 percent higher). The factory workers of El Paso, York,

Greenville, and hundreds of other locales were largely ignored, at least at this time. This was not an oversight, but the mark of a brilliant strategy.

OPPORTUNISTIC BEHAVIOR 101

Bargaining collectively rather than competitively allows workers to set higher prices for their services. We all learn this as children playing "Monopoly," in which cornering a market allows us to fix very attractive prices indeed. In the case of labor markets—in contrast to others such as, say, that for crude oil—there is a broad social consensus that this is well and good, for at least three reasons. First is the aforementioned belief that employers hold all the cards in such markets, and that competitive forces are insufficient to protect workers from exploitation. This is the "fight fire with fire" argument for collective bargaining, in which the market power of employers is met with equal or greater power from unions. Then there is a social justice rationale: even when labor markets are competitive and contain many employers bidding against each other for workers, justice is served by tilting the playing field in workers' favor in order to shift wealth from the owners of capital to laborers. Finally, some argue that unions provide valuable services both to employers and workers (by, for example, giving them a voice in managing the enterprise), thus offsetting unionized labor's higher costs.[6]

There's some validity to each of these views, at least in certain circumstances. When economists have studied the record of real unions over time, however, they have generally found less evidence of favorable effects on worker welfare than one would hope. In particular, dispassionate researchers (in other words, those not employed at union-funded institutes or think tanks) tend to find that unions (a) often win higher compensation for members, but that these premia vary considerably over time and across industries; (b) reduce employment in sectors they dominate; (c) have a near-zero effect on worker productivity; (d) reduce firms' profits by capturing returns that would otherwise flow to durable tangible and intangible capital; and (e) reduce capital investment and productivity growth.[7]

In sum, encouraging workers to "play Monopoly" can have unwholesome effects on a regional and national economy—like similar behavior in other markets, from oil to software. But set aside such concerns for a moment, for there's often something that unions can do in addition to set-ting monopolistic prices that has profound implications for firm decision making and urban form. After a "collective bargain" is reached and highly specialized productive assets are put in place, unions can take these assets hostage and capture *additional* returns from the owners of this capital. Economists have dubbed this "opportunistic behavior,"[8] and its ingenious nature can be illustrated with a simple example.

Suppose an entrepreneur devises a wonderful product that can generate revenues of, say, $100 million. First she needs to hire workers and construct a factory at a cost of $40 million each, or $80 million total (assuming away details like raw material costs, taxes, advertising, and so on, to keep the math simple without changing the thrust of the story). That'll leave her with a tidy $20 million return for her efforts to design the product, orga-nize its production, and bring it to market, so this thing looks like a go.

But while our entrepreneur posts help-wanted notices and breaks ground on the factory, the area's workers "get organized" in order to bargain col-lectively. They demand higher wages that will raise her total labor bill to $50 million. This would reduce her net to $10 million. Hmm. If she can earn more on other ventures, she might just say "no thanks" and walk away (with obvious implications for the local economy and the workers them-selves). But, thinking that half a loaf is better than none, she accepts those terms, signs a contract with the union, and builds the factory—a decision, by the way, for which she garners an award for socially responsible man-agement from a local business school for creating jobs at a "living wage."

Now the plot thickens. As her product starts to roll off the assembly line, the workers sit down at their machines and simply stop working. Major buzz kill for our entrepreneur, who was anticipating recouping her investment in the plant and capitalizing her next project. Instead, she's shocked to hear the union's demand: put another $20 million into our pension fund, or we will occupy the factory indefinitely.

This seems totally unacceptable. The math doesn't work. Even if she sells all her output and collects the expected $100 million in revenues, she's in the red to the tune of $10 million after deducting the costs of the factory ($40 million), her workers' above-market wages (another $50 mil-lion), and this unexpected $20 million pension contribution.

She explores legal options but gets no help. Yes, her contract with the union forbids such "wildcat" job actions, but there's also some hazy language about worker safety, and some of the guys on the line are complaining about carpal tunnel syndrome. Plus, litigation to put a stop to this would drag on a while—by which time she might be out of business—and the outcome is uncertain. The marketing department offers no reason for hope, either: raising product price to pump up revenue is ruled out because competition in this product line is intensifying by the day.

So our chastened entrepreneur curses under her breath, smiles bravely, and says, "Deal—now back to work." This won't make her business profitable, but it will minimize her loss. If she refuses the union's ultimatum or closes her factory, she's out its entire $40 million cost. A $10 million loss is the lesser of those two evils. Indeed, she might murmur a quiet word of thanks that the union didn't demand as much as, say, $49 million for its pension fund. That would have inflicted a $39 million loss, but even that would have been better than shutting down the whole operation. She is sadder, poorer, and wiser.

In real life, of course, entrepreneurs might not submit to such opportunism very easily. In addition to appealing to courts for help (and "shopping" for an appropriate jurisdiction where the interpretation of labor and contract law might be more sympathetic), they might try to wait out the strikers in the hope that the latter's pockets might be emptied before the firm's, or they might hire scabs—which could necessitate the deployment of "security personnel" to fend off the strikers seeking to take a facility hostage. In practice, these tactics and more have been attempted in job actions, but all are costly and risky. They might reduce the returns to opportunism, but do not alter the fundamental fact that specialized capital is vulnerable to appropriation by unions, and is thus more secure when and where unions are less powerful.

THE BIRTH OF THE RUST BELT

Though firms in Detroit and other northern industrial cities had kept unions more or less at bay for the first third of the twentieth century, the onset of the Great Depression created an extremely favorable ideological and political environment for unionization. The erroneous but widespread belief that falling wages and prices were a *cause* of the Depression rather than necessary adjustments to restore growth in employment and output contributed (alongside other factors) to the passage of several pieces of federal legislation that encouraged the cartelization of labor and product markets.

The National Labor Relations (or Wagner) Act, which eliminated many of the strategies commonly used by firms to defend the value of capital, was especially important. It took labor disputes out of the courts and vested enforcement of the Act in a politically appointed board, prohibited several "unfair labor practices" judged to be obstacles to organization, and enforced exclusive bargaining and union pay rates for all workers— whether union members or not—in board-certified bargaining units. But taking away a few defenses against the ever-more-sophisticated tactics of unions just increased firms' reliance on the remaining ones—especially *strategic redeployment of productive capital to less vulnerable locations.* Over time, this would have dire consequences for union towns.

The Wagner Act was signed into law in July, 1935; in August, the newly chartered UAW held its first convention in Detroit. The union correctly judged that piecemeal, plant-by-plant organizing efforts could not generate the market power needed to raise autoworkers' wages—again, already among the highest in American industry—to the desired heights. It cast its lot with those advocating industrial unionism, which sought to organize all the workers within a given industry into a single union (in contrast to craft unionism, in which various skilled trades unions could coexist within a firm), and set its sights on the industry's largest enterprise: GM.

It's hard to overstate the tactical brilliance of the UAW's campaign to monopolize GM's labor force. In late 1936, union officials learned that the company had only two factories producing the dies that stamped out the body components for all its cars. If they could take control of these the entire company would grind to a halt; in effect, *all* the firm's assets could be taken hostage by offensives against just two of its facilities. GM had placed them in Cleveland and Flint, away from Detroit's increasingly militant labor climate. Flint, especially, was a "company town" that seemed defensible. Only a fraction of its forty-seven thousand GM autoworkers had joined the UAW; city officials and police were in GM's pocket and its spies were everywhere. One union organizer, upon checking into a Flint hotel, was greeted with a phone call telling him to get out unless he wanted to be "carried out in a wooden box."[9]

In late December 1936, the union's own spies learned that GM planned to move the all-important dies out of Flint, and the UAW quickly initiated the Great Flint Sit-Down, the turning point of which was the Battle of the Running Bulls. GM tried all the usual counter-measures during what would turn out to be a forty-four-day "siege from within," from injunctions issued by friendly local judges to the earlier-described assaults by police. All failed. And without the crucial supplies from these plants, production slowed or stopped everywhere else. Eventually, GM's output fell from fifty-three thousand cars per week before the sit-down to fifteen hundred, and 140,000 of its 150,000 workers were idle.

On February 11, 1937, GM capitulated and recognized the UAW as the exclusive bargaining agent for its unionized workers. A sit-down strike at the union's next target, Chrysler, won a similar agreement the next month. Thus legitimized, within a year UAW membership grew from thirty thousand to five hundred thousand—fully half in Detroit. Henry Ford was a tougher nut to crack, vowing that the UAW would organize his company "over my dead body" and attempting to use violence and intimidation to fend off organizers. But an April 1941 sit-down strike at the huge River Rouge Ford plant finally led to his surrender. Reportedly, he had planned to break up his company and sell the plants for scrap rather than sign a contract with the UAW, but Ford's wife threatened to leave him if he did not cooperate with the union so that the family business survived and their son and grandsons could continue to run it.

Labor historian Sidney Fine therefore judged the 1936–37 GM sit-down strike "the most significant American labor conflict in the twentieth century."[10] It not only gave the UAW the means to capture a large portion of the returns to the auto industry's capital in succeeding decades, it demonstrated to laborers and employers the tactics that could lead to successful cartelization of labor supply in other industries.

Iron and steel workers' unions, for example, had been moribund for decades, but in March 1937, U.S. Steel (of Pittsburgh and Gary), its management fearful of the same sort of upheaval that had cost GM so dearly, signed a contract with the union that would become the United Steel

Workers. Smaller firms—Republic (of Cleveland and Chicago), Bethlehem (of that city and Baltimore), Lackawanna (of Buffalo), Youngstown Sheet and Tube, National (of Weirton and Detroit), and Inland (of Chicago)—attempted the Ford approach of violence and intimidation, including the Memorial Day Massacre of 1937 (in which Chicago police opened fire on strikers and sympathizers approaching the Republic mill, killing ten). Like Ford, however, by 1941 all had capitulated.

In sum, at the onset of World War II most of America's great industrial firms—which were concentrated in cities throughout the East and upper Midwest—now faced labor cartels. These cartels consolidated their power and flexed their muscles even during the war, when (in the popular imagination) the nation was strongly united and all pulled in the same direction. Their main tools of opportunism were the wildcat strike and sit-down. When wartime exigencies required auto plants to be retooled to produce military output on which lives depended, the UAW had made a no-strike pledge. Nevertheless, in 1943 there were 153 wildcat strikes in its plants, and in 1944 there were 224 involving over half the workers in the industry. Across all sectors, according to Bureau of Labor Statistics data, in 1943 alone over thirteen million man-days of production were lost to strikes—equivalent to idling over fifty-three thousand full-time workers (roughly three army divisions) for the year.[11]

Increases in employers' labor costs and reductions in their degree of management control would be significant but gradual. In the aftermath of the war, during which America's industrial rivals' productive capacity had suffered heavy damage that would be restored only slowly, firms were insulated to a great degree and for a considerable time from the competitive consequences of monopolistic pricing and opportunistic behavior by their unions. It was still possible to point to the U.S. auto industry as a reasonably healthy sector, even as many of its firms went bankrupt (so long, Hudson, Nash, Packard, and Studebaker) and it consolidated into a "Big Three." The survivors, in the public mind, were not headed to eventual bankruptcy themselves but laudably "sharing their prosperity" with workers.

But these firms and most others in capital-intensive industries in the post–World War II era were changing their behavior in ways that standard economic theory would predict—and that would ultimately help create what became known as America's Rust Belt. Union actions, clearly, were not the only reason that industrial cities would decapitalize, depopulate, and become poorer in the second half of the twentieth century, but they certainly merit inclusion on the list.

GOODBYE, AGGLOMERATION

As the owners of fixed capital began to understand fully its vulnerability to "hostage taking" in the post–New Deal economy, they made some countermoves. Though unions continued to operate with near-military discipline and still held the upper hand in their adversarial relationship with management, they soon found their opponents retreating to more defensible environs—followed by a stream of refugees.

In the decade following World War II, GM spent $3.4 billion, Ford $2.5 billion, and Chrysler $700 million on new facilities, almost all in rural areas "as a means of reducing wages and inhibiting union militancy in manufacturing cities like Detroit."[12] Detroiters decried these "runaway shops," but many simply followed the capital and the jobs it supported. From 1947 to 1958, manufacturing employment in Detroit fell 40 percent, a net loss of 134,000 jobs. Accordingly, between the 1950 and 1960 censuses, the city's population fell by 180,000, or 10 percent. The engine that had powered Detroit's rapid growth in the first half of the twentieth century was now operating very powerfully in reverse—and well in advance of the racial tensions of the 1960s, the completion of the interstate highway system, or the onset of globalization popularly assigned much of the blame for flight, sprawl, and deindustrialization.

And Detroit's experience, of course, just illustrates more dramatically and rapidly the trends unfolding in other industrial cities. Unfortunately, city- or metro-area data on the extent of unionization are not available for the decades of the 1950s and 1960s, but data on the extent of unionization in urban areas from the early 1970s make clear that the strength of unions was negatively and significantly related to subsequent population changes in core cities.[13] Cities with above-median unionization rates lost, on average, 7 percent of their residents from 1970 to 2000; those with below-median unionization *grew* an average of 32 percent over that period.

Faced with above-market prices for labor, the threat of opportunism, and work rules that limited their flexibility, industrial firms did not just flee. They reconfigured production in important ways. For example, using land intensively in urban settings (rather than extensively in rural ones) previously had enabled firms to realize enormous benefits of industrial agglomeration. Now they reduced their reliance on the more-expensive labor input and substituted capital and land, the relative costs of which had fallen.

In describing the resulting trend toward sprawling, more heavily auto-mated plants in low-density areas, observers have generally supposed that these technologies were new and superior and that adopting them was inevitable (given "capitalist greed"), if unfortunate. But the availability of cheap land outside cities was not new or unknown to capitalists, and neither was the ability of capital to substitute for labor. These adaptations were not made because a bolt of lightning had struck capitalists and in-formed them of the existence of low-cost rural sites and labor-saving de-vices, but because firms were confronted by a new array of input prices. Had the relative costs of labor, land, and capital not changed, it is entirely possible that many manufacturers would have decided not to eschew the many benefits of urban location and agglomeration.

We'll never know—nor will we know whether any technological spill-overs of the kind described by Marshall might have, over the decades, made U.S. industrial firms more innovative and globally competitive. Defenders of unions such as the UAW generally blame the declining fortunes of heavily unionized industries on bad managers selling poor products. They rarely contemplate whether such results become more likely once the "myster-ies of the trade" are no longer "in the air" but spread all over the map. Once trespass and appropriation of the value of physical capital by unions became (de facto) legal, it was inevitable that this capital would decamp for more secure locales. Its owners' main failure was in overlooking how much this strategic redeployment might cost them in other respects.

What we do know is that the consequences of capital flight and reduced labor demand were dire for the residents who remained in America's rap-idly deindustrializing cities. Figure 4.1 shows a scatter plot and trend line linking a metro area's level of unionization in 1973–75 to the subsequent

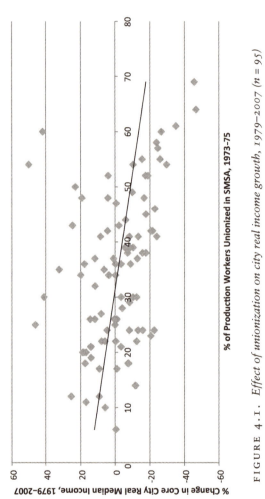

FIGURE 4.1. *Effect of unionization on city real income growth, 1979–2007 (n = 95)*

SOURCE: U.S. Bureau of the Census, *County and City Data Book*, various editions; R. B. Freeman and J. L. Medoff, "New Estimates of Private Sector Unionism in the U.S.," *Industrial and Labor Relations Review*, vol. 32, no. 2, pp. 143–75; author's calculations. Used with permission of the Cato Journal.

(1979–2007) change in its core city's real (inflation-adjusted) median income. Just as with population changes, the correlation is negative and significant. Cities with above-median unionization rates got poorer, their real incomes falling an average of 7.6 percent over the relevant period; those with below-median rates of unionization saw 4.5 percent *growth* in their real incomes.

It would be simplistic to say on the basis of this negative correlation that muscular unions are fatal to the destiny of cities. In any economy, there are always myriad forces interacting to influence key outcomes; the declining incomes observed in many heavily unionized cities might simply be an unhappy coincidence. At the very least, however, *there's no evidence that unions consistently deliver shared, widespread prosperity to their host communities.* Once capital starts to flee these communities, population densities start to fall, the benefits of urban agglomeration are discarded, and less-healthy cities seem an inevitable result.

LAST ONE OUT, TURN OFF THE LIGHTS?

Today, of course, much of Detroit is in ruins. Its median household income, once 29 percent above the national level, is now 44 percent below it; its poverty and crime rates are over three times the national averages. And while it would be nice to say that Detroit's experience is an aberration and other Rust Belt cities are on the rise, most are simply less *un*healthy. Of course, dry statistics on population or income do not convey the enormity of the problems that result from or are compounded by diminished economic opportunities in cities.

Sociologist William Julius Wilson has written forcefully of the social and cultural consequences of the "spatial mismatch" between labor demand and supply that was a by-product of urban deindustrialization.[14] Abundant industrial capital had long made American cities an economic launching pad for generations of immigrants, but its flight left the most recent migrants to cities—especially blacks participating in the "Great Migration" from the rural South to northern cities over 1916–70—with far more limited economic options. For many, Wilson has argued, this has meant persistent joblessness; such detachment from the labor force and limited exposure to the working- and middle-class populations that followed the capital out of cities have contributed to the creation of an urban underclass. For this population, flight of capital and jobs kicked off an unwholesome cycle that has adversely affected a host of social variables, from family formation to education attainment to the propensity to engage in crime.

It is noteworthy that the steep decline of America's deindustrializing cities occurred despite renewal efforts of astounding magnitude funded by remarkable infusions of cash from state and federal government coffers. Throughout the post–World War II period, incalculable billions were spent clearing slums and erecting public housing; installing transit lines that served ever-dwindling populations; or subsidizing the construction of convention centers, hotels, sports facilities, or other infrastructure in troubled inner cities. Each new public investment was touted as a "game changer" that would stanch the outward flow of population, jobs, and wealth—but little actually improved.

Economist Edward Glaeser has criticized this strategy as fundamentally flawed: "Scores of close to worthless urban projects have received government funding not because any cost-benefit analysis has justified them but because of hazy claims that they would make some once-great area thrive again."[15] The problem, he argues, is that such expenditures are misdirected. They are, primarily, attempts to *save places* rather than *help people*—and if many simply no longer want to live in a particular area, the money spent on renewal projects that are effectively attempts to bribe them to stay in place is simply wasted. Glaeser recommends people-based rather than place-based programs, such as enhanced education programs that will enable children to earn more when they become adults, wherever they choose to live. If that's outside the Rust Belt, so be it.

His approach is certainly correct as far as it goes. And he is undoubtedly right that many of the federal and state dollars thrown at urban infrastructure in declining areas could have been better spent. But perhaps Glaeser is excessively pessimistic about the fate of some places. We need to ask: Are the population declines in post-industrial cities such as St. Louis, Detroit, Cleveland, Buffalo, and many others really irreversible?

The answer is that we really don't know. Sure, winters are cold in the Rust Belt; maybe the advent of air conditioning has permanently altered people's willingness to endure summer heat and humidity in Sun Belt lo-cales. Or maybe technological advances have so fundamentally changed the American economy that ready access to natural capital in the form of lakes, rivers, forests, and mines no longer matter much for business (and therefore residential) location decisions. But we can't know these things for sure, because we really haven't addressed some underlying conditions that, alongside changing tastes and technology, may also be contributing to these cities' downward trajectories.

Recall: dreary Boston lost 30 percent of its population over 1950–80, almost as much as Cleveland or Buffalo (down 37 percent and 38 percent, respectively). It would have been tempting to write the place off and start devising programs to manage its decline. But as we saw in the last chap-ter, a statewide tax revolt radically altered Boston's future, transforming it into a boom town. A lower property tax rate made the city friendly to new capital investment; more important, the fact that this rate was secured by a popular referendum protected property owners over the long haul by tying the fiscal hands of potentially opportunistic public officials well-versed in the art of "Curleyism." The Hub's population grew 10 percent over the next three decades.

Boston didn't need sun to make people want to live there—just as San Francisco and Oakland, thanks to California's tax limitation initiative, didn't need drastically improved schools or miraculously safer streets. These cities simply needed more secure property rights: business- and home-owners had to know that their leaders' long-established habit of appropriating large portions of the value of their investments in fixed capital was at an end.

But, as we have seen in this chapter, the tax environment for investment in commercial or residential capital is not all that matters for the viability of an industry and its host city. The laws and regulations guiding relations between the owners of capital and labor also will have profound impacts, for good or ill. And since most of these appear to be determined at the national level, one might think that there's very little that state or local policymakers can do to correct problems in this area. Happily, though, as we'll see in the next chapter, this presumption is false.

CHAPTER 5

A Better Climate

KEN IVERSON made his first visit to a steel mill in 1947, while studying metallurgy at Purdue University. Because most other industrialized countries were recovering from the devastation of World War II, "Big Steel" was riding high in the United States, producing more output than the rest of the world combined and banking profits that made life very comfortable indeed for executives and unionized workers alike. A class trip to U.S. Steel's Gary, Indiana, facility seemed like a good way to learn the state of the steelmaking art.

What Iverson saw, however, was a dinosaur: massive, slow moving, and destined for extinction. "We were going through the plant," he later recalled, "and we actually had to step over workers who were sleeping there."[1] The highest-paid industrial workers in the world, enjoying an afternoon nap surrounded by capital equipment that, unbeknownst to them and the young students conscientiously taking notes, was fast becoming obsolete. Germany and Japan were not only energetically rebuilding their industrial capacity but experimenting with new production methods that would compete successfully with American mills that made raw steel in huge blast furnaces. The upstarts often used smaller-scale technologies, including electric-arc furnaces that recycled scrap into simple steel products at a fraction of the cost of their U.S. rivals.

By 1962, Iverson was working for a small company with a checkered past: Nuclear Corporation of America traced its origins to Ransom E. Olds, who had founded the Oldsmobile division of GM and later a startup he called REO Motor Company, producer of the famous but unprofitable REO Speed Wagon. REO went bankrupt in 1938 and reorganized, but continued to leak oil through the mid-1950s, when shareholders used what little cash the company had left to reorganize as Nuclear. Their strategy was to acquire distressed companies and turn them around; the name was taken from a tiny nuclear services consulting company that was their first takeover target. They missed more often than they hit, however, and veered toward bankruptcy again in 1965. The conglomerate's only reliable profit center was Vulcraft Corp., which made steel joists and girders in a small plant in Florence, South Carolina. Iverson ran it.

Desperate, Nuclear's board put the thirty-nine-year-old in charge of the entire outfit. He moved its headquarters to Charlotte, North Carolina, to be close to Vulcraft yet have access to a larger city's transportation infrastructure and banks, and then took the gamble of his life. He toured new mills in Europe and knew he had seen the future of steel. Vulcraft bought expensive steel ingots from European or U.S. producers and fabricated its products from them; Iverson wanted to start with cheaper steel, and to do that he had to make it himself. He mortgaged the company to buy a German-designed electric furnace that had never been tried commercially. Within nine months he built what would be called a "mini-mill" in Darlington, South Carolina, melting and purifying scrap (often junk cars) and turning out extraordinarily cheap raw steel that could be sent on to fabricators such as Vulcraft.

Iverson had not only saved his little company but revolutionized the U.S. steel industry, which seemed unable to fend off those pesky, innovative foreign competitors. Imported steel's share of U.S. consumption quadrupled between 1962 and 1982, from 5 to 20 percent, and would go higher. But Iverson's Nucor—he changed the company name in 1972 to reflect its distance from matters nuclear—not only could compete, but usually beat foreigners' prices. Nucor built a new mini-mill almost every year, made strategic acquisitions, and grew spectacularly. By 2000 it was America's largest steel company, ending U.S. Steel's century-long hold on that rank.

The management philosophy at the heart of this success was simple, egalitarian, and old-fashioned. Iverson, who died in 2002 at age seventy-six, kept the layers of company bureaucracy to a minimum, trusted his local managers and workers with considerable autonomy, and eschewed visible signs of status differences. During most of his tenure, corporate headquarters in Charlotte consisted of rented space in a strip mall and the executive dining room was a deli across the street; execs always flew coach to business meetings. Most important, though, everyone's compensation was strongly linked to performance. Nucor's non-union workers' base wages were well below those in the big, integrated steel companies, but with bonuses that ranged from 80 to 150 percent of base pay, they could out-earn unionized workers if productivity warranted. Usually, it did. If demand lagged, Nucor effectively shared the pain, with shortened work weeks for all; under Iverson's stewardship, no Nucor worker was ever laid off.[2]

Duplicating the incentives, flexibility, and decentralized decision making that fueled Nucor's rise might have been exceedingly difficult—if not impossible—in a highly unionized, bureaucratized setting like that of Big Steel (or Big Autos, or Big Anything). Of course, as the company grew from nothing into something, the United Steelworkers made several attempts to organize its workers, but always failed. The union faced an uphill battle because Nucor's facilities were small relative to those of the integrated firms, geographically scattered, and located in areas where sentiment ran against the collectivist ethos of Big Labor. In effect, Iverson's 1947 field trip had warned him of the vulnerability of large-scale, capital-intensive industries. Such operations were like castles to which an opposing army—as GM had learned in the Great Flint Sit-Down—might successfully lay siege. In contrast, he dispersed his forces widely, like guerillas in more easily defensible encampments.

As this strategy was imitated in other industries, of course, it had enormous implications for the American economy and the destiny of states and cities. Conversion to smaller-scale, less-centralized production methods kept some domestic industries, like steel, from being utterly vanquished by foreign competition. But embarking on this survival strategy also meant forgoing some potentially important productive benefits, such as the gains from agglomeration discussed in Chapter 4, or those from vertical integration or larger-scale production. The mini-mills proved to be economical recyclers, for example, but the steel they produced was not suitable for all uses; the big integrated operations still had a role to play, if they could be made more efficient. Mini-mills were a nice Plan B given the evident problems of Big Steel's Plan A, but that raises a question: Is it possible to make Plan A viable again in *any* industry? Can large-scale, integrated production thrive in America again—and if so, can it happen in urban areas?

In this chapter we further explore this issue and its consequences for cities, beginning with a more detailed assessment of the behavior of firms such as Nucor and proceeding to a discussion of methods by which the benefits of a more competitive labor market might help revive America's basic industries—and the Rust Belt cities from which they frequently fled.

DEFENSIBLE PLACES AND THE "RIGHT TO WORK"

Nucor isn't the only company that has scattered new factories throughout the South since the 1960s. While GM, Ford, and Chrysler, for example, were slashing employment in Detroit and elsewhere, Nissan was building huge plants in Tennessee and Mississippi, Mercedes-Benz in Alabama and Georgia, BMW in South Carolina, and Honda and Hyundai in Alabama.

This trend has led many to assume that these firms were simply attracted by better weather and cheaper land and labor; that the old industrial Northeast faces insurmountable competitive disadvantages vis-à-vis the Sun Belt. There's some truth to this, of course. All else equal, some might prefer to spend January in Darlington (mean temperature 44° F) rather than Pittsburgh (29° F). But, of course, *all else is not equal*. Setting aside the issue of the quality of life in a small southern town versus the big-city North—surely a controversial topic—this presumption ignores some other obvious trade-offs. As was noted in Chapter 4, for decades firms happily ignored cheap rural land in order to capture urban agglomeration's benefits, have better access to information and other inputs, and more easily tap bigger markets for their goods. And lower-wage labor can sometimes be less productive and profitable, as well: skills (the "mysteries of the trade") matter. It's worth noting that when Nucor's Darlington furnace commenced operation, most of its new workers had never been in a steel mill before; at their first sight of molten steel, many ran out of the building in terror.

What's more, the Sun Belt was not the only beneficiary of the strategic relocation of a great deal of America's industrial capacity throughout the post–World War II era. Nucor has steel-making facilities not just in the Carolinas and the Deep South, but in Brigham City, Utah (average January temp: 26° F), Crawfordsville, Indiana (25° F), and Norfolk, Nebraska (23° F).

What these sites have in common is not superior weather but a *better climate for business*. For example, all are in states where the ability of labor cartels to form and appropriate the returns to capital are somewhat limited—that is, they're in "right to work" (RTW) states in which workers have the legal right to decline to join the union (and, as well, decline to pay union dues) even at formally unionized firms. In the jargon of labor law, RTW states prohibit the "closed shop"—in which all workers at a firm must join the union and pay dues (or be fired) once a majority of them vote to be represented by that union—in favor of the "open shop." Clearly, the term *right to work* is a misnomer, as state RTW laws do not guarantee anyone a job, but simply remove union membership as a condition of employment.

RTW foes correctly point out that such laws create a free rider problem for unions. They must hire organizers to convince workers to let them bargain on their behalf, retain negotiators to perform that task and lawyers to write the necessary contracts (which specify not only wage levels but also work rules that govern relations with management), and pay staff to police these contracts and administer the employer-employee relationship in myriad other ways. Then non-members might simply invoke the RTW law to benefit from all the work done on their behalf without kicking in their fair share of the costs in the form of dues. Since the 1935 National Labor Relations Act requires that private unions must provide contract benefits to all employees, whether members or not, non-members may indeed "ride for free." And if they do so, the union's costs will be spread less widely, so members' dues will rise and tempt more to free ride.

Defenders of RTW laws often assert that this problem is of minor concern, and that in any case RTW serves a larger moral purpose, preserving an individual's right *not* to be compelled to give financial support to an organization with which he or she may disagree, either politically or philosophically. True enough—but an argument that is sometimes invoked insincerely, for when proposed RTW laws come up for public debate it's hard to believe that the corporations write large checks to their lobbyists chiefly because they're worried about their workers' rights under natural law. More likely, employers see the free rider problem as one of the chief attractions of RTW laws—a way of cramping union organizers' style. In at least one important respect, unions are just like businesses: if they have a tough time recovering all their costs, they may operate on a more modest scale, or not at all.

Surprisingly, though, there's little hard evidence that RTW laws keep union wolves from capitalists' doors. Some studies have found evidence that organizing activity diminishes after a state adopts RTW, but most have concluded that a new RTW law's net effect on a state's unionization rate is modest, reducing membership by as little as 3 to 5 percent, all else the same. The consensus seems to be that a state's adoption of an RTW law reflects prevailing (negative) attitudes toward unions, and that such legislation is a key *signal* that the state is favorably inclined toward business—and not just with respect to labor law, but regarding tax and regulatory policy, too.

With that in mind, economists have looked hard at how RTW might affect business location decisions and local economies. The evidence suggests that the presence of an RTW law is attractive to employers—especially those in the labor-intensive manufacturing and construction industries—and that adoption of RTW significantly improves employment prospects and wage growth. Two warnings about this evidence are in order, however. Discussions of RTW laws—indeed, of all issues related to unions—are contentious. There are big bucks at risk for both labor and business, of course, but even those without a direct stake in these contests often see these issues through an ideological lens in which one side is good and the other evil. This can yield more heat than light and invites "advocacy research" in which data are carefully mined for preordained conclusions. In addition, even dispassionate study of the topic isn't easy to do well. There's a lot going on simultaneously with respect to labor markets and investment decisions, and it will be easy to misattribute to RTW some influence that might well belong to some other factor. Caveat emptor. In what follows, I will try to summarize what I think is known, though these issues are far from settled.

RTW, BUSINESS CLIMATE, AND ECONOMIC PERFORMANCE

There are now twenty-four RTW states. A dozen are in the South, but seven are in the upper Midwest and five in the Rockies or the West. Most of these states adopted RTW legislation in the late 1940s and the 1950s (following the 1947 passage of the Taft-Hartley amendments to the Wagner Act). Only five states have passed such a law since 1961, most recently Oklahoma in 2001 and Indiana and Michigan in 2012. And on the surface, at least, it's easy to see why RTW advocates get excited about these laws' potential to stimulate economic development: from the late 1960s through the onset of the Great Recession in 2007, RTW states have outperformed non-RTW states on many key economic measures. Two reports for the Mackinac Center for Public Policy (which, while nonpartisan, long advocated RTW as a way to revive Michigan's industrial sector) tallied the raw data and concluded that, over this period, RTW states enjoyed greater growth of employment and output, lower average unemployment rates, larger reductions in poverty rates, and smaller increases in income inequality than non-RTW states.[3] And while per-capita disposable incomes are slightly lower in RTW states (a reason foes say it is a "right to work *for less*"), incomes have grown faster there, implying convergence of living standards.

But such descriptive statistics might be misleading. Perhaps the RTW states' geographic locations, demographic characteristics, or other key trends (such as changes in transportation costs) or policies (such as tax rates) are responsible for their superior performance. Robert Newman performed the first careful assessment of RTW laws' influence on industry migration, examining state-level employment data from the 1960s and 1970s and controlling for various national and local characteristics.[4] He found strong evidence that RTW positively affected job growth over that period, especially in labor-intensive industries. Further, this was not just "a southern thing," as northern RTW states also grew more rapidly than the national norm, and non-RTW southern states less rapidly. A spate of RTW studies followed, and a careful review by William J. Moore concluded that "RTW laws have a significant, positive influence on industrial growth and economic development,"[5] though, again, since they likely signal an overall favorable business climate, RTW laws alone should not be considered a panacea.

The most bullet-proof study of RTW's potential impact is by Thomas Holmes, who ingeniously looked at trends in economic activity along the borders between RTW and non-RTW states.[6] The logic here is that making apples-to-apples comparisons requires one to focus on localities that differ as little as possible from each other, apart from RTW. This method is like investigating the age-old nature-versus-nurture question by looking at identical twins raised in different environments; if they behave differently, you can't blame the nature (genetic) part. Holmes found that, over 1947-1992, manufacturing employment grew much more rapidly on the RTW side of a border: within twenty-five miles of a border, for example, employment grew 61 percent more on the RTW side. In sum, where the climate, culture, topography, access to transportation, and quality and quantity of labor differed little, employers were much more likely to expand in the environment where RTW (no doubt proxying for other favorable policies, as well) reassured them about the security of the returns to their capital investments. What's more, this growth effect was not limited to the southern states: in the Great Plains region, manufacturing employment in RTW localities within twenty-five miles of the border grew 90 percent more than those on the non-RTW side.

When I examined the effects on states' economies of broader indicators of business climate—not just RTW, but other labor market institutions and government-imposed costs—I found strong and favorable effects on the measured poverty rate.[7] Indeed, in the period studied (the 1970s), improvements in business climate, especially when this strengthened the local manufacturing sector, more consistently reduced poverty than did increases in public aid or vocational education spending.

Of course, it's possible that the RTW party is over—that prospective gains attributed to it and other capital-friendly policies happened to coincide with shifts in the U.S. economy that have run their course, and that this policy tool now has little capacity to spur local economic development. To consider such qualms, it will be useful to study some recent adopters of RTW.

BOOMIN' BOISE

The major media don't pay much attention to Idaho—it is, after all, in what the pundits call "fly-over country." But this state of 1.6 million (as many as reside in Manhattan, but spread over thirty-six hundred times more acreage) can teach us a lot about the possible causes and consequences of RTW legislation. To some extent, Idaho has been running a controlled experiment for us. It's not geographically blessed in terms of climate, access to natural or man-made transportation infrastructure, or proximity to major markets. Its RTW law passed after most of the precipitous national decline in private-sector unionization already had occurred, perhaps mitigating any presumed competitive advantages of RTW. And Idaho made no other major policy changes providing incentives for firms to relocate to or increase their investments there during the relevant period. If RTW can make a difference here, maybe it can make a difference anywhere.

Much of the political impetus for RTW likely came from Idahoans' awareness that their three RTW neighbors (in contrast to the three non-RTW states with which they also share borders) enjoyed healthier labor markets and faster growth. But Big Labor inadvertently helped kickstart the campaign. In 1984, employees of the Bunker Hill Mining Company had voted for wage and benefit cuts to keep the century-old but financially troubled firm from going bankrupt. Union bosses back in Pittsburgh overruled the concessions, however, and fifteen hundred jobs were lost. Anti-union sentiment grew, and an RTW bill was introduced in the legislature in 1985; it passed after much rancorous debate in 1986 and (though challenged in court) took effect in 1987.

The results have been encouraging. Emin Dinlersoz and Rubén Hernández-Murillo compared Idaho's performance to that of its neighbors (to control for overall national or regional economic trends) for the decade before and after implementation of the state's RTW law and found strong evidence of favorable effects on manufacturing employment, the number of manufacturing establishments, and their average size. In the decade before adoption of RTW, Idaho's manufacturing employment growth rate was actually negative, even lagging that of two of its three non-RTW neighbors. In the decade after, its employment growth rate leaped upward to 3.7 percent annually, comparable to its now-fellow RTW neighbors Nevada (4.3 percent), Utah (3.1 percent), and Wyoming (2.7 percent), three times the rates in non-RTW Montana and Oregon (1.2 percent), and nine times that in Washington (0.4 percent).[8]

What's more, Idaho's RTW law seems not only to have encouraged growth in the number of manufacturing establishments (the annual rate of increase rising seven-fold, from 0.6 to 4.1 percent), but also in their size. This is consistent with evidence found by Holmes in his national sample, and is important because it tells us something about how RTW laws reassure investors about the security of their property rights in large-scale, capital-intensive enterprises. As we saw in Chapter 4, there can be enormous efficiencies in massive, vertically integrated facilities—but such investments also might be taken hostage and their returns appropriated more readily by a powerful and opportunistic union. Apparently, capitalists are more willing to take that risk when an RTW law complicates unions' lives, potentially diminishing their incentive to organize workers or reducing their access to cash and foot-soldiers even if they've done so.

And investors notice. Steven Abraham and Paula Voos examined the stock prices of Idaho-based firms in the period before and after passage of RTW.[9] The logic of such "event studies" is that after controlling for forces that cause normal market fluctuations in the price of a firm's shares, additional (or "abnormal") price movements attendant to a particular event reflect investors' beliefs about how it will affect the future viability and profitability of that firm. Abraham and Voos found that the cumulative average returns to shares in Idaho firms increased by 2.4 percent thanks to its RTW law. They obtained similar (indeed, somewhat stronger) results for Louisiana's adoption of an RTW law in 1976.

Idaho's enhanced economic and employment growth also significantly improved the fortunes of its largest city, Boise (which, if you want to blend, you will pronounce BOY-see rather than BOY-zee). Its population has increased by two-thirds since the 1990 census, though that was partly a result of annexation of some surrounding unincorporated territory. But the city did not merely sprawl outward: its population density rose 7 percent between 1990 and 2000, even as it increased its land area 38 percent.

And Boiseans' median household income, which had been 3.1 percent below the national figure in 1990, moved 1 percent above it by 2000. Measured poverty in the city fell from 6.3 percent to 5.9 percent, and the fraction of families enjoying incomes more than twice the official poverty level rose by three percentage points. Labor force participation ticked upward, and unemployment has been consistently below the national average. What's more, as Boise has boomed, its residents' quality of life has been rated highly by diverse sources, earning top-ten rankings from various places-rated surveys, raves from *Inc.* magazine as a hot destination for business entrepreneurs, and excellent grades (sixth among U.S. cities) on Earth Day Network's "urban environment report." Critics are welcome to argue that all of this is purely coincidental and has little to do with RTW or other elements of Idaho's business climate—but it hardly supports the notion that RTW laws mean that workers inevitably settle "for less."[10]

OKC IS, WELL, OKAY

Another RTW experiment has been under way for a little more than a decade in Oklahoma, where the field of political battle over the law was similar to that in Idaho. Three of the states with which Oklahoma shares a border are RTW and three non-RTW, and Sooners' awareness that their RTW neighbors seemed to have an easier time attracting businesses and creating jobs doubtless contributed to the eventual success of the campaign. Nevertheless, it was a long, hard slog from the first introduction of RTW legislation in 1993 to its adoption via a statewide referendum (which passed 54-46) in 2001.

Nationally, of course, the succeeding decade was not an easy one, economically. In addition, unions fought Oklahoma's RTW law in the courts until 2003, narrowing the window for evaluation. And recently the region has benefited from an energy boom that likely explains more of the year-to-year variation in Oklahoma's economic performance than a change in its business climate. So we need to take the data for this period with a grain of salt, though there nevertheless seems to be more encouraging evidence that RTW can aid a troubled economy—or, at the least, does no great harm, as its critics usually claim.

Though manufacturing employment fell in Oklahoma (mirroring the national trend) over 2003–10, its total private-sector employment rose 3.2 percent but was flat in its non-RTW neighbors and fell 1 percent nationwide. Oklahomans' total compensation (wages plus benefits and bonuses) in private-sector jobs rose 12.2 percent more than inflation, well above the 3.4 percent rate for the United States as a whole. Such income increases were possible in part because of significant increases in labor productivity: in manufacturing, for example, output per worker increased 22 percent more in Oklahoma than it did in non-RTW states over that period.

And, as in Idaho, the state's improving economic climate carried benefits for its largest city. The population of Oklahoma City (OKC) surged 15 percent between the 2000 and 2010 censuses, and its residents appear to have coped with the Great Recession reasonably well. They started the decade (pre-RTW) with a median household income 17 percent below the U.S. average and ended it 15 percent below. While the national poverty rate went up 0.9 percentage points, OKC's went up 0.2. The city's civilian job base grew 16 percent, versus 9 percent for the nation as a whole, and its labor force participation rate grew three times faster. Not great, but in all respects above average—which, outside Lake Woebegone, not everyone can be.[11]

Also encouraging are some small changes in the city's educational profile. In the past decade, the fraction of OKC residents over age twenty-five who are high school dropouts has fallen 3.1 percentage points (from 18.7 to 15.6 percent), while the proportion of college grads is up two percentage points (from 15.9 to 17.9 percent). Tiny changes, assuredly, but worth watching, for it might signal that making a place more hospitable to physical capital investment can also be welcoming to those with useful stocks of knowledge and skills. Economists Edward Glaeser and Albert Saiz, especially, have stressed the importance of highly mobile human capital in determining the fate of urban areas.[12] Since human and physical capital are partners in production, however, it should not be surprising that friendliness toward the latter can strongly affect the location decisions of those possessing the former.

TRIFLING NO LONGER

Despite its status as a certified boom town, Charlotte suffers from an inferiority complex. This might date as far back as 1791, when George Washington called it a "trifling place." Or it might be the standard insecurity felt by the nouveau riche when vying for social acceptance from Old Money—an insecurity fed by the media in top-tier cities. When, for example, Charlotte spruced up its business district to entertain fans attending the NCAA's Final Four basketball tourney in the 1990s, the *New York Times* sniffed that it was a "Potemkin Village with a drawl."[13] And a *Washington Post* report on the city's rise to prominence was dismissively titled "Charlotte: It's Got a Football Team and a Bright Future. All It's Missing Is Personality."[14]

Poor Charlotte: so busy creating jobs, making money, and improving residents' quality of life that it hasn't had time to develop an identity. But that hasn't kept it from lapping its northern rivals. In 1950, the city's population was a mere quarter that of Buffalo; today, it is three times as large. The *Times* joked in 2000 that you know you're a Buffalonian if "half your friends moved to Charlotte, N.C., and the other half went to Raleigh."[15] In every census since World War II, the Queen City's population has increased by 20 percent or more (though some of that growth, to be sure, came via annexation of nearby unincorporated areas).

Far more important is the fact that on most measures of economic and social welfare, life in Charlotte has improved steadily relative to national norms. Between 1970 and 2010, average (inflation-adjusted) family income grew much faster there than in the nation as a whole (30 percent versus 21 percent). This in part reflects rising stocks of human capital. The city's school dropout rate fell from 17 percent in 1970 to 7 percent by 2010, and though both figures are slightly above national averages in those years, Charlotte now has a higher proportion of adults with high school diplomas and bachelor's or master's degrees than the United States as a whole. In addition, the city's rising incomes reflected both brisk labor demand and strong work effort: it added almost three hundred thousand jobs over that period (a growth rate almost three times the nation's), and by the 2010 census its labor force participation rate exceeded the national average by 7.3 percentage points. Its measured poverty rates for both whites and blacks are below their national averages, a rare attribute indeed for the central city of a metro area.

Credit for Charlotte's boom usually goes to its emergence as a major financial center: it is now second only to New York as a bank headquarters city. This surprising development got under way in the 1980s, when the federal government began loosening restrictions on interstate banking. Entrepreneurial Charlotte bankers, led by the legendary Hugh McColl, entered the resulting "race to be the biggest" with gusto. Local banks merged and used their assets to acquire regional banks, and those in turn became national players and gobbled others, culminating in NationsBank's acquisition of Bank of America in 1998 and the stunning relocation of the latter's top brass from sophisticated San Francisco to (gasp!) the Bible Belt. But Charlotte's banking sector didn't so much lead the city's growth as run alongside, supplying financial capital to the state's and region's thriving manufacturing, construction, transportation, trade, and service sectors. It's easier to become a financial center when there's abundant and growing business nearby to finance. McColl, after all, had only become CEO of NationsBank in 1983, by which time Nucor's Ken Iverson had been revolutionizing the American steel industry for over two decades. And the latter's sense that closed-shop states and their generally inhospitable business climates should be avoided was, evidently, widely shared by others making firm-location decisions.

Throughout the Sun Belt—or, more accurately, in RTW states, sunny or not—rates of job creation and income growth have far exceeded those in states less friendly toward capital investment. This was especially true in manufacturing: between 1970 and 2000, non-RTW states lost 2.3 million manufacturing jobs, but RTW states *created* 1.4 million. It's true that the decade following, which includes the Great Recession, saw declines in manufacturing employment in many (though not all) RTW states, but the prior fateful decades profoundly altered the geography of the American economy. Primary industries are cornerstones of a well-balanced regional economy. It's common to say that every new manufacturing job creates three to four additional jobs in related businesses—such as the banks that financed Nucor's first mini-mill, for example, or the firms that served their workers. Recent economic research suggests that talk of such a large "multiplier" effect of basic industry might be an exaggeration—but not by much.[16] In any case, the job-creation record is clear and convincing: since 1970, overall employment growth in RTW states has been half again greater than in non-RTW states.

And that, in turn, has created more boom towns. There were 270 U.S. cities with populations over 100,000 in the most recent census. Those in non-RTW states added 6.7 million residents between 1970 and 2010, but those in RTW states grew *more than twice as much*, adding 14.6 million residents. (It's also worth noting that cities in California—a non-RTW state, but one that reassures homeowners and businesses about the security of their capital investments by means of a statewide property tax cap, as discussed in Chapter 3—added 7.3 million residents over this period, which means that the cities in non-RTW states other than California collectively *shrank*.) Charlotte, which has tripled its population since 1970, actually trails Houston, Phoenix, San Antonio, and Austin in absolute population gain in that time. All told, 53 cities in RTW states have added at least 100,000 residents over the last four decades. Sunny locales predominate, of course, and some have benefited from other endowments of natural capital, but others—such as Nashville (up 201,000 residents), Lincoln (108,000), or Wichita (105,000)—are simply experiencing the kind of steady growth that a relatively benign business climate can foster. The only large city in an RTW state that lost appreciable population during this period is New Orleans (down 249,000 residents), about which more will be said in the next chapter.

THE POLITICAL PATH TO RTW

It seems apparent, then, that RTW and similar policies that reassure owners of fixed and durable capital that their assets are less vulnerable to hostage-taking by opportunistic actors can be a useful tool of economic development. What's more, the protections and signals conveyed by RTW might be especially important for localities seeking a balanced economy in which citizens lacking graduate degrees in computer science, biotechnology, or finance have a decent chance to secure lucrative employment in expanding manufacturing or construction sectors. Finally, RTW may have value in dampening the growth of union power in the public sector, enabling state and local governments to chart a more fiscally responsible path—another subject for the next chapter.

The question, then, is not whether to pursue RTW, but how to achieve it in the face of implacable, well-funded, and pugnacious opposition by Big Labor—aided by its admirers in the media and academe, many of whom are guided by the conviction that greater union power always and everywhere enhances social justice as it alleviates poverty (despite evidence to the contrary like that in Figure 4.1). What's more, the political deck will be stacked against RTW initiatives for a more mundane reason: the majority of the electorate simply won't care much about it. This will be very different from statewide debates about property tax limitation, in which roughly two-thirds of voters may be homeowners and thus see a direct link to their well-being. By contrast, union members rarely constitute as much as 20 percent of any state's labor force these days, and capitalists are a trivial fraction of the electorate. The rest of us may simply tune out because we don't think we have anything at stake and it's too time-consuming to learn about this complex issue (a phenomenon called "rational ignorance") or take a side ("rational abstention"). In such cases, the interest group with the most at risk and the most cohesive organization—likely the unions—will be the odds-on favorite in the political arena.

Nevertheless, Idaho, Oklahoma, Indiana, and Michigan have managed successful RTW campaigns relatively recently, and they have some key lessons to teach us. In general, it's fair to say that getting RTW done politically takes considerable time, effort, and money, but it is "do-able," and its advocates' chances improve if (a) there's growing public awareness that nearby states with RTW are faring relatively better than the home state, (b) there's some bipartisan support among elected officials, (c) the business community is willing to work for change, (d) there are some media outlets that understand the issue and support the campaign, and (e) the fraction of the local labor force that is unionized is waning.

Patience and persistence will be virtues. In Oklahoma, RTW advocates worked through several state election cycles, getting RTW voted upon each time so that legislators would have to go on record and then could be held accountable to voters. Unions generally rely on delaying tactics; their political minions bury RTW legislation in committee and ultimately wear down its advocates. In some cases, if it appears RTW legislation might pass, unions have shifted their strategy and offered to put RTW on the ballot for a public referendum.

RTW advocates generally think ballot initiatives favor the unions. Since 1950, for example, only one state (Kansas) other than Oklahoma has won RTW via that route. Once RTW is put up for a vote by the public, unions do, indeed, have major advantages: local affiliates can pull in cash and volunteers from national offices, so they will often outspend their opponents and put many more boots on the ground to rally support among voters. And they will use aggressive scare tactics in their publicity—even going beyond the usual assertions that RTW inevitably leads to big wage and benefit cuts (including loss of health insurance) among union members and non-members alike. A 1964 Oklahoma referendum failed in part because of a well-circulated pamphlet that showed a black youth under attack by a police dog in Selma, Alabama, captioned "These are Civil Rights in Right-to-Work Alabama."[17]

But economists favor referenda because they can be useful in mitigating the effects of special interests in at least some circumstances. In particular, when there is little political competition within a jurisdiction, it may actually be more desirable to put an RTW initiative on the ballot for a public vote than to try to get elected officials to fall in line. This is because of the "rational ignorance effect" in which voters do not daily monitor the actions of their elected representatives because it's simply too costly to do so, relative to the benefits. As a result, well-funded and -organized interest groups such as unions can unduly influence these officials without much chance the general public will learn about it—unless political competitors are around to publicize the back-room wheeling and dealing. In sum, the stronger that unions' hold is over the dominant party in a state, the more likely it will be that RTW advocates are best advised to do an end-run around entrenched pols and go the ballot initiative route—and, of course, prepare a voter-education program that will be ready for the inevitable scare tactics.

Getting RTW into law assuredly won't be easy, but a careful study of the states that have done so should leave one upbeat about what such policies can do. Rust Belt states and cities with underperforming economies don't have to fight a fruitless battle against the forces of globalization or close up shop and buy their residents bus tickets to the Sun Belt to improve their standards of living. These areas can become more competitive by improving their business climates, and RTW is simply the most obvious and effective step in that direction. It is, like an efficient approach to local taxation, a key way to protect, and therefore to encourage, private investment in productive capital. In the next chapter, we'll address some issues that arise when such capital is publicly or communally owned.

CHAPTER 6

Things Fall Apart

IN THE FALL OF 2004, before the name "Katrina" evoked grief and anger, Beth LeBlanc and her neighbors on Bellaire Drive in New Orleans had a problem. Their back yards had become wading pools, and they worried that this had something to do with the contiguous 17th Street Canal levee—which helped contain the waters of nearby Lake Pontchartrain.

"We called the Sewerage and Water Board, and one of their guys tested the water and said it was coming from the canal," LeBlanc told reporters. "They sent repair crews out. They tore up sidewalks and driveways. Things got better, but it never got dry. So I keep wondering why no one ever came out to ask about it. No one from the Corps of Engineers. No one from the Levee Board. The Sewerage and Water Board never came back."[1]

Many months too late, Jerry Colletti, New Orleans operations manager for the U.S. Army Corps of Engineers, admitted a catastrophic failure to communicate: "If someone had told us there was lake water on the outside of that levee—or any levee—it would have been a red flag to us, and we would have been out there, without question. [But] we have nothing on that, nothing at all. That's something we should have been told about." The half-foot of lake water in Beth LeBlanc's yard was a sign that the levee might be fatally undermined. The agencies responsible for maintaining the levee system were supposed to share such information and take quick action to remedy problems. But in this case, said Mr. Colletti, one or more of them "dropped the ball."

Then came Katrina on the morning of August 29, 2005. The eye of the Category Five hurricane—the third-strongest ever to make landfall in the United States—missed the heart of New Orleans by twenty miles, and initially the city seemed to have survived with limited damage and flooding. But the worst was yet to come. Storm surge from the Gulf of Mexico and pressure from the elevated waters of the Mississippi River and Lakes Borgne and Pontchartrain tested the city's defenses against flooding. The

17th Street Canal levee and many other crucial pieces of its flood control system failed the test. By the evening of August 30, floodwaters covered 80 percent of the city's land area. All told, Katrina and its aftermath caused over eighteen-hundred deaths and property damage of as much as $100 billion. By most measures, Katrina tops the list of the most destructive storms in American history, and the failure of New Orleans' levee system has been called the worst civil engineering disaster in U.S. history.

Investigations by professional engineers, government officials, and the insurance industry later documented a complex array of problems that contributed to Katrina's horrific toll.[2] There were over fifty major breaks in the city's levees and floodwalls. Some were caused by "overtopping," in which water levels rose above barriers and produced erosion that subsequently led to breaches; others were caused by design flaws and poor construction or maintenance that led to failure below specified capabilities. The bottom line is that the physical capital on which New Orleans depended for its citizens' safety was not up to its assigned task—and all those who were responsible for the condition of that capital had a lot to answer for.

Beth LeBlanc's experience showed that those charged with maintaining New Orleans's 101 miles of levees sometimes failed to address reported problems, but it's more shocking how little they did to detect weaknesses in this crucial infrastructure. The *Times-Picayune* reported how nonchalantly officials inspected the city's defenses against flooding—which, shockingly, they did but once a year: "Records of the annual Levee Board and [Army Corps] inspections show that they are fairly hasty affairs, with dozens of officials piling onto a convoy of vehicles to drive along the levees, stopping at various points for visits of 15 to 30 minutes. They review areas between stops from the cars."[3] These drive-by inspections generally took under five hours so that those involved could enjoy lunch before adjourning until next year. After assessing the safety of over twenty miles of levees per hour, they doubtless had healthy appetites.

Every public official of every agency linked to the Katrina disaster has vowed to do better in the future, of course. Avoidable deaths, incalculable suffering, and widespread devastation tend to focus the mind and energize even the most indolent of bureaucracies. But how could the entities charged with building and maintaining New Orleans' defenses against nature have become so dysfunctional in the first place? How could a city whose very existence depends on a fail-safe system of levees, floodwalls, canals, and pumps have managed that capital so poorly? The answer, it turns out, can be found in the pages of history and the immutable laws of political economy.

PUBLIC GOODS AND PUBLIC CHOICE

The urbanites of antiquity (and their rulers) considered protective walls to be the most valuable and important type of civic asset. A city with nothing to keep out plundering hordes would have been inconceivable to them. During China's Zhou dynasty, in fact, the written character for wall was the same as that for city.[4] These days, of course, people's well-being depends on a vast array of such assets—not just walls or levees, but streets and highways, subways, water and sewer systems, and myriad other physical capital often referred to as infrastructure or public works.

It is commonly—and erroneously—assumed that public (or governmental) ownership of such assets is a necessity, either because creating or maintaining them would be too expensive for a private firm or individual to afford, or because such an owner could not be trusted to serve the public interest. Down through history, however, there have been many examples of privately produced public works—even when it was clearly difficult to make a buck in the bargain.

One example dates from America's earliest days, when private companies built and operated turnpikes (toll roads) connecting urban centers. The first opened in 1794 and linked Philadelphia, Lancaster, and points in between. Wherever such roads were built, the costs of transporting goods fell significantly, trade flourished, and land values and workers' wages rose. It soon became clear, however, that these turnpikes weren't making any money for the capitalists who had paid to build them: toll revenues were almost always far below promised levels because it was so easy to, literally, free ride. Commercial travelers often circumvented toll booths via short detours ("shunpikes"), and the charters granted to the turnpike companies usually specified many toll exemptions for noncommercial uses (such as travel to worship) that were easy to claim and hard to refute.

Despite their lack of profitability, however, private tollways continued to be built into the 1830s, and many operated until the turn of the twentieth century. In the early 1800s, New England had 3,750 miles of private roads managed by 238 companies, and New York had 4,000 miles, New Jersey 550, and Pennsylvania 2,400—most yielding very low returns for their shareholders. But investors continued to fund these projects because people well understood the aforementioned indirect benefits of the toll roads and because these early capitalists seemed to have a cooperative spirit. And if they didn't, they were encouraged to buy stock in these companies by social pressure. Governments can toss you in jail if you don't pay your taxes, but your neighbors can shun you if you don't subscribe to a stock issue that will help increase the value of their land or labor.[5]

Over time, however, it became common to assume that *only* government could successfully finance, produce, and operate these sorts of facilities. In part this reflected the fact that the power to tax (and penalize nonpayers) seems a much more efficient way of solving the problem of free riding than any methods available to private firms. But it also jibes neatly with economists' notion that *not* charging for certain things—called pure public goods—will enhance social welfare. These goods have the unique characteristic of "nondepletability": a levee, for example, can protect me from floods without reducing the amount of protection available to you (assuming, of course, our area is not too crowded); the cost of protecting an additional person is zero.

In such cases, we actually *don't want to exclude anybody* from consuming the public good—as might happen if any price is charged at all, since some might be unable to afford to pay—because that would withhold from them a valuable benefit that can be delivered without any additional social cost. Only the government, it is commonly argued, has the wherewithal to supply public goods and allow people to enjoy them for free—though, again, there are many contrary examples (such as television broadcasters who give their programs away to viewers while recovering their costs from advertising sales). But even if we grant to government a special role in securing provision of such goods, two major challenges remain.

How Much Is Enough?

The first problem to solve is determining which public goods are worth producing and which are not. It's true that *once public goods exist* added people can consume their services at zero added cost, but building them costs money—usually, a lot of it. There has to be a limit on use of taxpayer dollars to those projects for which up-front production costs are exceeded by ultimate benefits, and there are questions about whether the democratic process is up to this task.

We can't just rely on majority voting to make these weighty decisions, because "one person, one vote" means we can't express the *intensity* of our preferences for a particular public good or infrastructure investment. You may value an expansion of our city's flood-control capacity ten times more than me, but my casual "no" vote on the ballot question cancels out your enthusiastic "yes."

Many infrastructure projects promise broad, indirect benefits at modest cost, yet are deep-sixed by NIMBY-ism (for "not in my back yard"). In other cases, extravagantly expensive projects sometimes win approval because they deliver small but concentrated benefits to well-connected special interests. There is simply no consensus among economists about whether the political marketplace generally overproduces public works (that is, government is "too big"), underproduces them ("too small"), or delivers the optimal amount ("just right").

Good Enough for Government Work

Even setting aside such abstractions, though, there are questions about how efficiently the government will *operate* any facilities in which it chooses to invest tax dollars. The problem, again, relates to property rights. Once we have installed a socially beneficial civic asset, we now own it collectively, through our government. We taxpayer-owners would like the politicians and bureaucrats we hire to manage these assets to do so very efficiently, since resulting savings might flow to us as tax relief or fund service improvements. But there are so many collective owners that any such individual benefits would be small, so we don't have much incentive to closely monitor these managers or organize effectively to modify their behavior even if it seems obvious they're wasting our money or otherwise "dropping the ball." And their incentives to be efficient are unfortunately weak, too.

It's widely credited that placing ownership of key assets in the hands of government is wise and good because a public enterprise "doesn't need to make a profit." This makes economists grumble, because the pursuit of profit in private enterprises often leads to substantial cost savings, superior quality, and higher rates of innovation.[6] But it's also not quite correct to say that those managing public enterprises don't pursue "profit": rather, they are simply constrained in what they can do with any gains they might realize by exercising their managerial discretion. True, they can't get rich by improving the bottom line, raising share prices, and cashing bonus checks from happy shareholders. This does not mean, however, that they'll ignore other opportunities to feather their nests. Bureaucrats might find it rewarding to augment their staffs and enjoy more power or leisure. Politicians might use the revenues flowing to public enterprises as piggy banks they can use to buy the votes of key interest groups. Making an enterprise "nonprofit" does not necessarily make it, and those who run it, virtuous. Again, the failure of New Orleans' flood control infrastructure provides some lessons.

POLITICAL MYOPIA

With an average elevation one to two feet below sea level, the Gulf a mere hundred miles away, the Mississippi flowing through its center, and Lake Pontchartrain on its northern border, New Orleans has always faced the threat of catastrophic flooding. Before Katrina, the greatest test of its defenses against nature was the Great Mississippi Flood of 1927. In the summer of 1926, heavy rains throughout the Midwest had inundated over twenty-seven thousand square miles, causing 246 deaths across seven states. On April 15, 1927, with the Mississippi already at dangerously high levels along New Orleans's riverfront levees, the city was hit by fifteen inches of rain in nineteen hours. Unfortunately, its pumps were electric, and the power grid went down early in the storm. Rainwater flooded much of the city inside its protective walls, and the river threatened to top those walls at any moment. Desperate to head off complete disaster, officials dynamited a levee upriver, sacrificing some rural areas to flooding. In combination with unintentional levee breaks which dispersed floodwaters elsewhere, that was enough to keep the Big Muddy on the proper side of the city's levees.

Their narrow escape taught New Orleanians a lesson—and created a political opportunity. It was now obvious to all how much their lives and property were in the hands of the Orleans Levee Board, which had been created in 1890 and made "primarily responsible for the operation and maintenance of levees . . . and other hurricane and flood protection improvements surrounding the City of New Orleans." The public's willingness to grant the board power and money were at an all-time high, so its structure and mission were altered radically via an amendment to the state's constitution, called Act 292. But, remarkably, instead of the board being given greater focus and accountability, its duties were broadened: in addition to looking after levees, it could "dedicate, construct, operate, and maintain public parks, beaches, marinas, aviation fields, and other like facilities."[7] Why spread the board's resources more thinly? Why tell it to mow grass at parks and operate yacht clubs in addition to—or instead of—protecting the city from floods?

To a calculating politician—and there have been few more calculating and corrupt pols in history than the man behind Act 292, Louisiana governor Huey Long, "the Kingfish"—there was a simple reason. Long knew that the unquestioned need to rebuild and improve New Orleans's levees guaranteed that the board's budget would soar. Allowing it to get into other lines of business meant these dollars could be doled out in many more politically advantageous ways than previously possible. Votes could be bought by delivering public works projects to new jurisdictions. Kickbacks could be solicited from vendors other than those few involved in levee construction or maintenance. More patronage employees could be hired once the board took on its new, more labor-intensive pursuits.

Long did all of the above. He seized control of the Levee Board shortly after the 1927 flood, installing as president one Abraham Shushan, a loyal minion experienced at using the government procurement process to enrich himself and deliver the votes of key constituencies to his boss. Though skilled at draining cash from the board, Shushan wasn't quite smart enough to keep himself out of jail in the process. In 1939 he was sentenced to thirty months for arranging kickbacks while refinancing the board's debt.

Over the years, stories of Levee Board malfeasance became legendary. In 2005, NBC summarized "a pattern of what critics call questionable spending practices by the Levee Board—which, at one point, was accused by a state inspector general of 'a long-standing and continuing disregard of the public interest.'" Former board member Peggy Wilson recalled that at one meeting, "I raised my hand and I said, 'Excuse me, I'd like to ask a question. When are we going to talk about levees?' And they told me that that was not on the agenda." A former president, Billy Nungesser, described the board as a "cesspool of politics, that's all it was. [Its purpose was to] provide jobs for people."[8]

But the key thing to observe here is not just that corruption happened. We fallible humans may be tempted to do fraudulent things as long as we live and breathe—and in both the public and private sectors. The issue here is deeper and more subtle than lawbreaking, and has to do with the nature of durable but depreciable assets such as levees, streets, bridges, water systems, and other key elements of a city's infrastructure. Let us refer to it as the Magoo Principle, in honor of the venerable cartoon character who is so profoundly nearsighted that he is constantly on the brink of disaster—though always luckily escapes harm.[9] It can arise in the public sector as a result of electoral uncertainty. And it can cause problems even when no laws are broken.

Think of your house. You know the roof might leak at some point. If you're smart, you'll schedule periodic inspections and perform repairs promptly before small problems turn into big ones; you'll put money aside for such tasks and to prepare for the roof's eventual replacement. You call it a rainy day fund, but in accounting jargon it's your capital maintenance budget, and it's a key part of proper asset management. You know that if you raid that fund for, say, a trip to Vegas and there's no money left on the rainy day, you'll have only yourself to blame—and far more costly damage to cope with than if you'd kept up with needed maintenance in a timely manner. So you resist the temptation to be shortsighted.

If you're running City Hall, different logic applies. Failure of some city infrastructure may be years away, but in the meantime you face an election. You might lose, and you know how the laws of politics operate: when stuff happens, whoever is in office at the time usually gets credit or blame. You determine, therefore, to make good stuff happen on your watch even when it carries risk of big future problems. If polls say your re-election bid is a coin flip, you will heavily discount the possible political cost of those future problems as you make policy decisions today. After all, there's a 50 percent chance *your successor* will be the target of tough questions about why something wasn't done to prevent the problems when they arrive. If you win—well, you'll cross that bridge when you come to it. So even if there's a maintenance budget for City Hall's roof, you might raid it for things that buy votes *now*. Are public employee unions offering support in exchange for a wage increase or more generous pension benefits? Done. Just "defer maintenance" on the roof, or the levees, or the water system. Or raid the maintenance budget to build new infrastructure while ignoring the old. Owners of construction companies will show their gratitude with campaign contributions; their workers will support you at the polls.

The likelihood that you'll pay any political price for your cynical application of the Magoo Principle goes down as the life expectancy of the infrastructure on which you are deferring maintenance goes up. Which is why New Orleans's levees were perfect for such exploitation: in most cases, they're simply huge piles of earth, depreciating very slowly. And the probability of a Hundred Year Storm arriving to test those levees is, for a near-sighted pol, too small to worry about.

In the blame game that played out in the weeks and months after Katrina, fingers pointed everywhere and nowhere. There was minimal discussion of the generations of Louisiana politicians who had turned the Orleans Levee Board into a "cesspool of politics" rather than a bulwark against disaster—and no way to make them pay a political price in any case, since most were retired or, like Long and Shushan, dead. Surveys aimed at gauging public sentiment about who or what was responsible for the disaster never identified any political decision makers other than those unlucky enough to hold office when the storm hit. Most polls focused on the *response* to the storm by various officials and entities (which was, by all accounts, disastrous in itself) rather than causes of, or preparedness for, the flooding. When attention was turned to the latter, it is remarkable how diffuse—even forgiving—sentiment turned out to be. Yes, President George W. Bush's job approval took a hit, as did that of some local officials, but in one major poll a surprising 38 percent of respondents blamed "no one" for the storm's awful toll, with the remainder pointing to various officials and multiple levels of government.[10] That is the awful appeal of the Magoo Principle: when the consequences of bad political behavior are long deferred and others will be blamed when those consequences arrive, we should expect a lot of bad behavior.

And we've gotten it—all across America. There are eighty-four thousand dams in the United States, and the Association of State Dam Safety Officials rates four thousand of them "deficient." The Environmental Protection Agency has identified four hundred thousand brownfields sites that await cleanup and redevelopment. The Federal Highway Administration estimates that two hundred million trips are taken daily across deficient bridges in the nation's cities, and traffic congestion wastes roughly $101 billion in time and fuel annually. The National Education Association estimates the cost of bringing our crumbling public schools into good repair at $270 billion. The American Water Works Association claims that public water systems will require more than $1 trillion in funding over the next twenty-five years to bring them up to acceptable standards. And so it goes. The American Society of Civil Engineers (ASCE) issues a national infrastructure report card and totals up the cost of catching up on all the deferred maintenance we've been engaging in for many years. Most recently, they assigned a grade of "D+" to the overall condition of our collectively owned capital and asserted that we need to spend $3.6 trillion by 2020 to bring these assets up to "satisfactory" condition.[11] Even allowing for some inflation of this estimate (engineers, after all, stand to benefit from such spending), we've got a lot of work to do. Clearly, the infrastructure failure in New Orleans is not an isolated case—just the most dramatic and tragic example of what can happen when our public officials exploit the Magoo Principle. The question is how to stop them.

TOWARD A CAPITALIST INFRASTRUCTURE

An idealist might observe that the simplest way to keep public capital in good shape is with far-sighted, disciplined budgetary practices. Local governments just need to set up the aforementioned capital maintenance budgets and use them only for their proper, assigned purposes. Those budgets should be sacrosanct and infrastructure moneys kept in a "lock box" that opportunistic politicians can't treat like an ATM every time there's a budget crisis or a key interest group demands new spending.

Sometimes this approach actually works. Just not often enough, as the ASCE report card documents and as anyone with a discerning eye can see. When the head of China's sovereign wealth fund visited the United States in 2010 to evaluate investment possibilities, he told a gathering of big-city mayors that America appears to have a "socialist infrastructure."[12] It was not a compliment, but a straightforward observation that we behave as if too poor to upgrade our rickety bridges, potholed streets, and aged subways. Far too frequently, our elected officials raid their capital budgets and borrow from the future in order to pursue short-term political goals. We might *try* to make these budget lines off limits; we might speak of "sequesters" or "trust funds" designated for specific purposes. But the temptation to circumvent such limitations is always strong, and where there's a political will there's usually a way. Perhaps it's best not to hope politicians will leave the lock box alone, but simply to take it away from them entirely.

One radical way to do so is to take public capital private. Private owners try to maximize the value of their assets, and doing so usually requires taking the long view. Even if you don't plan on living in your house for more than a year or two, you'll probably consider the effects on its resale value of repairs or improvements that will endure for many years after you've sold the property. And, obviously, private owners face no risk of being voted out of office, so are less likely to discount the future costs of short-sighted decisions about maintenance in the same way office-holders often do. Humans are not perfect, of course; we all have a tendency to be short-sighted in at least some of our choices. It's just that if *we* will suffer the consequences of such choices rather than some unknown successor, the odds that we'll be far-sighted improve greatly.

But putting crucial infrastructure into private hands seems problematic on many fronts. First and foremost, how could we ensure that these assets will serve the broad public interest rather than line the pockets of their private owners? When "greedy corporations" (a term which, in the minds of many, is redundant) rather than public-spirited elected officials and dispassionate civil servants control such assets, surely the quality of the services these facilities provide will fall, prices will skyrocket, and access will be limited to the well-heeled.

Except—every day and all over the world, hundreds of millions of people happily consume high-quality, low-price goods often presumed to be best supplied by public entities but which are, in fact, provided by private firms. As one example, consider drinking water and the facilities with which it is produced and distributed, doubtless one of the more important elements of any area's infrastructure. To see how private water supply works in practice, we might look to a country not normally identified as being friendly to market capitalism—France, where the majority of the population obtain their tap water not from local governments but from for-profit companies.

At about the same time Americans were guilting investors into building useful but unprofitable toll roads linking the country's scattered trading centers, the French were relying on the private sector to build and operate the infrastructure to bring clean water to the residents of many cities and towns—including Paris, which granted the Perier brothers an exclusive franchise to do so in 1782. In the decades that followed, the water business was a bit of a political football. Some municipalities opted for private provision of some sort, others operated their own systems (as is common in the United States), and a few that had once encouraged private firms nationalized them. That's the fate that eventually befell the Periers. After some years of municipal operation, however, Parisians found that the price of their water had quintupled and quality had suffered, so eventually the city privatized its system once more.[13]

Such varied experiences gave French policymakers and voters good data about what worked and what did not, and the current popularity of private, for-profit water systems in France is eloquent testimony to their feasibility. Indeed, that country's expertise—three of the five largest water suppliers in the world are French—has fueled rapid growth in water privatization elsewhere. Just 5 percent of the world's population was served by private suppliers in 1999, but that market share doubled by 2006 and is expected to reach 20 percent by the year 2025.

This market is especially interesting because, at first blush, it appears that a central virtue of competition—the need to win customers by offering them a combination of price, quality, and convenience that is superior to that of rivals—will simply not be present. Rivalry here seems impossible given the way this good must be produced and delivered. To bring water from some distant reservoir to your kitchen, lots of pipes and pumps must be installed. This is expensive—and would be doubly so if we wanted two firms to compete for your business via separate systems. It's much cheaper to install just one set of pipes serving everyone. But then customers would be prey to confiscatory pricing by a single seller undisciplined by competition. So it seems we are on the horns of a dilemma: we can have wasteful, duplicative capital investment in order to invite competition, or abuse by a monopoly.

The usual ways of resolving that dilemma are either public ownership and operation of the monopoly or, if private ownership is tolerated, subjecting this "public utility" to rigorous price regulation. The first approach is based on the theory that our elected representatives can be trusted not to abuse us; the second on the idea that regulators will be good at identifying and enforcing a price schedule comparable to that which would prevail under competition. Economists have been testing these theories for some time, and unfortunately neither is well supported by the evidence. But luckily, as we've seen, the French have been hard at work on a third way aimed at bringing the benefits of competitive provision of key services such as water supply without trusting elected officials to be far-sighted and disciplined about their budgets, and without devising complicated regulatory schemes that often turn out to be unsuccessful.

The key is that there need not be competition *within* a market to serve consumers' best interests as long as there is competition *for* that market. Economists now refer to the process by which naturally monopolistic markets such as water systems can be efficiently served by private firms with minimal regulatory meddling as *franchise bidding*, but the French employed this process well before anyone used that name. To be sure, it involves cooperation between the public and private sectors.

The public sector's role is to auction off the right to serve the relevant market—creating, for example, a local water franchise or concession, as the French referred to it. In a nutshell, the municipal government specifies a contract detailing what it wishes produced, to what quality standards, in what amount, and for how long. Then the auction is held, but the winner is *not* the party offering to pay the highest fee for the right to be the monopolistic seller, but rather the firm *offering the best price to consumers of the ultimate product* while meeting all specifications about quality contained in the contract. That is, this auction will not feature bidders offering millions for the right to sell water at extravagant prices to a captive clientele. Instead, it will be won by the *low* bidder (in terms of, say, cents per gallon it promises to charge customers while the contract is in force). In the case of water supply, the technology of production and distribution is sufficiently straightforward that such contracts can be drawn up and enforced at manageable cost, and as long as the bidding is not rigged it will produce a winner that can satisfy consumers' demands at the lowest attainable prices and costs of production.

Equally important, from our point of view, the capital maintenance budget necessary to keep the required infrastructure in good order must be part of the bidders' calculations about how much (or little) they can afford to charge for their output, or they will not be able to satisfy the terms of the contract. As a result, *this budget will be out of reach of political Magoos* and controlled by the private firm that wins the auction.

About 80 percent of Americans are served by government-owned and -operated municipal systems, but the rest obtain their water from their own wells or one of six thousand private companies, most of which get high marks for price and quality of service from customers and local public officials alike. A good sign is the frequency of repeat business. In the United States, only 10 percent of cities that have privatized the ownership or operation of their municipal systems have subsequently deprivatized. The comparable figure worldwide is about 8 percent. It seems that the efficiencies promised by competition for the market are realized in the great majority of cases. One survey of U.S. systems found reductions in operating costs ranging from 10 to 40 percent in privatized facilities. And quality improved: prior to privatization, two-fifths of sampled facilities were out of compliance with federal clean drinking water standards, while one year after entering into public-private partnerships, all were in compliance. Case studies of privatizations in Africa, Asia, and Latin America are similarly encouraging with regard to operational efficiency but also to equity, with the poor generally benefiting from greater access to network services in areas served by private concessions.[14]

INCENTIVES AND INNOVATION

Clearly then, the energy and expertise of private companies *can* be harnessed to manage key infrastructure in the public interest. A well-designed and -executed franchise bidding system has the potential to both enhance the efficiency with which some public goods are provided and protect their capital maintenance budgets from raids by short-sighted politicians.

It's gratifying also to report that many U.S. cities are embracing this approach—often in surprising ways. Tulsa's zoo, for example, was recently privatized to avoid loss of its accreditation (following the tragic deaths of two of its giraffes). Under private management, fund-raising efforts were stepped up, staffing levels increased, deferred maintenance problems corrected, and the zoo reaccredited. Thus inspired, similar concessions are (as this is written) under consideration for zoos in Los Angeles, Grand Rapids, Santa Ana, and Evansville; other cities are hiring private entities to operate their animal shelters. Seventeen municipalities employ a Maryland-based company to operate their public libraries. Many more hire concessionaires to maintain parks and operate recreational facilities such as public golf courses and youth centers.

One especially important illustration of the nature and sources of potential gains from privatization of public assets comes from Indianapolis. That city has a unique environmental problem: it discharges its wastewater into a small, non-navigable river (the White) that runs through the heart of downtown. By the early 1980s, its two water treatment plants (one built in the 1920s, the other in the 1960s) were out of date, in decay, over capacity, and technologically unable to meet the stringent standards of the 1972 Clean Water Act. The initial fix, in 1982, was over $600 million (in today's dollars) worth of upgrades, funded in large measure by the federal and state governments.

Less than a decade later, however, another quarter-billion dollars were needed for Indy's wastewater collection and treatment system, which was still suffering from the long-term decay wrought by the Magoo Principle. This time, however, the city could not rely on other people's money for the improvements, and the political will to raise sewer usage rates by the amount necessary (an estimated 37 percent) was lacking. So newly elected mayor Stephen Goldsmith decided to see if privatization might provide a way out of the corner into which the city had painted itself.[15]

The political obstacles were formidable. Regulators feared that a private firm would sacrifice environmental quality in pursuit of profits. Public employees' unions were certain that talk of "cost reductions" and "efficiency gains" was code for wage cuts and job losses. In addition, there seemed little reason to hope that privatization would do much good. Two consultants' reports on the treatment plants concluded that they seemed reasonably well run; one estimated that private management could, at most, trim about 5 percent from operating costs.

Nevertheless, Goldsmith and the City-County Council plowed ahead. They opted not to sell the treatment plants outright, but put a five-year concession contract up for bids. The winner was the White River Environmental Partnership (WREP), a consortium that included one of the big French water companies, a Denver-based environmental management company, and the city's own (private) water supplier. WREP's winning bid was not 5 but 40 percent below the city's prior costs. Actual savings exceeded initial projections, with utility, maintenance, and capital costs all coming in well below budget. And environmental quality *improved*: the number of effluent violations decreased from about seven per year under city management to one. Though some of these efficiency gains did, indeed, come from a one-third reduction in operational staff (which led the union to fight the privatization tooth and nail in both the courts and media), the city provided a safety net for displaced workers by offering them a severance package or transferring them to other positions as they became available; within a year all had been placed. Those that remained actually banked higher wages, experienced fewer workplace accidents and injuries (which, in turn, cut workers' comp insurance costs), and reduced the frequency with which they lodged grievances with their union.

But Indianapolis did not realize such dramatic gains in the performance of its wastewater treatment system by merely eliminating some redundant staffers. WREP had access to the technical expertise of the best engineers in the world; more important, it had a *strong incentive to heed their advice*.

Under city management, innovative ideas—simply figuring out better ways to operate or adopting new technologies—usually went nowhere because they brought nothing back to the innovator. Any realized cost savings would revert to the city's general fund to be spent on other constituencies. With shareholders and managers operating under a long-term concession contract, however, such savings would go to the bottom line and fuel dividends, bonuses—and even the aforementioned higher wages. Indeed, once workers are freed of unions' work rules and across-the-board compensation formulae, they frequently offer up the most useful suggestions about how to get their work done better for less—and find private managers far more willing to listen than their public-sector counterparts.

A key lesson is that vesting property rights in private owners seeking profits can unlock unimagined (even by expert consultants) efficiencies in many enterprises' operations. Foes of privatization often invoke firms' "greed" as a reason to rely on public production of goods and services, but this ignores the fact that public managers and employees are human, too; self-interested behavior was just as common at Indianapolis's wastewater treatment plants (and Tulsa's zoo, and myriad other places) *before* privatization as after. This behavior just took unwholesome forms: the pursuit of ease or job security rather than efficiency, for example, or budget- rather than profit-maximization. People don't become selfless just because they work for a government agency. Creating a class of owners who may claim any residual income generated by the origination or adoption of better ideas simply rechannels the natural impulse to act in one's self-interest in more productive directions.

It's not surprising that the consultants hired to study Indianapolis's proposal to privatize operation of its wastewater plants could conceive of no great prospective gains, for they were not in a position to realize them. We work hardest to solve knotty problems when we will gain tangibly from their solution. *Incentives matter.* That is one of the bedrock principles of economics, and in the next chapter we will discuss a few more that can improve the efficiency with which cities' communally owned assets are managed and, so, enhance the quality of urban life.

CHAPTER 7

Three Simple Rules

INDIANAPOLIS, like Charlotte, is a successful city with insecurity issues. Locals sometimes refer to it as "IndiaNoPlace." But it is an *exceptional* place. Squarely in the Rust Belt, it has not emptied out like deindustrialized Detroit, Cleveland, Buffalo, and St. Louis, or even endured managed decline like Pittsburgh or Cincinnati. Since 1950, its population has roughly doubled (though a good portion of this growth resulted from consolidation with some inner-ring suburbs, about which more will be said later). All the other cities named have lost at least 40 percent of their residents in that time.

The contrast to Detroit is especially interesting. In the early years of the auto industry's development, each city was home to many carmakers contending for market leadership. For a time, those in Indianapolis—which included premium brands such as Stutz, Duesenberg, Cord, and Marmon— seemed to have a fighter's chance. In 1909, construction of the Indianapolis Motor Speedway reflected Hoosier optimism. When local products bested the competition on the track, eager consumers surely would beat a path to the victors' showrooms.

But Detroit held insurmountable advantages. It was blessed with important natural capital in the form of proximity to key raw materials and waterways that could be used to move them cheaply. As its firms grew they benefited also from agglomeration and scale economies that enhanced their competitive advantages. A Model T or Chevy might never outrace a Bearcat or impress onlookers like a "Duesy," but they were more affordable and reliable. Those virtues won market share if not trophies, and clinched Detroit's status as *the* Motor City: it boomed to twice Indianapolis's size by 1910 and was four times bigger by 1930. The Great Depression's onset made life difficult for all manufacturers, of course, but the Indy firms' focus on luxury models was especially problematic. By 1937, all the city's major automakers were out of business (though some suppliers and assembly plants for Detroit-based firms remained).

In the decades since, Indianapolis has proved that losing one key driver of an urban economy need not halt forward progress. Generations of civic leaders have worked hard to diversify the city's job base and manage its key institutions effectively. Their philosophy was best summarized by William Hudnut, who served four terms as mayor from 1976 to 1992: "To become competitive, we . . . trained our sights inward and concentrated on internal management of local government, knowing that our first job was to run the store well."[1] Not all the city's initiatives have been resounding successes, and it has not been immune to the myriad problems prevalent elsewhere in the Rust Belt. But it has certainly coped with deindustrialization, suburbanization, and other urban headwinds of the post–World War II era far better than the city that won the battle for supremacy in the auto industry. Today, Indianapolis is 16 percent larger than Detroit, its residents enjoy a median household income 54 percent greater, and its homicide rate is one-third as high.

The example of Indianapolis, then, offers some guidance for cities trying to restart their stalled economic engines. Of course, a good portion of the city's success is attributable to simple avoidance of policy blunders common elsewhere. It has not, for example, much tried to play the role of "Robin Hood" by aggressively pursuing redistributive programs that ratchet up tax rates and repel residents and investment to neighboring locales. And it has benefited from tax and labor climates more protective of property rights than is typical of other Northeast and North Central states.

But Indianapolis has also benefited from creative and courageous initiatives of its own. In particular, its political leaders have maintained a favorable climate for growth and investment not by relying heavily on special tax inducements or development subsidies (though these have not been unknown) but rather by focusing on economic fundamentals. They understood how three key forces at work in most markets—competitive conduct, scale economies in production, and price signals—could be harnessed to improve the operation of the government sector. As we'll see, each of these forces works better when certain key property rights are defined optimally. In this chapter we'll examine how this was done in Indianapolis, and then highlight a couple of broader applications.

RULE 1: ELIMINATE MONOPOLY,
CULTIVATE COMPETITION

When Stephen Goldsmith succeeded William Hudnut as mayor in 1992, Indianapolis was already poised to be a leader in the privatization of urban public services. Hudnut was a fan of management gurus such as Peter Drucker and W. Edwards Deming—he gave staffers books by the former and took cabinet officers and city-county councilors to seminars featuring the latter—and had worked hard to build an entrepreneurial culture in city agencies. His mantra was, "Do it better. Improve the delivery system. Become more efficient. Streamline and downsize. Do more with less. Privatize. Bring in competition. Break up the traditional government monopoly."[2]

This meant redrawing some turf boundaries: just because an activity had long been done by government workers did not mean they "owned" it. In his early efforts to implement Hudnut's philosophy, however, Goldsmith learned two important lessons. First, competition is the key that unlocks all else; privatization, by itself, need not "do it better." And it's possible to eliminate government monopoly without ending government employment.

Goldsmith's first attempt to do more with less involved the city's Department of Public Works (DPW), which spent a distressingly large portion of the revenue it collected in sewer charges just mailing out bills.[3] He approached the Indianapolis Water Company (IWC, the city's private water supplier), asked if they'd take on the billing duties, and was disappointed to learn that while they'd be happy to do so their price was only 5 percent below the DPW's cost. This produced an "aha!" moment: replacing a public monopoly with a private one won't get you very far.

So Goldsmith contacted every utility in central Indiana and asked for competitive bids for the sewer account. Newly motivated, IWC came back with a better offer: they would do the billing work for 30 percent less than the DPW—and also identify underbilled or delinquent sewer users, collect the missing revenue, and share the proceeds with the city. The resulting contract generated millions in budget savings.

A second key lesson came when Goldsmith put maintenance of some of the city's streets up for competitive bids. It seemed a logical step. Building such infrastructure is usually done by private contractors rather than city employees, so why not contract-out repairs to that capital? To Goldsmith's surprise, the city's unionized Department of Transportation (DoT) workers wanted to bid. And to his chagrin, they pointed out that they were competitively handicapped by political patronage: roughly one third of the staff in DoT's street repair division were highly paid "supervisors" who had been appointed, in part at least, because they were loyal supporters of Goldsmith's party.

To his credit, the mayor laid off or transferred half of those supervisors, provided the DoT workers with a consultant to help them prepare their bid, and then applauded when the city employees outbid their private competitors and won the concession with a price that promised 25 percent savings relative to prior costs. But they delivered more. As one worker put it, before bidding for the work, "we didn't give a hoot what anything cost," but once a competitive system was in place "we got efficient real quick."[4] In short order, the average productivity of work crews soared by two-thirds, from 3.1 to 5.2 lane miles serviced per day.

Such experiences led Goldsmith to argue that the word *privatization* should give way to *marketization*. It may be true that private firms are, on average, more efficient than public agencies in supplying goods and services, but what's true on average may not hold in any specific case. There's no reason to assume government workers can't compete when they are offered a chance to do so. The key to doing more with less is to create a market in which *everyone* has an incentive to act entrepreneurially and put their energy and creativity to work figuring out better ways to get things done.

Aside from the budget savings that can be obtained when workers start to "give a hoot" about cost and efficiency, encouraging pubic employees to compete alongside those in private firms can allay some voters' fears that contracting-out is a dark conspiracy against government workers and their unions. An open and inclusive bidding process will inform these voters (and their representatives) very directly about how expensive monopolies can be. If government agencies' bids are competitive, it's all to the good—or if voters see that their bids are millions more than the private alternatives, then public sympathy is much more likely to rest with the latter.

RULE 2: EXPLOIT ECONOMIES OF SCALE

Much discussion of Indianapolis's success in avoiding the decay and flight that has afflicted other Rust Belt cities focuses on its "Unigov" (for "unified government") system. On January 1, 1970, by act of the Indiana General Assembly and without any public referendum on the issue, the boundaries of the city of Indianapolis were made contiguous with those of Marion County. Overnight, the city's territory expanded five-fold (from 82 to 402 square miles), its population grew by 260,000 (to 740,000 residents), and its voter rolls expanded by 113,000 (to 406,000).

Such consolidation of the urban core with its surrounding suburbs is commonly advocated by those with a redistributionist bent. The idea is that central cities are far poorer than the suburbs to which well-off residents have fled, and annexation of these areas will provide a city government with the broad, deep tax base it can use to better tend to the needs of its "left behind" populations. Of course, those affluent suburbanites generally dislike being treated like cows to be milked; when they have any say in the matter, city-suburb mergers meet with vigorous political opposition. Though much admired in progressive circles, such mergers don't often happen.

That Indianapolis pulled it off reflects the fact that all and sundry understood that Unigov was definitely *not* motivated by any sort of redistributive plan. If one assumes (fairly or unfairly) that Republicans are less inclined than Democrats to engage in progressive transfers of income or wealth, it's noteworthy that the Unigov law was passed and implemented while the mayor, governor, and clear majorities in the state Senate, House of Representatives, and city and county councils were Republican. In fact, Democrats denounced the plan as "Unigrab," arguing that consolidation would dilute the political influence of the city's poorer residents—and thus *forestall* redistributive efforts.

Whether that was, indeed, an unspoken motivation for the program is unclear. What its advocates did say was that they saw consolidation as an efficiency measure. In Hudnut's words, it was "precipitated by reformist zeal for better services at lower cost."[5] Unigov's advocates saw considerable waste resulting from "fractionated" government agencies, and pointed to the area's five different transportation authorities and sixteen independent special-purpose municipal corporations operating over various jurisdictions. Ultimately, Unigov centralized management of many (but by no means all) local government services, creating six departments (Public Safety, Public Works, Metropolitan Development, Parks and Recreation, Transportation, and Administration) under a mayor elected countywide. For various reasons—primarily to overcome opposition to Unigov based on the perception that it would reduce local control in undesirable ways—the county courts, school districts, several of the municipal corporations, and a few neighboring towns were excluded from the governance structure of the new consolidated city.

How might delivering public services with fewer, larger agencies cut costs? The basic principle at work—scale economies in production—was identified as far back as 1776 by Adam Smith in *The Wealth of Nations*. In Smith's famous description of a pin factory, output soared when workers became specialized and the necessary tasks were divided among them. Government agencies are clearly not much like factories, but some of the same principles apply. When, for example, workers in a small enterprise are required to move among distinct tasks and perform various roles, their attention may be divided and their proficiency may fall. They might become "jacks of all trades and masters of none." Greater division of labor might also reduce capital costs. If, for example, workers in separate jurisdictions must both answer phone calls and enter data on computers (and assuming that these tasks do not overlap), the amount of each type of equipment needed might be cut significantly by setting up one phone bank and one data center, each staffed by specialists. In addition to such "technological" economies, larger enterprises can often benefit from "pecuniary" economies. Buying supplies in greater bulk, for example, may qualify the purchaser for volume discounts.

But how could the advocates of Unigov know that such savings would actually be realized? They couldn't. And it's important to note that enterprises can experience *dis*economies of scale. Perhaps, for example, excessive specialization and division of labor so bores workers that they become inattentive and less efficient. But there was actually very little risk that consolidating many municipal agencies into fewer, larger ones would ultimately increase the total cost of government services. If available scale economies are exhausted, there's simply no reason to expand further and experience diseconomies, for the agency can default to prior (optimal) configurations of its operations, effectively locking in constant returns to scale.

In any case, Unigov delivered the goods. One independent review identified almost $6 million (in today's dollars) in budget savings in just the first year of implementation due to elimination of duplicative positions, bulk purchasing, and streamlined contracting. Broadening and diversifying the city's tax base also contributed to an improved bond rating and reduced borrowing costs. Within a few years, Indianapolis began to consistently rank among the top handful of the fifty largest U.S. cities in measures of fiscal strength, financial management, and staffing efficiency.

RULE 3: AVOID LYING PRICES

Clearly, marketization and consolidation enabled Indianapolis's political leaders to run their store better. To understand the entrepreneurial culture that prevails among city officials, however, we should not overlook how the products on the store's shelves are *priced*. It's common for many of the services provided by government to be bundled together and a single price charged for all, in the form of each constituent's total tax bill. Whether it is a historical accident, politically expedient, or the result of brilliant economic thinking, however, Indianapolis goes very far in the opposite direction.

For example, the city-county features one of the most complicated and detailed property tax systems in the United States, with sixty-three different tax areas. Within each, a property owner's total bill might include several special levies to fund a variety of services and programs. It seems confusing but is, in fact, a good thing: an array of honest prices that help consumers of government services know what they're paying for and how much. By *un*bundling its package of products and putting price tags on them, local officials and their constituents communicate more effectively about what's valued and what's not. Consumers armed with better information about the cost and quality of government services might see better options elsewhere in the store (or across the street) and move along, so sellers have strong incentives to offer value. The "zeal for better services at lower cost" that animates many of Indianapolis's elected representatives might be a by-product of the way these services are priced.

In any market, prices always serve two crucial functions: they send signals to buyers and sellers about how each should behave, and they allocate (or "ration") the good in question. And prices discharge these responsibilities better or worse depending on how honest they are—which is to say, depending on how closely they correspond to the true, real costs of producing goods and delivering value to consumers.

As one example of the consequences of dishonest or *lying* prices,[6] consider events in the gasoline market in New York in the aftermath of Superstorm Sandy. Given widespread power outages, many stations couldn't operate, so Governor Andrew Cuomo—either naively thinking that this would alleviate shortages quickly or cynically betting that there was political gain in giving something away—announced that people could claim up to ten gallons of "free" gas at several government-supplied fueling locations. Chaos ensued. Large crowds queued up, and National Guard troops were needed to keep order. And it soon became clear that the available supply wasn't being allocated efficiently or fairly. At a zero price, folks who attached relatively *low* value to gasoline had an incentive to queue up for it, and many got in line ahead of those with more urgent demands—such as first responders and drivers of emergency vehicles. Different sites attempted different ways of rationing more effectively, some banning distribution to "civilians," but to little avail. The program was quickly canceled.

But state officials still could not abide "price gouging." They threatened to prosecute sellers who raised prices above pre-Sandy levels and imposed an odd-even rationing scheme (allowing those with license plates ending in an odd number to purchase gas one day, those with even numbers the next). Still, queues were lengthy, since at the artificially low price level, buyers (or at least those who had time on their hands) had little reason to economize on their use of the scarce and valuable good; hoarding flourished. And with their prices fixed, suppliers had little incentive to transport added supplies to the market (at added cost) from other areas. In effect, by telling buyers and sellers that the gas available in the affected area was still cheap, officials were lying. As with most lies, the consequences were harmful—here, an unnecessary shortage of an important good, misallocation of the supplies that were available, and additional inconvenience and misery for people who had already suffered far more than their share.[7]

When it comes to government services, lying prices are commonplace—just less so in Indianapolis. In one recent report on property taxes, for example, the Marion County treasurer reported that across the aforementioned 63 political jurisdictions and districts, residents might face as many as 60 applicable levies, yielding a 3,780-cell matrix of possible tax rates, depending on where the taxpayer chose to live. And property taxes are just one of several prices of government that one might consider in making this choice; user fees for specific services also vary widely.

To illustrate one virtue of such a well-defined price system, consider the levy for Indianapolis's Flood Control Special Taxing District. Plainly, the possibility of flood damage is not randomly or uniformly distributed. Riverfront property faces high risk, while tracts on high ground face low or zero risk. If you were to bundle the total costs of flood control together with the costs of all other services provided by the local government and then divide these costs among all taxpayers with a single, lump-sum tax bill, you would have lying prices. The apparent cost of building in the flood plain would seem lower, and that of locating out of harm's way higher, than the true costs. You'd see too much development in risky areas and too little on high ground. Over time, as the subsidized flood plain became more populous, you'd also see the expenditures required to avoid floods or cope with their damage rise to non-optimal levels. It would be much better to signal to those considering living in the flood plain that such a location decision carries an extra cost. Then and only then could you be confident that those who choose riverfront property value it as much or more than the costs of mitigating the risk of flooding.

In short, Indianapolis's unique and complex system of multiple tax districts with varying rates and user fees performs the signaling and rationing functions of a good price system much more effectively than is common in the market for government services. It is far from perfect, of course, but it does make residential location decisions there much like a trip to a store, where shoppers can compare hundreds of products and choose the combination of quality and price that best suits them. And that, in turn, puts local officials into a far more competitive frame of mind than is common among political leaders elsewhere in the Rust Belt.

TAKING IT TO THE STREETS

Avoiding the damaging effects of lying prices often faces two formidable obstacles: "fractionated" local government (in Mayor Hudnut's expressive phrase) and a deep-seated feeling among elected officials that voters can't handle the truth.

Consider the enormous waste of time and gasoline—to say nothing of the toll on Mother Earth—resulting from our commitment to "free"-ways. In Los Angeles, for example, congestion delays increase average commute times by *36 percent*—adding a full hour and forty-eight minutes to a normal five-hour weekly commuting schedule.[8] In a year, that's ninety hours wasted creeping, beeping, and polluting. One would think Angelenos (and New Yorkers, San Franciscans, and other residents of cities with similar congestion) would very much want to solve this problem. And they do: ask them how to make their commuting lives better, and most will loudly demand that more roads be built.

Except—there's no evidence that this actually works—or works for long. An unfortunate fact of commuting life, first noted by Anthony Downs as he observed the results of years of frantic freeway construction, is known as Downs's Law: on commuter routes, peak-hour traffic rises to meet capacity.[9] In short, we respond to the availability of extra space on the road by filling it up. The reason: *lying prices*. And in this case, those lies induce us to take actions that are costly not just to us, but others.

At five in the morning, for example, your route to work is a public good—that is, non-depletable, in that your use of it doesn't really diminish the amount available to me as we both cruise along at the speed limit. If, however, you start your drive to work at eight-thirty, you might be the straw that breaks the freeway's back. Traffic flowed nicely until your arrival, but now the road is over its optimum capacity and everyone slows down as a result. You're unhappy because you might be late; you're paying a cost of your decision to commute at the peak of rush hour. But everyone else also pays, which economists refer to as a "congestion externality" because you imposed a cost on those "external" to your action. Of course, you're free to argue that everybody else is imposing the external cost on you, since any of them could have slept in, thereby eliminating the cost for all. In fact, economists are careful to say that all externalities are reciprocal in nature, so fixing blame is pointless; the goal is to solve the externality problem. And charging a price (in money rather than in time wasted) can do exactly that.

Making the freeway "free" only makes sense at off-peak hours or whenever demand is below the road's capacity to carry traffic at optimum speeds. The problem is the rest of the day, when a zero price sends bad signals to potential users, inviting everyone who attaches even a trivial value to using the road to give it a shot. That's a prescription for gridlock. One recent survey totaled up the typical delays nationwide and concluded that Americans waste $121 billion annually in congestion-related fuel and time costs.[10] There's no free lunch, and pretending there is can be a horribly expensive, inefficient, and even inequitable way to ration a valuable good.

The solution is to (a) coax those who *least* value the road at peak times *not* to use it, thus reserving space for those who value it most, and (b) make those high-valuing users pay for the privilege. Tolls do both. The prospect of avoiding a toll might get more commuters onto buses, induce more carpooling, or give employers incentive to adopt flex-time so their workers can commute during off-peak (and off-price) periods. Absent reliable signals about the value of scarce freeway space and honest prices for it, no one has much incentive to change habits that lead to chronic congestion.

The problem, of course, is that people in general don't like the idea of paying for something that is customarily free. Never mind that Americans are, in fact, paying that aforementioned $121 billion. We apparently think we can make that go away, in defiance of Downs's Law, by lobbying for more lanes to be built. In the meantime, we seem to like the *illusion* of a zero price, because every time anyone proposes greater reliance on tollways and congestion pricing, the response is overwhelmingly negative.

Eventually, though, some enterprising U.S. city is going to try what the clever Swedes did to overcome resistance to using tolls to alleviate Stockholm's chronic traffic problems. In 2000, a parliamentary commission recommended treating the city's congestion in the usual way: more roadbuilding. But the cost—roughly half of the national government's capital budget for the next decade—was so high that other approaches, including always-unpopular tolls, made their way into the public debate. As a condition of joining a ruling coalition, Sweden's Green Party won a promise that the government would simply *try* congestion charges in Stockholm.

This blunted the opposition to charging for that which is commonly free. Even some enemies of tolls were looking forward to the trial period to demonstrate how unfair and inefficient it would be to price road capacity; it was called "the most expensive way ever devised to commit political suicide."[11] Nevertheless, an intrepid group of transit experts and government officials designed a system that charged varying amounts to those traveling in and out of Stockholm from 6:30 A.M. to 6:30 P.M. on weekdays. There were no toll booths to slow travelers down, however: transponders in cars were linked to bank accounts and charges collected automatically, as is done in the United States with systems like the EZ Pass along some East Coast interstates.

The trial began on January 3, 2006, and the results were immediate and visible to the naked eye. The next morning's headline in a leading Stockholm newspaper said it succinctly: "Every fourth car disappeared." Accompanying before-and-after photos showed a clogged arterial highway pre-toll and the same spot flowing freely under the new pricing system. This was not a fluke. Over the six-month study period, monthly reductions in the numbers of vehicles passing the toll cordons averaged 21 to 30 percent. The average time wasted in traffic jams fell one-third in the morning and one-half in the evening peak hours. Exhaust emissions fell 10 to 15 percent. Road safety improved. Equity effects were generally favorable, since much of the toll burden was shouldered by employed, affluent drivers and lower-income commuters benefited from expanded public transit capacity funded by the tolls.

But these were outcomes that economists had long predicted. What was surprising was how *public opinion* swung from negative to positive as the pricing system's favorable effects became apparent. A few weeks into the trial, the Swedish prime minister announced he'd changed his mind about tolls and now supported them. About 35 percent of respondents in subsequent polls said they'd done the same. That was—barely—enough: once the trial was concluded and the evidence processed, Stockholm residents voted 53-47 in favor of continuing the congestion charges; in August 2007, the system was reinstituted and made permanent.

Clearly, then, honest prices can be extremely effective in allocating scarce resources such as road capacity. People well understand the signals that such prices transmit and are quite capable of modifying their behavior in wholesome ways in response. What's more, as they do so they ultimately appreciate how congestion pricing can yield personal benefits. That so many Swedish commuters changed their minds indicates they realized that the value of time saved under the toll system repaid them for the requisite monetary outlays or other inconveniences. Surveys showed that a lot of the car trips that disappeared during rush hours were discretionary shopping trips or other leisure activities that were easy to reschedule or do without.

In addition, congestion pricing can yield financial benefits for localities. Tolls convert the time and fuel wasted via "rationing by waiting" into revenue streams; they monetize the efficiency gains that result from traffic jams avoided. Though the startup costs of installing toll equipment can be substantial, over time this investment can generate surpluses that can be used for other needed public goods, especially complementary transit infrastructure. In New York, for example, the Metropolitan Transit Authority was merged (in 1968) with the Triborough Bridge and Tunnel Authority so that surplus toll revenue could be invested in subway repairs and improvements, helping rescue that system from physical and fiscal decline.[12] Still, however, the city is not pricing away congestion externalities the way it ought: not all its bridges and tunnels are priced at all, or in both directions, so opportunistic truckers and commuters often plot circuitous "free" routes through clogged surface streets to save cash, instead spending their and others' time, gas, and air quality.

Monetizing the value of scarce curb space is another possible source of funding for urban public goods. Drivers often cruise crowded city streets in search of "free parking" (yet another lying price). In some congested neighborhoods, 30 percent of the traffic consists of drivers searching vainly for underpriced curbside spots rather than paying a fee sufficient to ration this scarce good more effectively.[13] So far, San Francisco, Los Angeles, and New York have been the leaders in experimenting with metering technology aimed at better equating the demand for and supply of parking on public streets, installing sensors to measure space availability in problematic areas and providing smartphone payment apps and electronic signage with rate and availability information. As with tolls, the unpopularity of such pricing systems tends to diminish over time as consumers see its benefits.

LEVELING THE LEARNING FIELD

Ninety percent of American children attend public elementary and secondary schools. But these schools get very low grades from consumers. A recent Gallup poll found that only 37 percent of respondents rate public schools "excellent" or "good," versus 78 percent for independent private schools, 69 percent for church-related schools, and 60 percent for charter schools.[14] How do the public schools maintain their near-monopoly status in many communities? Another lying price, of course. Send your child to his or her assigned public school, disappointing though it may be, and it's "free." Go private and you're on the hook for tuition, while your taxes pay to educate others' kids.

It's been known for a long time that the public schools are underperforming—probably since a 1975 *Newsweek* cover story titled "Why Johnny Can't Write," but certainly since a 1983 presidential commission shocked parents with a scathing report titled *A Nation at Risk*. So lots of money has been thrown at the problem, more than doubling inflation-adjusted per-pupil spending on public education since 1975. Nevertheless, teens' scores on the National Assessment of Educational Progress have remained stubbornly flat, and a 2012 report from Harvard's Program on Education Policy and Governance ranked the U.S. twenty-fifth of forty-nine countries regarding student achievement.

Marketization would therefore seem to have enormous potential to enhance performance in this vital sector. This is especially true in some large cities, where greater population density, mass transit infrastructure, and a rich endowment of established church-related schools increase the chances that students could access competitive institutions. The best evidence is clear: in education as in much else, monopoly is the enemy of quality and cost effectiveness, while competition is their ally.

Even when private alternatives are largely absent, competition *between* public systems has beneficial effects on educational performance. Many public systems are huge and dominate an enormous area: New York's covers the five boroughs and enrolls over a million students, L.A. Unified serves almost seven hundred thousand, and the entire state of Hawaii is a single school district. But some metropolitan areas—Indianapolis and Boston are good examples—contain many independent school districts within a short distance of each other. In such areas, families can vote with their feet and locate in the districts that offer the best value. In turn, those districts and their political leaders have a stronger incentive to safeguard school quality. In 2000, Caroline Hoxby compared public school performance in areas with lots of interdistrict choice to that in areas with essentially none.[15] She found that eighth grade reading scores in competitive areas were 3.8 national percentile points higher, tenth grade math scores 3.1 points higher, and twelfth grade reading scores 5.8 points higher than those in noncompetitive districts. What's more, the competitive districts got these superior results while spending 7.6 percent *less* (per pupil) than the no-choice districts. And public schools in areas blessed (for historical reasons) with a large market for private schooling show similar gains in test scores. When they fear losing business to rivals, the public schools can, indeed, do more with less.

Milwaukee was a trail-blazer in using vouchers to help its poorest students escape underperforming public schools. Starting in 1990, families with incomes below 175 percent of the poverty line could apply for vouchers to be used toward tuition at accredited private schools. Generally, the voucher amount was less than two-thirds of the public system's per-pupil spending. The district lost half of the voucher amount every time a qualifying student left for the private sector, so it had a reasonable incentive to get better—especially when the city's self-imposed cap on participation was raised to 15 percent of district enrollment. And, indeed, the threat of voucher-related loss of enrollments led to improvement in *all* the potentially affected public schools, but the stronger the degree of competition was (measured here by the fraction of eligible families in a district), the greater was the gain in students' test scores.

Charter school legislation has been somewhat easier to obtain in the political marketplace than vouchers, and the results have been similarly encouraging. Arizona and Michigan have been early leaders in these efforts. Hoxby has found that in the former, fourth grade reading and math scores improved by 1.4 national percentile points per year in schools that faced competition from charters. In the latter, the improvements were even greater: 2.4 added percentile points in fourth grade reading and 2.5 points in math. That can add up. For example, if impoverished and largely minority Detroit (whose public schools now face some competition from charters) can continue such relative gains, it would close its students' achievement gap with affluent Gross Pointe in less than a generation.

Of course, monopolies never yield their dominant positions without a fight, and the political opposition to competition in this market from teachers' unions, bureaucrats, and ed-school academics has been well-funded and no-holds-barred.

Cyberspace is full of agenda-driven "studies" defending the education status quo (while advocating ever-more-lavish funding), denunciations of marketization as "elitist" and contrary to our democratic ideals, and vitriolic assaults on "profiteers" exploiting our children while lining their own pockets.

All of this is more than a bit ironic, since the monopolists are themselves defending some very lucrative turf: they control streams of tax dollars that fund generous compensation schemes and retirement benefits, set work rules that make life on the job more pleasant, and define curricula that require students to conform to their tastes about what should be learned and how. It would be naive to suppose that they will easily give all this up just to enhance student learning or lighten the burden on taxpayers.

Nevertheless, the campaign to loosen these groups' stranglehold on the education market—waged variously by reformist politicians, philanthropists, and entrepreneurial educators tired of the failures of prevailing approaches—has made significant progress. Vouchers, which can reduce or eliminate the public schools' price advantage and are thus of greatest value to poor parents, now exist in seventeen states. In 2002, the Supreme Court's ruling in *Zelman v. Simmons-Harris* removed a legal impediment to the growth of such programs by establishing that the federal constitution does not bar parents from applying vouchers to religiously affiliated schools. In a few states with constitutions that are more restrictive on this score, education tax credits are helping close the public-private price gap. And forty-one states and the District of Columbia now allow charter schools, though some of these publicly funded but semi-autonomous institutions are so constrained in their management, staffing, and curriculum decisions that they are virtually indistinguishable from the public schools with which they are nominally competing for students.

The question is how to bring marketization to locales where the opposition is most deeply entrenched. One answer might be to employ the same strategy used by former Indy mayor Goldsmith to bring greater efficiency to street maintenance: simply put the work up for competitive bids, allowing unionized public employees a fair chance to keep their jobs if they can deliver better results.[16] Where it is politically infeasible to create competition *within* the market—by empowering parents with vouchers they may spend at any of several private schools vying for their business, for example—it may be possible to realize gains via competition *for* the market.

In a nutshell, public officials could identify the most dysfunctional schools in their district, engage parents in setting improved standards for student performance and other school characteristics, and specify an amount to be paid to the eventual contractor. Bidders would then compete not by offering lower prices but better quality. This strategy, while it foregoes some potential cost savings associated with marketization, blunts criticism that students in targeted schools would be shortchanged by "greedy education entrepreneurs," and that marketization is mere union-busting. As a practical matter, the education monopolists do not actually *own* the schools they operate—they just behave as if they do, and absent market pressure can mismanage them without much consequence. Even if this contracting approach is just applied to a few schools within a much larger district, such an apparently minor rearrangement of property rights might encourage all others to raise their game.

There are, in sum, many steps great and small that city governments might take to perform their traditional functions more efficiently. Unfortunately, however, it's often less fun to "mind the store" and give customers better quality, service, and prices than to attempt to remodel it entirely, a topic to which we must turn in the next two chapters.

CHAPTER 8

No Little Plans

IN 1997, SUZETTE KELO bought her first house, a century-old cottage overlooking the Thames River in New London, Connecticut. On the day she moved in, she wrote, "I have never been happier in my life than I am right now, sitting on the porch rocker watching the water go by."[1] It was a fixer-upper, but she loved the fixing, even studying Victorian architecture to make sure her restorative touches were historically appropriate, right down to its color (pastel pink). She put down roots and joined her neighbors in renewing, as best they could, an area that had seen better days but which they were determined to improve and make their lifelong home.

The city's movers and shakers, however, had more grandiose ideas. The New London Development Corporation (NLDC), a "public-private partnership" created to "combat community deterioration," recruited Pfizer, the multinational drug firm, to build a research facility nearby. The plan included a waterfront hotel, a conference center, retail stores, and new residences on the adjoining ninety acres. That would require bulldozing Ms. Kelo's old Vic, and many others. As one company executive put it, "Pfizer wants a nice place to operate. We don't want to be surrounded by tenements." And the NLDC wanted to pump up the city's tax base and bring in new jobs. Aided by state grants, it began buying property, telling any owners reluctant to sell that the city would eventually condemn their homes and acquire them through its powers of eminent domain.

Most left. Ms. Kelo and a few other "tenement dwellers" went to court. Such cases usually revolve around money, as the Constitution's Fifth Amendment establishes government's authority to take property for public use as long as just compensation is paid. The New Londoners' lawyers, however, saw the case as an opportunity to test some controversial legal principles. Not only was the NLDC not quite a government agency, but the use to which it intended to put the land it was taking did not appear very "public"—as a new school or road might be. The plaintiffs' goal was not to ratchet up the price the NLDC had to pay them, but to stop the land seizure entirely.

They failed. In a 5-4 decision written by Justice John Paul Stevens, the Supreme Court ruled that "[p]romoting economic development is a traditional and long-accepted function of government. There is no basis for exempting economic development from our traditionally broad understanding of public purpose." In a vigorous dissent, however, Justice Sandra Day O'Connor noted that almost any lawful use of private property—such as the "nice place" Pfizer wanted for its lab—could generate some incidental public benefit. Construing the words "for public use" in this way, she argued, would "not realistically exclude any takings," and thus "not exert any constraint on the eminent domain power. . . . Nothing is to prevent the State from replacing any Motel 6 with a Ritz-Carlton, any home with a shopping mall, or any farm with a factory."[2]

Public sentiment favored the dissenters; subsequent events vindicated them. Years after the decision, the land the NLDC had seized stood vacant, and Pfizer's research facility was shuttered when it was acquired by another drug company. In 2012, New London's mayor formally apologized to those displaced in the name of renewal that had never come. Partly as a result of *Kelo*-related backlash, forty-three states passed legislation aimed at preventing takings based on economic development rationales. Suzette Kelo lost the battle for her home but clearly helped advance a wider war against local governments' expansive use of their eminent domain powers.

The tragedy is that this has been a "hundred years war," and for most of it the owners of private property have been in retreat. *Kelo* merely observed precedent. In 1954, the Supreme Court had given local officials virtual *carte blanche* to take property for renewal purposes in *Berman v. Parker*, which upheld the District of Columbia Redevelopment Act of 1946. This etched in stone some principles that had evolved over prior decades: that "substandard housing and blighted areas" were "injurious to the public health, safety, morals, and welfare," that these areas should be eliminated "by all means necessary and appropriate," that "the ordinary operations of private enterprise alone" could not do so, and that "redevelopment pursuant to a project area redevelopment plan . . . [was] a public use."[3]

Clearly, however, stripping people such as Suzette Kelo of their property rights—even when a sizeable check is cut and there are grand plans for the property taken—can have a significant downside. The mere threat of such takings will have a chilling effect on private owners' plans to upgrade residences and businesses in areas targeted for "rescue" by planners. What's more, relocation of residents of those areas may carry hidden costs, as it rends the social fabric of neighborhoods. Finally, those "project area redevelopment plans" may grossly misallocate the scarce capital available for investment in a city because the takings and subsidies inherent in such efforts distort price signals and substitute the tastes of planners for those of market participants. In this chapter, we'll examine how the desire to save cities via planned redevelopment has so often damaged their viability in these three important ways, and develop some guidelines for more "organic" renewal efforts.

FROM REGULATION TO DEMOLITION

Slums have many causes, but the simplest is the passage of time. As structures age, they commonly decline in utility and value. This can be mitigated by regular maintenance, of course, but older buildings tend, ever-so-slowly, to "filter down" to lower-valued uses and lower-income users. In the extreme, this can degrade entire neighborhoods to the point that they become known as slums or blighted areas. If tax policy is benign and owners have appropriate incentives to maintain their properties, this process can be self-limiting. Or, it can be reversed entirely: the value of depreciated structures may fall so low that their owners will profit by upgrading them, recycling them to higher-valued uses and higher-income users—a process referred to (often pejoratively) as gentrification.

However slums develop, their existence has long troubled people of good will. Living conditions in slums are usually so far below what is considered decent and tolerable that organized campaigns to improve them date as far back as the mid-1800s. The publication of Jacob Riis's *How the Other Half Lives* in 1890 energized these efforts. Riis was a talented photographer, journalist, and social reformer, and his provocative photos and accounts of life in the squalid tenements of Manhattan's Lower East Side helped transform concern into action. Soon New York passed aggressive new housing laws aimed at reducing overcrowding and improving living conditions by capping building heights and lot coverage and mandating larger rooms, higher ceilings, bigger windows, metal fire escapes, and indoor plumbing in each apartment. Many other large cities followed suit.

When these regulations were enforced, however, tenants often joined with their landlords to *resist* relocation from structures declared substandard. If this surprised the reformers, they seldom reconsidered their approach. It was easier to assume that these slum dwellers—most of them semiliterate immigrants—simply didn't know what was good for them. Perhaps, though, they were managing their lives in ways the reformers could not grasp. Riis himself noted with astonishment that despite working long hours in dreadful conditions, the objects of his concern commonly deposited more than half their modest incomes in banks.[4]

Why not buy better housing or enjoy more leisure? Because they had more important objectives. It's not that they didn't want bigger, better-ventilated apartments or private bathrooms. It's that they didn't want these things if it would keep them from sending money to a starving cousin in County Cork, buying a trans-Atlantic steamship ticket for a brother in the Warsaw ghetto, or starting a small business. The new regulations would raise their rents and force them to spend some of their limited wealth in ways they would not have chosen. So, naturally, they resisted. The tenement laws consoled the reformers, but the *net* effects of their campaign were not necessarily socially beneficial, for improving slum-dwellers' physical surroundings would not enhance their overall welfare if it impaired their ability to achieve other goals.

In any case, more stringent housing regulations did little to eliminate slums. By the 1920s, many tenement dwellers had moved "up and out" thanks to brisk wage growth, but their economic and geographic mobility was of small comfort to the reformers. The abundant stock of high-density urban housing that dated from the late 1800s inevitably filtered down. Immigration restrictions imposed during and after World War I somewhat dampened demand for these cheap, low-quality accommodations, but domestic migrants—whites from impoverished Appalachia, blacks from the rural South—arrived to fill them and pursue opportunities in the booming industrial cities of the East and North. So, since tighter building codes and regulations seemed incapable of ending urban blight, it was time to escalate the battle.

The reformers' new strategy was slum clearance and construction of publicly owned and managed housing projects. Their success in getting this program approved and funded owes as much to interest-group politics and historical happenstance as to their intellectual energy, which came from utopian visionaries and progressives with an interest in architecture and urban planning. Many were environmental determinists, believing that more beautiful surroundings—high-amenity housing; orderly, planned neighborhoods—would both please their residents and *transform* them. Their plans often featured large tracts dotted with high-rises or geometrically arranged low-rises, with much acreage left open for green spaces that would improve the health and uplift the spirits of residents. They took it on faith that private markets would never produce decent housing that the poor could afford, but avoided incendiary socialist rhetoric. Instead, they warned that slums were cancers that could spread to healthy urban tissue, and armed themselves with studies purporting to show that slums not only damaged their residents' well-being but were a drag on municipal budgets, consuming far more in governmental services than they generated in tax receipts.

Such arguments won favor with Chamber of Commerce types who wanted to move the poor away from downtown because they thought this would enhance business. Fiscally conservative elected officials also saw slum clearance as a way to increase cities' tax bases and cut outlays. What everyone needed was a way to pay the steep acquisition, demolition, and rebuilding costs inherent in the reformers' grand plans. When the Great Depression arrived and the federal government began looking for ways to stimulate the macro-economy, their problems were solved. Thanks to the National Housing Act of 1934 and the Wagner-Steagall Housing Act of 1937, dollars for slum clearance and public housing began to flow.

The results were not a complete and unmitigated disaster, but they came close. A key element of the 1937 law ensured that it would have a trivial effect on housing affordability. The monkey wrench in the works was a political compromise needed to win enough votes for passage. Landlords

correctly anticipated that increasing the supply of apartments would reduce rents and their incomes. At their insistence, the legislation stipulated
equivalent elimination: each unit of public housing constructed required
the demolition of a preexisting unit of private housing. Therefore, overall
housing supply could not increase and private-sector rents would not fall
as a result of this program.

As cities bulldozed neighborhoods they considered blighted and erected
public projects in their stead, though, *some* lucky citizens indeed got
cheaper housing. Rents were based on ability to pay—often just 20 percent of income—and the lure of these subsidies meant there were long
waiting lists for space in public housing. But the buildings themselves
usually were neither built to high design standards nor well-managed by
the local public housing authorities, and economically mobile working-
and middle-class tenants often exited in pursuit of greater amenity. The
authorities then found it even harder to maintain their properties while
subsidizing an increasingly poor clientele, and things began to spiral out
of control. There were, of course, some public housing success stories,
but by the 1960s it was already clear that many of "the projects" were
worse than the slums they had replaced: more economically and racially
segregated, poorer, and beset by social problems of a nature and level unimagined by the reformers.

The short, tragic life of one of the more infamous tests of their theories,
the Pruitt-Igoe project in St. Louis, is illustrative. It won design awards
from *Architectural Forum* prior to its opening in 1954. Construction of
its 2,870 apartments cost $36 million, or $12,500 per unit at a time when
the median single-family home in the United States had a market value
of about $11,000. But this premium price did not buy much amenity: in
order to encourage mingling in common areas, apartments were kept small
and "skip-stop" elevators delivered residents only to every third floor.

This proved unpopular: even with sizeable rent subsidies, Pruitt-Igoe's
occupancy rate peaked at 91 percent in 1957 and headed steadily downward thereafter. As it did, crime, vandalism, and the drug trade flourished.
By 1965, the project was one-third vacant; by 1971, it housed only six
hundred and almost half its buildings were boarded up. It had neither
pleased nor transformed its residents; they had transformed it. Its architect

noted sadly, "I never thought people were that destructive."[5] By 1976, its thirty-three towers were demolished. During the 1980s, most of the new vertical slums in other cities were imploded as well.

EXILE ON MAIN STREET(S)

This record of profound failure led to some salutary changes in policy toward housing the poor. In particular, the Housing and Community Development Act of 1974 amended Section 8 of the 1937 housing law to allow localities to grant qualifying applicants rent vouchers, which could be used to cover the difference between private market rents and recipients' capacity to pay for housing (now defined as 30 percent of income). This enabled tenants to search for units that best suited their needs, harnessed the forces of market competition to their benefit, and reduced municipalities' role in the property management business, for which the evidence suggested they were ill suited.

But slum clearance efforts actually gathered steam because, by the late 1940s, the housing reformers' movement had been hijacked—by their allies. Downtown business interests still liked the idea of leveling nearby blighted areas, but argued it would be better—not least for their cash flow—to replace tenements not with public housing but with shiny new office towers, upscale apartments, convention centers, or hotels. City planners agreed, since implementing redevelopment policy would empower them: it seemed obvious that deciding which areas to bulldoze and determining their "best and highest use" could not be done piecemeal but required a general plan, one that would spell out "future land uses of the whole city."[6] Local politicians jumped on board when it became clear that Uncle Sam would underwrite renewal efforts with large checks. Title I of the Housing Act of 1949 authorized the federal government to help cities buy and bulldoze property in designated redevelopment areas and turn it over to private developers, and allocated $1.5 billion (about $15 billion today) to do so; much more would follow.

Slum-dwellers themselves, whose plight had proved so useful in getting urban redevelopment policy on the books and opening the money spigot, almost became an afterthought—though rhetorically, project proponents always invoked their interests. Promised tax receipts from an improved central business district would ritually be said to give cities the wherewithal to fund services and programs of value to the poor. Surveys appeared showing that those relocated generally enjoyed higher-quality housing—a "significant increase in both the cleanliness and orderliness of the dwellings."[7] There was a trade-off, however: one careful study of those displaced by Boston's West End project found that almost nine of ten were paying higher rents, with the median increase a staggering 73 percent.[8]

No matter: since a large proportion of the costs of renewal efforts came out of Uncle Sam's pocket—constituting yet another lying price that made it seem irresistibly cheap to uproot entire neighborhoods in the name of economic development—cities swung the wrecking ball with gusto. By 1967, the projects enabled by the 1949 housing law had leveled 400,000 housing units and built just 10,760 low-rent dwellings to replace them.[9] By 1973, 992 cities and towns had implemented 2,532 redevelopment plans, at which point the Nixon administration cut off funding for the program. It wasn't just that Nixon was cheap, but that the program was visibly counterproductive. Once planners designated a tract a redevelopment zone, investment within its borders ceased. Why spend money improving your property when it will be taken in a few years at a price determined by a bureaucrat? Renewal efforts thus frequently resembled an attempt to fill a bathtub with the drain open: in any given area, as much capital might flow out as the redevelopment authority (and its subsidy-seeking private partners) might pour in.

Whether Title I, on net, added significantly to cities' stocks of physical capital has never been carefully studied. One thing that is clear and undeniable, however, is that it produced an intra-urban diaspora: from 1949 to 1973, about two million people were displaced from their former residences by Title I–funded projects.[10] Roughly two-thirds of these were the most recent arrivals in cities: black migrants from the rural South. Thus it became popular, among critics of redevelopment policy, to refer to urban renewal as "Negro removal." There is no way to judge whether this was, as some allege, frequently the program's intent. It is clear, however, that its effects have often been devastating—though in ways not fully appreciated.

TEARING THE SOCIAL FABRIC

As much as urban renewal policy was lauded by cheerleaders in the media, academe, and the aforementioned interest groups during this period, it was decried and contested by those in the path of the bulldozers. Again, some of this resistance stemmed from relocatees' awareness that they were likely to be forced to a less-preferred budget allocation: higher-amenity, higher-cost housing would mean less saving or spending on other goods. In addition, there was the trauma of being uprooted from surroundings that, unappealing as they might seem to outsiders, might have considerable value to their inhabitants. Psychologists speak of "place attachment" and describe it in terms similar to our affection for and connection to other people. In the same way that loss of a loved one involves significant psychic costs, so might movement from even a slum dwelling produce genuine grief.[11]

But use of government's taking power also carries risk of another, perhaps greater cost to individuals and society: loss of social capital. Sociologists sometimes explain this concept by simply pointing out that *relationships matter.* When people interact frequently with each other they form connections; these can develop into bonds of trust that enable them to do things that might otherwise be impossible—or possible only at a higher cost. Executives, for example, often invest a great deal of energy developing their "networks." This is because these intangible assets can be every bit as important in meeting the challenges of business—and everyday life—as education (human capital), a healthy bank account (financial capital), or a computer (physical capital).

Obviously, what we now call social capital has existed since people began gathering in tribes. Scholars' awareness of it, however, is embarrassingly recent. And because measuring it faces serious obstacles—it can't easily be counted like years of schooling or readily valued like bank balances or machinery—assessments of its importance and impact are limited in scope and reliability. Most studies of the phenomenon measure it by combining various indicators of the extent to which people are connected or have formed bonds with each other—such as the level of participation in religious or political groups, membership in social organizations, the extent of voluntary activities, or the frequency of work-based socializing—into some sort of "social capital index." Clearly, this approach has its flaws, and research on how the stock of social capital varies over time or across regions remains a subject of debate.

Still, the evidence suggests that social capital is crucial to people's welfare. It can, for example, influence economic outcomes just as strongly as other forms of capital. Personal networks are often as or more important than formal employment agencies or other entities in securing a job, and contribute to the success of firms, especially startups, by enhancing access to credit, helping identify opportunities for growth, and stimulating innovation and knowledge transfers. Political scientist Robert Putnam avers that "where trust and social networks flourish, individuals, firms, neighborhoods and even nations prosper."[12]

The presence or absence of social capital seems to play an even larger role in non-economic spheres. Educational attainment, for example, is favorably affected by parents' and students' stocks of social capital—particularly for children from otherwise disadvantaged backgrounds. Social cohesion and health are positively correlated; some studies have found that people with strong social networks have mortality rates one-third to one-half those of people with weak social ties.[13] And higher levels of social capital lead to lower levels of crime (after controlling for other possible influences on such activity). Relationships, connectedness, and bonds of trust among family, friends, and neighbors apparently make it easier to develop and enforce social norms and controls that have a variety of wholesome effects.

No wonder, then, that slum clearance plans were met with resistance far more often than acceptance. To outsiders' eyes, a neighborhood might seem rundown, but its residents' stocks of invisible social capital might be considerable. Over time, they might have built up trust in their neighbors—and their neighbors in them—or developed a nearby network of potential employers or employees, suppliers, customers, child-care providers, or mentors. Some of this capital might be portable, of course. An address change doesn't necessarily force one to abandon one's church or circle of friends. The costs of maintaining these relationships might go up with greater geographic separation, however, and clearly *some* proportion of this capital will be destroyed by relocation.

That we have no measures of the value of this squandered capital, or the impact of its tragic loss on the health and welfare of those uprooted during this period, does not mean we should dismiss or forget these considerations today. It is quite possible that a nontrivial share of the social and economic problems associated with urban poverty in the second half of the twentieth century originated in just such indifference to the importance of social capital. We must never repeat this error.

CAPITAL ALLOCATION: WHO DO YOU TRUST?

Entrepreneurs pursue profits by buying low, adding value, and selling high; this principle applies in real estate as much as it does in any other industry. So it's hard to see how the idea took root that developers would be uninterested in buying cheap property, upgrading it, and profiting from its sale—a process that might be called "organic urban renewal." But take root it did, despite ample evidence that private firms were happy to perform this task and often did so on a reasonably large scale and to wonderful effect.

Manhattan's Tudor City provides one enduring example. By the mid-1920s, many of the upper- and middle-class residents of the East Side had moved to suburban locales, from which they could commute by rail to nearby Grand Central Terminal and jobs in mid-town. The tenements in the area that would become Tudor City—all the blocks between East 40th and 44th Streets and First and Second Avenues—had therefore filtered down to an "ethnically diverse, working-class" population.[14] Property values were low partly because of the area's undesirable neighbors: an elevated rail line clattered along Second Avenue, and east of First Avenue were slaughterhouses that often produced a stench that East Siders described as "unbearable" (an example of what economists call negative externalities). Had this been the era of Title I–funded renewal, officials probably would have formulated a plan to level and reconstruct the entire area—including, perhaps, relocating the nearby industries and all their jobs—on the premise that otherwise there would be no hope for an improved East Side. A developer named Fred French, however, saw an opportunity for profit.

In a single month late in 1925, French's company put together the largest redevelopment tract theretofore assembled in Manhattan, buying over a hundred buildings covering five acres at a cost of $7.5 million (about

$100 million today). Holdout problems—the most oft-cited rationale for the need to use eminent domain, in order to keep greedy or opportunistic owners from stalling a socially beneficial project—were largely overcome by using buying agents who kept the plans for a new development secret, by paying prices that sellers found attractive, and, ultimately, by leaving a handful of unwilling sellers alone and their properties intact.

As to the unpleasantness arising from the industries nearby, French mitigated those by means of artful design, arranging his ten new structures facing westward and incorporating private parks and innovative traffic flow patterns to make the residents of his "city within a city" less mindful of their noxious neighbors. And because French was trying to attract tenants rather than modify their behavior (a la Pruitt-Igoe and its "skip-stop" elevators, for example), he and his architects created value for potential customers in every way they could. The project's pleasing Tudor Revival architectural style and careful arrangement of structures and green spaces created a distinct sense of place. Diverse businesses were integrated into the plan to make living in Tudor City convenient. Ads highlighted the presence of restaurants, shops, a gym and bowling alley, daycare and a kindergarten, a library, and laundry and valet services. To compete with the suburbs in appealing to upscale residents, one of the development's two private parks was for a while configured as a golf course—on 42nd Street!—that was illuminated at night.

But tenants of modest means were not ignored. The larger structures included studio apartments designed to be shared by young people working entry-level, white-collar jobs; each included two fold-out ("Murphy") beds, two closets, a kitchenette, and a bathroom, and rented for $60 a month in the late 1920s (equivalent to about $800 today).[15] As a result, Tudor City was immediately popular and immensely profitable. By 1930 it housed forty-five hundred residents, many times the number who had occupied the ramshackle low-rises it replaced. Its designs were widely praised and it ultimately won status as a landmark historic district.

Of course, once the Great Depression arrived it became difficult for anyone to make much money doing anything. Real estate tycoons—including French himself—became good at lobbying for subsidies and "public-private partnerships" as a way to create jobs, revivify cities, and improve their bottom line. And those arrangements outlived the Depression because they suited the political elites as much as the tycoons, and because it was easy to take taxpayers along for the ride.

Buying High, Selling Low

The 1949 housing law permitted local authorities not only to sell sites acquired via eminent domain to private developers, but also to sell for *less* than they had paid—and put Uncle Sam on the hook for two-thirds of any difference. This buy-high, sell-low method of subsidizing economic development remains common today: the land the NLDC took from Suzette Kelo and her neighbors was to be leased to a developer for a mere $1 per year, for example. Why would such giveaways be necessary if renewal areas were to be transformed from low-valued uses to better and more lucrative ones?

In recent decades, the go-to rationale for subsidies has been the *spillover benefits* of redevelopment (here, positive externalities). If, for example, a developer wanted to build a four-star hotel next to a downtown business district but found that acquiring the tract and building on it would cost more than could be earned in revenue, the project would be a loser for the developer—but not necessarily for society. Perhaps the hotel will stimulate nearby businesses, generating income or job growth worth *more* than the developer's deficit. In that case, a redevelopment authority could ensure the realization of these external benefits by buying the tract and discounting it to the developer just enough to make the hotel project profitable.

Accordingly, it's routine to talk up spillover benefits in selling taxpayer-assisted renewal projects to the public. Economic impact studies promising abundant job creation, income growth, and new tax receipts now accompany every redevelopment plan of any size. Convincing evidence that these positive externalities are significant—if they eventuate at all—is scant, however. In recent years, for example, cities large and small have spent billions subsidizing the construction of downtown stadiums and arenas in order to attract visitors to nearby hotels, bars, and restaurants. Inevitably, these facilities are touted as game-changers that will spark a boom via a strong "multiplier effect," as the dollars those visitors spend recycle through the urban economy. Economists have been studying these investments for a long time, though, and generally find no evidence of favorable impact to employment, wages, or other key variables. The problem is that such projects often just rearrange consumer spending geographically—attracting it to one area but diverting it from others. Unless a facility attracts many visitors from outside the region, its net impacts are likely to be trivial.[16] And if promises about spillover benefits from sexy, high-profile sports facilities are all too often empty, why should we give much credence to claims about more mundane projects like a new office park or strip mall?

In any case, the frequency with which subsidies were doled out under Title I (and subsequent legislation) raises some suspicions about redevelopment authorities' motivations. In principle, buy-high, sell-low tactics should be necessary only *at the margin*. In any troubled city, there ought to be plenty of areas where low-valued properties can be transformed to higher-valued uses. Only when an area's value as renewed is lower than that in its current form *and* the spillover benefits offset this deficit is this rationale operative and a subsidy necessary to realize prospective social gains. In fact, though, subsidies almost always are paid to developers in large-scale renewal projects. Rarely if ever does the government authority merely act as a broker, assembling a tract and passing it along "at cost" so that the developer(s) can add value.

Perhaps then we should entertain a more cynical view of cities' relentless commitment to grandiose, heavily subsidized urban renewal plans: that this reflects rent-seeking behavior by developers and their enablers in the public sector. In the ill-chosen jargon of economists, rents are not what tenants pay for their apartments but, rather, undeserved profits, often obtained by manipulating government rule makers. The owner of a department store, for example, might bank higher profits by getting the local town council to impose a restrictive zoning law that prevents a rival from locating nearby; the resulting monopoly profits for the incumbent store would be called rents. In the context of urban renewal, the use of eminent domain might enable redevelopers to capture rents by limiting initial owners' bargaining power and undercompensating them. Additional subsidies would be icing on the cake.

But what's in it for the local pols and bureaucrats who do their bidding? Clearly, they can extract their pound of flesh—that is, *share* the rents that they alone can create. The responsible politicians, for example, can bank on contributions from the developers of the tracts they will acquire on the cheap and subsidize, and votes from the construction unions who will do the work (at very attractive rates, as the bill for Pruitt-Igoe showed). Almost as gratifying, perhaps, is that by exercising control over the urban development process in this way the local officials become enormously powerful and prestigious. Organic, Fred French–style renewal leaves politicians and bureaucrats out of the development loop. But a willingness to use eminent domain and subsidies to pump up the returns on renewal projects puts these officials in the middle of every major deal. The executives of private-sector development companies might cash enviably large paychecks, but refereeing the urban redevelopment game can give humble civil servants the rush of being the people without whom big deals cannot get done, big profits made, and cities rebuilt. Hard to resist that.

Making Losers Look Like Winners

Once politicians, bureaucrats, appointed boards, and well-connected corporate "partners" are put in charge of allocating much of the scarce capital that's available to be invested in a struggling city, there are serious doubts about how well that investment will serve the public interest and reflect citizens' preferences—no matter how many open hearings officials include as part of their planning process. And injecting federal or state subsidies into the renewal process just puts those doubts on steroids.

The first problem is the obvious one, noted earlier in other contexts: a lying price often causes people to buy things they otherwise wouldn't. A half-off coupon will tempt the most virtuous of us to break our diet at the all-you-can-eat buffet. And during the Title I era, when federal taxpayers paid two-thirds of the subsidies flowing to developers, cities had a huge incentive to overdo urban renewal—to seize, bulldoze, and rebuild to excess.

Do some hypothetical math on the four-star hotel in the earlier example. If it costs $100 million to acquire the site and build a hotel worth only $90 million, it's a loser; it merits subsidy only if spillover benefits exceed $10 million. But suppose those positive externalities are worth only $5 million. The project's still a loser, but the availability of federal subsidies will make local officials eager to start the bulldozers. A $15 million subsidy, of which only $5 million comes from locals and $10 million is "other people's money," will make it happen. It enables the developer to bank a $5 million profit (which he might generously share with those who greased the political skids for him), while local taxpayers break even (that is, the spillover benefits match the local one-third share of the subsidy). This is a sweet deal for everyone but federal taxpayers, but perhaps we're not paying attention: polls show that less than half of us even know the name of our Congressional representatives, much less what they're up to on any given day.

The upshot is that the redevelopment playbook still in use in cities from New London to Seattle consumes great amounts of scarce capital (for hotels or convention centers, for example) that may have far more valuable alternative uses (better schools or roads). What's more, even when proposed projects do, in fact, hold out benefits in excess of costs, the current approach provides little assurance that the ultimate development will maximize prospective social gains or satisfy popular demands. The central problem here is that the combination of eminent domain, politically allocated subsidies, and design-by-bureaucracy essentially removes all honest price signals from the urban renewal process, fatally distorting decisions about what gets built, where, and how it looks and works.

These distortions begin at site acquisition, when the coercive power of eminent domain is substituted for voluntary transactions that occur at mutually agreed-upon (and therefore mutually beneficial) prices. Even if a Pfizer research facility would have been a winner for New London, for example, the fact that the NLDC could ignore signals from Suzette Kelo and her neighbors that they were unwilling to sacrifice their location-specific social capital or suffer the trauma of a move meant that the city had no real need to try to find a superior site.

Finally, once a tract is assembled and its fate is to be determined in the political rather than the economic marketplace, vastly different tastes and rules determine outcomes. In the political marketplace, unfortunately, the popular will often takes a back seat to special interests. Cities have, for example, collectively spent billions on stadiums—sometimes even after referenda have determined that voters oppose them—that pad the profits of fabulously wealthy owners of sports teams while other urban infrastructure crumbles. The problem is straightforward: such projects deliver concentrated benefits to the few, who therefore have a strong incentive to work the political system to their advantage, while spreading the costs among many, who therefore have little incentive (individually) to organize, lobby, and resist such misallocation of capital.

In sum, then, there's a lot to worry about when local officials heed the advice of twentieth-century architect Daniel Burnham to "make no little plans" which "have no magic to stir men's blood," and instead "make big plans . . . remembering that a noble, logical diagram once recorded will never die." Big plans may stir the blood, but as Pruitt-Igoe and other mega-projects have shown, they most definitely can die—and take large parts of their host cities with them.

A CENTURY OF LESSONS

The moral of this story is *not* that city governments should adopt a "Do Not Resuscitate" policy for their blighted areas and simply stand back, hoping for a miracle in the form of some modern-day Fred French. But physicians are taught that if they are uncertain about what's wrong with a patient and how to help, they should "first, do no harm." Redevelopment advocates must exercise similar caution and remember that their good intentions are no insurance against ill side-effects.

If we want cheaper housing for the poorest among us, we can't ignore the basic laws of supply and demand. Housing becomes more affordable when its supply increases relative to demand—*not* when more units are demolished than are created with renewal plans, and *not* when constraints are imposed on suppliers that raise their costs and limit buyers' range of choice. And if we want better living conditions in poor areas, the best course is not necessarily to have lawmakers write stricter housing regulations, but rather for cities to aggressively enforce the basic standards that already exist while efficiently providing the kinds of public services that ensure common areas are as clean and safe as possible. All too often, local governments accelerate filtering-down of the housing stock in aging neighborhoods by neglecting crucial services and infrastructure. Neither tenants nor landlords are likely to believe that their homes merit the investment of much energy or capital if City Hall won't bother to patrol and pave their streets, for example, or clean litter, replace lighting, and keep parks orderly and pleasant.

Improving the well-being of the poor also requires more awareness of some invisible but important elements of their lives. Yes, the condition of the physical capital that the poor inhabit matters, but improvements to the quality of this capital often come at exorbitant if hard-to-measure cost. When people are relocated against their will, we may tell ourselves that it's for the greater good, but we need to remember that such relocation forces them to less-preferred allocations of their limited budgets, traumatizes them, and destroys social capital that might have greater impact on their lives than the size or amenity level of their apartments. Fortunately, an ever-increasing number of states and localities have decided to tread more carefully in this area and vowed not to use eminent domain in pursuit of purely economic objectives; more need to do so.

But perhaps the main lesson of America's long and largely unhappy experience with "Big Planning" is that if government-guided redevelopment projects have any chance of success, it will be where cities have first taken steps to improve their economic fundamentals. When no Fred Frenches ever step forward to upgrade a city's residential or commercial capital stocks without major subsidies, that's a loud warning to redevelopment officials: *there's a basic problem here that needs to be fixed—now.* As noted earlier, subsidies are sometimes useful at the margin, when spillover benefits from a project are large enough to offset a prospective deficit associated with converting a property to a new use. But if entrepreneurs consistently complain that projects in a city will generate only red ink, then the city's overall investment climate needs to be improved via tax policy or regulatory reform that both improves returns and makes property rights to those returns more secure.

Officials often hope that subsidized investments here and there will produce a chain reaction that will spread more widely, but this rarely happens when the root causes of a city's repulsiveness to investment have not been treated. And the bald fact is that the amount of investment needed to keep a city viable and to maintain or improve its enormous and ever-depreciating stock of physical capital will swamp the financial capacity of any redevelopment agency. Subsidy-based renewal plans might delay the inevitable, but a city that cannot attract abundant investment on its own is, in the long run, doomed.

A city with sound investment fundamentals, on the other hand, will benefit not just from greater inflows of financial capital but from superior entrepreneurial energy and creativity. When developers compete with each other for customers, they often produce ingenious solutions to very vexing problems—as we saw and still see today in Tudor City. In contrast, a renewal program that relies heavily on the coercive power of local government and the availability of special breaks generates less wholesome competitive behavior by developers: for the favor of politicians, bureaucrats, and planners rather than tenants or buyers. As noted earlier, this empowers the political class; as we'll see in the next chapter, this power is not always used to good effect.

CHAPTER 9

Control Freaks

NICKNAMES FOR DECADES are often silly and misleading, but none quite so much as "the Swinging Sixties." Yes, there was self-indulgent behavior and taboo-breaking in those turbulent years, but most of the time Americans were very serious about identifying social problems and solving them. Eggheads wrote books about arcane policy issues that actually became best-sellers and moved people to action. Michael Harrington's *The Other America* spawned a federal war on poverty and Rachel Carson's *Silent Spring* spurred environmental awareness. James Baldwin's *The Fire Next Time* altered views on race, Betty Friedan's *The Feminine Mystique* became a cornerstone of the feminist movement, and Ralph Nader's *Unsafe at Any Speed* provided a brief for business regulation. If the "Mad Men" of Madison Avenue had coined a slogan for the period, it might have been "Something Must Be Done. Right Away."

On urban policy, however, one author marched in the opposite direction. Jane Jacobs was a working mother, writing about urban issues for *Architectural Forum* magazine while raising three children in Greenwich Village with her architect husband. She had no formal training in architecture, economics, or planning—indeed, no college degree—but this proved to be advantageous in her work, for she approached her subjects without preconceived notions or set theories, instead carefully observing real neighborhoods to learn what worked, what didn't, and what people actually wanted from their built environments. She saw that in cities, and especially New York, the impulse to "do something" had been given free rein for years, and concluded that this often did more harm than good.

Her nemesis and polar opposite was New York's planning czar, Robert Moses. Yale- and Oxford-educated, he didn't much care what ordinary people wanted, was confident he knew what they needed, and had given it to them good and hard, reshaping the city with hundreds of miles of new highways, thirteen bridges, two tunnels, innumerable parks, and thousands of units of public housing. His first encounter with Jacobs, in the 1950s, concerned one of his less ambitious proposals: to alleviate traffic congestion in Lower Manhattan by extending Fifth Avenue through Washington Square Park. As Jacobs and her neighbors fought the plan, Moses was dismissive, remarking, "there is nobody against this. Nobody, nobody, nobody but a bunch of . . . mothers."

But the mothers won. In November 1958, they held a "ribbon-tying ceremony" to celebrate the park's preservation. And, persuaded of the need to stop the bulldozers elsewhere, Jacobs spent the next three years writing her classic work, *The Death and Life of Great American Cities*. Her analysis proved devastating to Moses and other devotees of Big Planning. "Nobodies" had frequently resisted the improvements that renewal projects promised to deliver, but planners' arguments that they had to destroy parts of a city in order to save it usually prevailed. *Death and Life* documented the ineffectiveness of that approach and exposed the "anti-city ideals of conventional planning."[1] Where planners saw blighted structures, Jacobs saw valuable social capital. While they decried old neighborhoods' inefficient traffic flow and insufficient open space, she defended pedestrian-friendly small blocks and broad sidewalks. In place of their Le Corbusier–inspired towers surrounded by green space, she wanted low structures whose residents could keep "eyes on the street" to make them safer. And she advocated mixed-use development in place of the functional segregation that zoning authorities often employed to mitigate nuisance spillovers.

Thanks partly to Jacobs, wrecking balls became less prominent tools of urban renewal policy, and planners' gradual embrace of her key principles made many post-1960s projects more livable and likely to succeed. Of course, *Death and Life* was not perfect. Some of Jacobs's policy prescriptions were flawed; sometimes policymakers—and even fans—misinterpreted her. She criticized planners for their formulaic approach, for example, but was sometimes wedded to formulae herself, arguing that one hundred residences per acre were necessary to support nearby commerce but that two hundred per acre were too much, and so buildings should be limited to six stories. But imposing such density controls would limit housing supply and make cities more expensive and exclusive—outcomes Jacobs would have despised.

What's more, her apparent embrace of such rules made it easier for those holding the reins of power to ignore her discussions of "spontaneous order" in neighborhoods and her warnings that the most congenial and dynamic cities were those that allowed "unofficial plans, ideas and opportunities to flourish." For obvious reasons, they favored *official* plans, and many took from Jacobs that they simply had to take these down a notch and be more sensitive about imposing them on their constituents. And some of those constituents saw her preservationist principles as a license to stand in the path of *any* proposed change to the built environment and yell "stop!"

Then there were Jacobs's fellow public intellectuals of the day. Whether to rectify past wrongs, protect nature, or pursue justice, most argued that much tighter regulation of human behavior was needed. They urgently wanted the world to be a better place and were reluctant to entrust its progress to the wisdom of crowds and the chaos of markets. If Big Planning had already established a pattern of shredding property rights in "blighted" neighborhoods, these new activists and their tools of choice—growth controls, restrictive zoning, and more—would extend this pattern more broadly. Unfortunately, as we'll see, the results were frequently disappointing: cities that became less efficient and remarkably unfair.

THE GREAT EXPROPRIATION

Suppose you're approaching retirement. You've earned pension benefits that'll cover the normal expenses of life and accumulated a little nest egg—say, $180,000—to help you enjoy your Golden Years. Then you get a rude shock: your state government, seeking the means to provide important public goods, institutes a tax on wealth. You get a bill for . . . *$164,000*. So you go through the three stages of grief over misguided policy. Anger: "Not fair!" you sputter. Regret: "Why didn't I party more and save less when I was younger?" you wonder. Packing: you are *so* moving to a more wealth-friendly state.

Luckily, though, this example is just hypothetical. The 16th Amendment prohibits any "direct tax" on personal holdings. But even if it didn't, policymakers might worry about both the equity and efficiency of this sort of program. A tax rate north of 90 percent seems, well, confiscatory, and far lower rates might induce flight that could damage the state's economy.[2]

But what if we're talking about taxing something that *can't* move, and the tax is well disguised. If your wealth is in the form of land, for example, it's not portable. What if regulations reduce its value in small bites over several decades by preventing you from building anything on your acreage? The result might be the same—a nest egg worth $16,000 instead of $180,000—but you might not even know what had hit you. There's no bill for $164,000 in your hand, after all—just smaller gains than you otherwise would have realized. Could this make the whole thing both legally permissible and politically appealing? Yes and yes. Such schemes are quite common, praised in the media and academe, and popular politically. Opinion makers and voters usually overlook or are unaware of any wealth taken in this way, and focus on the public goods they assume are created as a result: forests preserved, family farms saved, emissions of climate-changing greenhouse gases reduced when commutes get shorter, and cities rejuvenated. Who would want to stand in the way of all that?

Not Oregonians. In 1973 the state adopted a growth management law that, its advocates promised, would deliver all of the above. Metropolitan areas were required to establish urban growth boundaries (UGBs) encircling populated areas, within which development would be allowed and beyond which was *verboten*. The theory was that this would improve environmental quality by limiting sprawl and channeling investment to already-urbanized zones. As those achieved higher densities and enjoyed economies stemming from more intensive use of infrastructure, residents would find that their living costs were lower (or at least no higher) and the quality of their lives improved by virtue of their access to the surrounding natural amenity.

Californians, ever the trendsetters, had limited development earlier, though not by state legislative action. Some growth controls were installed at the local level thanks to "not in my back yard" lobbying by established residents, but most resulted from action in the courts. According to legal scholar William Fischel, in the 1960s the California Supreme Court became "the most antidevelopment in the nation. . . . After 1967, virtually the only predictor of who would prevail in [land use cases] was whichever side the antidevelopment interests were on."[3] The court-erected roadblocks to growth were many and varied and thus less coherent and predictable than Oregon's lines on maps. In California it was sometimes harder to build in an urbanized neighborhood than where density was low, but in any case it became progressively more difficult and expensive to obtain the right to build than in earlier eras. And since the 1970s, several other states have more strictly regulated land use in order to limit sprawl, though urban containment policies remain the exception rather than the rule.[4]

Portland's UGB is regularly held up as a model. It was imposed in 1979, but initially 40 percent of the land "inside the line" was vacant. With so much available acreage there seemed little reason to force customers into high-density housing they might not want, so through the 1980s new developments averaged just two-thirds the density levels permitted by land-use plans. By the 1990s, however, less than 20 percent of the land within the UGB remained vacant, so the price of buildable sites soared. Just between 1990 and 1996, some lots went from $20,000 per acre to $200,000.[5] But many saw this as a favorable trend. Higher costs would force developers to use land more intensively, limiting sprawl and moderating home price inflation. As the trend toward ever-higher prices for developable land accelerated, however, doubts arose about this feel-good narrative. Not only was Portland fast becoming one of the more expensive housing markets in the nation, but its tight control of land use was having some interesting redistributive effects.

In 2010, policy analyst Wendell Cox gathered price data for land along a twenty-five-mile stretch of the UGB (roughly a third of its total length) and tabulated the figures that inspired our earlier hypothetical example: lots inside the boundary sold for an average of $180,000 per acre, while contiguous but nondevelopable land outside the line sold for $16,000 per acre.[6] Some of this difference, of course, might reflect sources of value unrelated to development rights, such as access to roads or other infrastructure. And even if such considerations were not in play, it's an exaggeration to say that all of the $164,000 per-acre price difference was "confiscated" from the owners of acreage outside the line. If Oregon's growth controls had never been put in place, the land from which rights had been stripped surely would be worth more, but its availability would also reduce prices of lots inside the line.[7] Nevertheless, it's clear that taking development rights away from those outside the limit line shifted enormous wealth from them at the same time it created windfalls for the lucky ones "on the inside." Similar stories were playing out in California and other locales where growth controls were most binding.

These sorts of transfers are potentially problematic on two levels. When it comes to shifting income or wealth around, economists first ask whether the redistributive program takes from those who are higher on the economic ladder and gives to those who are lower. Doing so enhances *vertical* equity (in the jargon), and most agree that that's a good thing—a key reason that Robin Hood–type policies, within limits, often enjoy broad support. But everyone agrees that the *reverse* is harmful. In this case, there's no evidence that landowners outside a growth boundary are, on average, more affluent than those inside it, and it strains credulity to suppose that all of those "outsiders" are richer than the "insiders." In at least some cases, then, it's likely that growth boundaries produce vertical inequities, like Robin Hood breaking bad.

Next, economists generally think it's unfair for policymakers to treat people who are on the same rung of the economic ladder differently, arbitrarily picking winners and losers. If landowners in a particular district are comparably rich (or poor), then drawing a line through it and showering those on one side with gains at the expense of those on the other side damages *horizontal* equity, and ought to be avoided if at all possible.

We might be tempted to shrug off these fairness concerns. We're talking about the landed gentry, after all, and there are those who think they deserve little sympathy. As Robert Moses once said (paraphrasing Lenin, who was paraphrasing Robespierre), "I hail the chef who can make omelets without breaking eggs." If it'll help save the planet, why not take some rights away from property owners? Unfortunately, though, landowners on the wrong side of a limit line are not the only ones damaged by growth controls. And there are some troubling questions about whether those controls, at least as implemented in practice rather than in theory, really are saving the planet.

GREENLINING

Decreases in the supply of buildable land need not lead to proportionate increases in housing costs. People can build up instead of out and mitigate the effects of higher land costs. But what happens to home prices under any growth management regime depends not just on the types of homes that are built but how many are allowed to be built relative to demand. And the evidence is quite clear that "managed growth" often translates into limits on supply that inflate housing costs. This is true for all income levels, but especially for those of modest means. Hello again, vertical inequity.

The best available method for monitoring volatile real estate markets is that devised by economists Karl Case and Robert Shiller, who tabulate the price of the *same* house each time it changes hands and adjust for upgrades or renovations. Their data on home prices go back to 1987 for fourteen metropolitan areas; they added a half-dozen cities to their sample by 2000. For some cities, they also report price changes for three "housing tiers": entry-level or low-tier homes, luxury or high-tier homes, and those in between.[8]

Between 1987 and 2012, Portland ran away with the Case-Shiller trophy for housing cost inflation, with average prices rising 242 percent. Finishing second, third, and fourth in this unwholesome race were—no big surprise—the California cities: San Francisco (up 210 percent), San Diego (198 percent), and Los Angeles (196 percent). By contrast, cities with less binding urban containment policies in place saw far more modest home price increases. For example, Portland's inflation rate was more than twice that of New York (117 percent) and Chicago (106 percent), triple that of Charlotte (82 percent) and Tampa (72 percent), and almost five times that of Las Vegas (51 percent).

More troubling is that the tiered data show that prices rose especially rapidly for *entry-level* homes in the markets with growth controls. In Portland, for example, prices of low-tier homes soared 405 percent between 1987 and 2012—more than twice the inflation rate for the city's high-end dwellings (194 percent). By contrast, the inflation rate for entry-level homes in Miami (104 percent) was one-fourth Portland's and below the inflation rate for its higher tiers. Ditto Tampa and (over the period for which Case-Shiller data are available) cities such as Phoenix, Chicago, and Atlanta. In the 1950s and 1960s, when lenders withheld credit from those living in poor, minority neighborhoods, such "redlining" was widely condemned and eventually prohibited. But imposing rigid growth controls in the name of environmental preservation—call it "greenlining"—has also made it difficult for working-class families to afford home ownership.

The culprit here is not exclusively urban containment policy, of course. Much else has gone on while Portland's UGB and California's anti-development judicial rulings have been in force. For example, once land and home prices started inflating in the late 1980s and their property tax bills became more painful, Oregonians capped their property tax rates at 1.5 percent in a 1990 referendum, Measure 5. Californians, with Prop 13, had revolted even earlier, of course. These initiatives not only increased home values via tax capitalization but likely fueled demand growth by protecting property owners against future wealth-reducing increases in rates.

But there's no getting around the fact that growth controls bear *some* portion of the responsibility for these cities' home price inflation problems.[9] Policies advertised as managing growth have, instead, squelched it and kept housing supply from rising to accommodate demand, pushing prices sky high. This was not supposed to happen. Portland's boundary, in particular, was to be accompanied by *spurs* to development within it: relaxation of density limits and a streamlined permit process among them.

Some of that has occurred. Just not enough—which shouldn't be surprising. Passage of urban containment legislation reflects, to a great degree, the political power of interest groups that, if not opposed to growth *per se*, are unsympathetic to it. These include many existing property owners, who tend to want higher-density housing and mixed land uses only in other peoples' neighborhoods, and who see housing price inflation not as a problem but as a source of capital gains. These interest groups don't go dormant once they've won limits on development. They get busy influencing the practical application of these policies. On the other hand, those most harmed by the unavailability of affordable housing—the young who have not yet entered this market, or potential migrants from other areas—are not at the political table. They can't or don't lobby and vote, so their preferences about these policies don't carry much weight with decision makers.

DO ECO-UTOPIAS WORK?

Even if we ignore equity and affordability concerns, growth limits raise other, potentially more pressing questions related to *efficacy*. Do containment policies contribute to urban vitality? How much do they improve the environment? Might similar environmental objectives be achieved at less cost?

Let's first acknowledge that cities in which growth controls tend to be most binding are attractive, successful, and livable—especially if you have money. Demand for housing in a particular city doesn't outrun supply and push prices upward unless there are compelling reasons to locate there. These demand drivers can, obviously, vary from place to place: they can take the form of amenities such as a vibrant culture, stunning scenery, and pleasing weather, or can be more mundane and economy-based, such as access to a unique resource or a low property tax rate.

Economists Joseph Gyourko, Christopher Mayer, and Todd Sinai labeled metro areas in which these kinds of attributes fuel brisk growth in demand for living space while supply is, for one reason or another, constrained as "superstar cities." This term is a bit misleading. Who, after all, doesn't want to live the life of a superstar? But Gyourko and his colleagues are worried that there's a downside to such status. Their model of urban development posits a not-so-virtuous cycle: in superstar cities, the limited supply of developable land "results in a rightward shift in the income distribution and rising land prices that are neither due to changes in the innate attractiveness of living there nor in local productivity, but follow from an increasing number of high willingness-to-pay families in the population."[10] Such cities, they submit, have become luxury goods, with lower-income families migrating out and higher-income families migrating in. They wonder whether this trend is sustainable, or whether superstars will lose their vibrancy and allure as they become resorts for the wealthy.

Urbanologist Joel Kotkin is less equivocal: he calls cities that have priced themselves out of reach of families of modest means not superstars but "boutiques," and argues forcefully that they fail to discharge one of the historic functions of American cities: to serve as engines of upward mobility.[11] The problem is that when middle- and working-class populations exit in pursuit of more affordable housing, many employers who depend on their skills follow, altering the mix of opportunities for those who remain. This yields an urban labor market characterized by high-salaried positions at the top of the economic ladder, low-wage jobs in retail and hospitality at the bottom, and few rungs in between. Over time, the result is slower employment and income growth and rising economic inequality. This is the opposite of Jacobs's vision of cities as places that are "constantly transforming many poor people into middle class people."

Further, it's not clear that greenlining produces environmental improvements of the magnitude hoped for. One problem is "leapfrogging." When growth limits send housing prices skyward, the search for affordable living space often simply takes people beyond the specified boundaries, occasionally yielding longer commutes and lower-density development than might otherwise occur. For example, Clark County, Washington—beyond Portland's UGB and not subject to its controls—added 233,000 residents between 1980 and 2010, versus 216,000 in the city itself (some of which came as a result of annexation of inner suburbs). So, despite its growth boundary, several billion dollars of investment in light rail lines, and generous subsidies for higher-density construction along their routes, commuting patterns in Portland aren't exactly eco-friendly. Indeed, census data show that the fraction of city residents using public transportation was actually lower in 2010 (12 percent) than in 1980 (16 percent). In the metro area as a whole, only 7 percent of commuters use public transit while 80 percent still drive. For the latter, the costs of congestion are painfully high. Car trips in Portland take about 28 percent longer than they would in optimum traffic conditions, the sixth highest figure among the nation's hundred largest cities. Portlandians waste forty-four hours and twenty-one gallons of fuel annually in traffic delays (respectively, 19 and 24 percent above the national average for large urban areas). And since stop-and-go produces more pollution than free-flowing traffic; each driver burdens Mother Nature with an extra 415 pounds of carbon dioxide (26 percent above average).[12]

These unhappy results generalize. Economists Matthew Holian and Matthew Kahn have examined driving patterns and gasoline consumption for a large sample of households across many metropolitan areas.[13] The good news: greenhouse gas (GHG) emissions go down as cities achieve higher density levels and attract a larger share of college-educated adults to their downtown areas. The bad: when cities impose stringent land-use controls that limit housing supply and raise prices in their core areas, those upscale college grads crowd out less prosperous residents and cause them to increase their reliance on autos and fossil fuels. Holian and Kahn estimate that less-regulated urban real estate markets can yield GHG emissions levels that are roughly 50 percent lower than those in center cities featuring high regulation.

Defenders of growth-controlled cities tend to brush aside such concerns. They note, first, that containment preserves farms and forests forever that would otherwise, in the words of folksinger Pete Seeger's 1960s anthem, be cluttered with "little boxes made of ticky-tacky" that "all look just the same." And if some souls still cling stubbornly to a lifestyle that features detached homes, lawns, and cars, well, perhaps if traffic becomes painful enough they'll learn to commute via light rail and pedal a bike to Whole Foods. Indeed, inefficiency in the market for scarce road space seems, to fans of growth controls, to be a strategy rather than a problem. Portland's Metro planning authorities, for example, have said that "transportation solutions aimed solely at relieving congestion are inappropriate," for that "would eliminate transit ridership."[14] But perhaps there are better ways of achieving the twin goals of a healthier environment and vibrant, inclusive cities.

HOME REMEDIES

Critics of growth boundaries and other regulatory approaches to sprawl tend to argue that they substitute coercion for choice, overriding the preferences of market participants in favor of those of planners. Depending on how much respect one has for the tastes of consumers versus those of planners, this might be seen as either a good or a bad thing. For their part, most economists are dubious about the effectiveness of this kind of "command and control" approach, preferring instead to focus on ways to see that individuals' choices are based on proper consideration of relevant benefits and costs and thus lead to equitable and efficient outcomes. That's why earlier chapters focused on avoiding policies (such as flight-inducing taxes) that bias these choices and produce behavior that can unnecessarily damage cities and the environment.

But even a city that is on firm ground in most such respects can benefit from policies which help ensure that individuals' city-versus-suburb location choices are, indeed, based on *all* relevant benefits and costs. The fact is that living in a low-density area or developing open space frequently involves exchanges at what we have called lying prices, or those that do not reflect true, underlying values. Fortunately, however, the distortions that might result from such exchanges are easily avoided or corrected.[15]

The first remedy has already been discussed, in the context of transportation infrastructure and congestion pricing (recall Chapter 7). The basic problem is that each person who chooses to reside in an area where roads and freeways are sometimes filled to or beyond capacity will not only waste his or her time and fuel in ever-worsening traffic delays but raise others' costs as well—a so-called congestion externality. And, per Downs's Law, building their way out of this problem is less likely to be successful than more honestly pricing road capacity, employing tollways that better ration the space available and send superior signals to commuters about whether and when to use it. Once it is clear that driving long distances from areas where land costs little isn't actually as cheap as it looks, development decisions will change in wholesome ways. Economists Alex Anas and Hyok-Joo Rhee have compared congestion tolls with UGBs and found the former to be "a very effective tool for reducing urban sprawl"[16] and far more effective than boundaries in managing traffic delays and associated pollution problems.

Honest prices can also reduce excessive sprawl that results from two other sources: hidden subsidies for the infrastructure often needed in new developments and failure to pay for the lost amenity value of open space sacrificed to development.

The first problem results from localities' tendency to charge builders the *average* cost of additional facilities required to develop new tracts rather than their *marginal* cost. Suppose, for example, a new project on the edge of town needs a firehouse to ensure its residents' safety. Traditionally, the town might finance construction of the firehouse by issuing a bond and paying it off with tax receipts collected from all its residents. But that involves a cross-subsidy: incumbent residents pay a large part of the capital costs of a facility that, absent the new development, they would not need or choose to build, while the new residents avoid some of these costs. Such mispricing makes living in older, developed areas more expensive than it really is, and living in newer areas less so, inviting leapfrog development and discouraging "infill" of areas where no new facilities are required. The straightforward fix is an *impact fee* equal to the incremental costs of firehouses, roads, water and sewage access, and so on, associated with new development. When builders incorporate that fee into the prices they charge, home buyers get a more truthful signal about the costs of the resources they're consuming—and an incentive not to overdo it.

Consumers need to consider one more cost, as well: the reduced amenity value to *others* of the land they are claiming. Studies have shown that homes near certain types of open space are worth more than otherwise-similar properties elsewhere, presumably because owners value the views or recreational opportunities to which they have ready access.[17] This is not true for all types of open space: proximity to tracts that neighbors do not expect to be preserved or open to them, for example, do not appear to enhance property values. But developing a public forest or other parkland is likely to reduce nearby residents' welfare, and the sale price of that land should include an "open space amenity tax" (equal to the loss of value elsewhere) to reflect this fact. Only if builders and their customers are willing to pay the full cost of the land they are consuming can there be confidence that a proposed development is socially beneficial.

THE GREAT AND POWERFUL IZ

Cities where housing costs are through the roof often proclaim they're working on it. Unfortunately, their treatment of choice is sometimes a member of the same genus of policies that gave rise to the problem in the first place: restrictive zoning.

Authorities don't have to post "keep out" signs (a la Portland's growth boundaries) to constrain development in certain areas. It's more common to tie builders' hands in subtle ways. Local zoning policies may, for example, specify that new homes must be sited on lots of at least two or three acres rather than the customary quarter or third of an acre. Some economists justify such restrictions as a wholesome defense against free riding by residents seeking a high level of public services without paying high taxes in exchange. Without them, a town with, say, a lavishly funded school system might attract developers offering cheap (and therefore lightly taxed) dwellings to families wanting to get their kids in those schools at a discount. An influx of such free riders would strain the town's budget and damage the schools' viability; in this view, restrictions are motivated by fiscal concerns and not to keep out the riff-raff or pump up the value of existing properties. But this idea of "fiscal zoning" seems more like a rationalization than a rationale. Often, minimum lot sizes on new developments are far larger than those of incumbent residents' properties. Further, they don't completely control in-migration: free riders might rent or share space in such communities. And at least with respect to educational services, most states have determined that spending inequalities are undesirable and distribute funds to ameliorate them. Accordingly, most economists refer to minimum-lot-size regulations and similar restrictions by a name that better captures their likely intent: exclusionary zoning (EZ).

On the other hand, some of the priciest enclaves in America embrace a policy that goes by the opposite name: *inclusionary* zoning (IZ). The idea is simple: builders may get permission to increase housing supply as long as they include some units that are "affordable." The percentages to be set aside vary by locality, of course, usually ranging from 5 to 25 percent of new homes in a project. Then the prices of set-aside units are controlled at levels determined by formulas related to a locality's median income level. A family earning $50,000 annually, for example, might be deemed able to pay $175,000 for a house of particular size. If the market value of such homes is $500,000 (not a stretch in growth-controlled regions), the builder would be required to forego $325,000 in revenue on this unit.[18] Under some IZ laws, she would be expected simply to make that up on (presumed) profits on her market-priced units. More often, localities offer carrots—fast-track permitting, fee waivers, and relaxation of density limits or growth controls—to help her break even.

Since IZ allows public officials to say they are providing affordable housing while simultaneously putting developers (rather than taxpayers) on the hook for the costs, the policy became very popular in the decade before the housing bubble burst. The problem is that IZ generally doesn't increase the supply of housing, and in some forms and at certain times actually reinforces its evil cousin EZ in *reducing* supply. There are always so few set-aside units available relative to demand—in San Francisco in 2002, for example, there were twenty-seven hundred applicants for a hundred available homes[19]—that it's fair to say IZ solves a housing affordability problem the same way that lotteries enable the poor to finance a cushy retirement: on a very limited and highly selective basis. For those keeping score, this is another horizontal inequity.

Then there's inefficiency. In its most stringent forms, IZ acts like a tax on development, so it should be no surprise that it generally does what taxes do elsewhere, depressing quantities exchanged. Two surveys of California real estate markets before and after the onset of local IZ ordinances suggest that these effects are sizeable. In thirty-three cities in northern California for which data were available, new construction fell by over ten thousand units in the seven years after IZ mandates took effect, compared to the seven prior years. In eight southern California jurisdictions, total output fell by more than seventeen thousand homes. IZ also pushed median home prices further upward and yielded relatively few "lottery winners" of below-market units: in the north, the median city added fifteen units of affordable housing per year, and in the south only eight.[20] These surveys did not, however, control for other possible influences on California construction activity, so the estimated effects might be too high—or low. A later study of IZ in Massachusetts and California that attempted to control for cyclic factors and other development limits, however, also found evidence that IZ "has constrained housing supply and increased prices."[21]

In sum, attempts to control development and sprawl often produce inequities and inefficiencies that are sometimes treated with further controls that yield—more of the same. It's certainly arguable that these unwholesome outcomes are just minor side-effects of a necessary and basically sound system of land-use regulation. There's no question that restrictive zoning, in principle, can solve otherwise nettlesome externality problems: homeowners who value serenity or environmental amenity want to know that their next-door neighbor will not go into business selling used cars or diesel fuel. If public officials occasionally go a bit too far in regulating the built environment, maybe we should be more understanding. Surely a city *without* zoning would be unpleasant if not unlivable, right? Let's see.

OUT OF CONTROL?

Houston is the largest city in the United States that lacks any zoning law or authority. To the naked eye, though, it looks just like other metropolises that reached adulthood after the car became king. It sprawls; it features neighborhoods of single-family detached homes; it has office parks and shopping centers; traffic jams are common. But it shows no evidence of the kinds of nightmarish externality problems assumed to be unavoidable without zoning. Car dealerships and filling stations are absent from leafy residential enclaves, these enclaves tend to have a certain amount of aesthetic consistency (for good or ill), and noxious factories cluster together.

In part this is because economic forces tend to produce some natural sorting of land uses: convenience store proprietors want to be in high-traffic areas, families with small kids do not, and many businesses like to be near complementary ones. The larger reason is that Houstonians actually have a very sophisticated program of land use regulation. It's just that they don't vest much regulatory power with planning boards (though they have one) and political officials. Such regulation has, in effect, been privatized: nuisance spillovers from one landowner's actions to a neighbor's property values are managed not by zoning authorities but by privately negotiated covenants, which are simply contracts that developers specify and which convey with the deed to each property, regulating the behavior of owners.

In designing these covenants, profit-maximizing developers start by identifying the most valuable use for a tract: deeds for land near a main drag might permit enterprises such as a gas station or strip mall, but acreage in a secluded, high-amenity area might generate more revenue (and social utility) if limited to single-family residences. Developers then have an incentive to devise covenant rules that can enhance property values over time—and not just by limiting externalities, but by specifying how tracts might be converted to higher-valued uses if and when circumstances change. The upshot is that Houston residents suffer from few of the problems of incompatible land uses commonly alleged to have predated the invention of zoning and benefit from many advantages of its absence.[22]

Consider first the task of allocating acreage among competing uses. Will bureaucracies and political actors be able to figure out that, as of now, it's efficient to reserve, say, 60 percent of available space for residential use and 40 percent for commerce? Market participants will be guided by relative prices and expected profits in making this call, allocating more land to the use in which bidders signal the most urgent needs via their willingness to pay the most. Absent this profit motive, political authorities may find the optimal allocation only by accident, for the hallmark of the public sector is that no one in it gets rich when responsible for good decisions, nor poor when responsible for bad ones. They are also freer to subscribe to planning fads, impose preferences, or cater to special interests. Zoning an excessive amount of land "residential," for example, will depress its relative price and deliver a subsidy to homebuyers (who may show their gratitude at the polls) at the expense of less-numerous landowners.

But even if zoned and nonzoned cities initially solve this land allocation problem equally effectively, we can depend on two enduring trends: things change, and the wheels of bureaucracy grind slowly. The 60-40 residential-commercial split that's optimal today might be way off the mark in a couple of years. But a "comprehensive rezoning" that brings all political stakeholders to the table to nudge the needle in the appropriate direction will be a lengthy and contentious process with a highly uncertain outcome. That's why many cities tip-toe into this minefield only every few decades. Good-government bastion Columbus, Ohio, for example, first imposed a zoning code in 1923, updated it in the 1950s, and then waited until 1992 to rewrite the rewrite.

As decades tick by, zoned cities might be straitjacketed by obsolete allocations or inundated with requests for adjustments or waivers. Nonzoned cities, by contrast, can make adjustments at the margin relatively easily, and with no political middlepersons demanding "commissions." This is because covenants are often written in such a way that property owners may cash in if a new, higher-valued, and more profitable use for their land arises; they're willing to sacrifice a bit of protection from nuisances in exchange for the right to realize potential capital gains. In Houston, a few single-family homes can be replaced by a mixed-use high-rise within a year, ensuring a more efficient allocation of capital and a very robust, adaptable market for property.

Presently, though, there's no *proof* that privatizing land use decisions delivers better short- or long-run economic outcomes, on average, than entrusting them to planners and pols. Among large cities, there's no "non-zoning average"—just Houston. Still, it's hard to argue that its approach has been a handicap. A century ago, it ranked thirty-seventh in population among U.S. cities and third in Texas. Since then, it has grown faster than every city with a 1910 population over fifty thousand. It now ranks as the fourth largest city in the United States, and no one would be surprised if it blew past Chicago into third place by the next census. There are, of course, many reasons for this growth that might be more important than land-use policy: proximity to oil fields, pipelines, and transportation infrastructure; a tech sector that leveraged federal dollars expended for the space program; national and regional shifts in population and economic activity; an overall business-friendly tax and regulatory environment. Note, however, that Houston's growth rate has even been twice that of its in-state neighbors, zoned Dallas and San Antonio—and unlike Portland and other western cities, its climate and geography are hindrances rather than helps. Houston is, simply, a dynamically efficient city that works, offering opportunity and affordability to an extraordinarily diverse populace.[23] Its land use policy is an important ingredient in this recipe for success, and its residents seem to get that: on three occasions, in the 1940s, 1960s, and 1990s, a zoning law referendum appeared on the ballot, and each time was defeated at the polls.

Which is not to say that repealing zoning is necessary to make other cities more dynamic. The problem is not what zoning was designed to do, but how it has evolved.[24] Once upon a time, it primarily served landowners' interests, a means to better specify the bundle of rights and obligations that come with ownership of property, thus mitigating externality problems and enhancing property values. Over time, the zoning mechanism became landowners' master, a means by which planners could realize their visions for the ideal city and an opportunity for political officials to broker deals that would enhance their power and prestige. This has often gone badly, misallocating resources and contributing to sprawl and environmental degradation, straitjacketing urban economies by discouraging adaptation and innovation, repelling much urban investment, and raising the costs of those investments allowed to occur. This has to change.

Cities striving for greater fairness in their treatment of property owners, enhanced levels of opportunity for their citizens, and improved efficiency in their operations need to loosen their grip on decisions about land use. They need to heed the price signals transmitted by market participants rather than mute them. In their development reviews, they must focus on avoiding nontrivial spillovers rather than on substituting planners' aesthetic or ideological preferences for those of builders and consumers. And they should streamline the review process, formulating clear boundaries on who has standing—and who does not—to comment on and object to development proposals.

Ironically, at the same time that many cities began regulating decisions about the uses of private property ever more tightly, they became much more *laissez-faire* about behavior in "the commons"—the streets, parks, and other public areas that people own collectively and trust to government management. As we'll see in the next chapter, this had tragic consequences for these cities' viability and the safety and quality of life of their residents. Fortunately, however, a great deal has been learned about ways to reverse this trend; all that is needed is the courage and wisdom to apply the lessons.

CHAPTER 10

Reclaiming the Commons

BY THE LATE 1980S AND EARLY 1990S, America's big cities were more dangerous than they had ever been. In 1990 in New York alone, 2,245 people were murdered—over 30 per 100,000 residents, roughly five times the homicide rate that had prevailed in 1960 and for several prior decades. The carnage was even worse elsewhere: Dallas's homicide rate was over 50 percent higher, Detroit's twice as high, and Washington, D.C.'s rate almost three times that of New York.[1]

Many feared that things would soon get even worse. The 1980s had seen the invention of a powerful and profitable new illicit drug, crack cocaine, and much of the urban violence was a result of rival gangs' attempts to carve out or defend marketing territories. The foot soldiers in these turf wars came from a growing cohort of violent juveniles. The baby boomers' babies were coming of age, and they were apparently more murderous than prior generations. Criminologist James Alan Fox, in a report for the U.S. attorney general, speculated that homicides committed by fourteen- to seventeen-year-olds, which had doubled in the 1980s, might double again in the next decade. That worry was widely shared. Political scientist John DiIulio forecast that "the demographic surge of the next 10 years will bring with it young male criminals who make the . . . Bloods and Crips look tame by comparison," and President Bill Clinton opined, "We've got about six years to turn this juvenile crime thing around, or our country is going to be living with chaos."[2]

Most policymakers, however, weren't optimistic about the likelihood of turning things around. Across the ideological spectrum, it was widely believed that the roots of antisocial behavior went deep. Liberals focused on racism, poverty, and inequality as the chief causal factors; their preferred treatments involved social and economic reforms designed to overcome a legacy of oppression and enhance economic opportunity. Conservatives argued that the culprit was cultural breakdown—newly permissive social mores, the decline of the family, rising dependency on transfer programs—and argued that only a "moral renewal" would stem the rising criminal tide. Few believed that their policy reforms of choice would become reality anytime soon or have immediate effect even if they did. In the meantime, there didn't seem to be much that could be done. Many academics held that enhanced law enforcement efforts would be fruitless, as too much criminal conduct was the by-product of forces out of the control of police. Criminologists Michael Gottfredson and Travis Hirschi, for example, wrote, "No evidence exists that augmentation of police forces or equipment, differential patrol strategies or differential intensities of surveillance have any effect on crime rates."[3]

Then, remarkably, our descent into chaos didn't just stop—it was reversed. By the new millennium, New York's homicide rate had fallen by over 70 percent, Dallas's by 60 percent, Washington's by half, and Detroit's by a third. Neither racism nor poverty had been eradicated; no great victories in the culture wars had been achieved. Economic conditions had improved slightly, but not enough to produce such a turnaround. Demographic trends also lacked explanatory power. What had changed significantly, though, were tactics on law enforcement and maintenance of public order—and the new approaches were widely adopted once their utility was demonstrated. Elite opinion about the potential of good policing, it turned out, had been very wrong.

TAKING BACK THE STREETS

In the late 1970s, Bill Bratton's colleagues on the Boston police force called him "Lord of the Dots." He was obsessed with crime maps, and diligently plotted the locations of murders, rapes, assaults, robberies, and auto thefts in the belief that such data would enable him to target and reduce the frequency of these major crimes. When he attended community meetings in his South End precinct, however, the most commonly aired complaints involved prostitution, after-hours clubs, public drinking, and trash-filled streets. Cops usually ignored these "quality of life" issues in favor of things they thought mattered more to public safety, but after one contentious gathering Bratton decided to literally start cleaning up Southie: he ordered his officers to spend a few days writing tickets and towing illegally parked cars so that street sweepers could clear away trash. While on ticket-writing duty, one cop got a tip from a resident about some suspicious behavior around the time of a recent break-in. The tip led to an arrest—and an end to a string of burglaries. Bratton took the lesson: listening to people and addressing visible signs of disorder in their neighborhoods could lead to bigger things.

At about the same time, some renegade academics reached the same conclusion. In 1979, sociologist Nathan Glazer critiqued the increasingly accepted—and, in some circles, celebrated—"public art form" of graffiti, arguing that tagging signaled the presence of predators in a neighborhood and that failing to address this symptom of disorder both repelled the law-abiding and invited more misbehavior.[4] In 1982, political scientists George Kelling and James Q. Wilson extended Glazer's argument with an article in *The Atlantic Monthly* titled "Broken Windows: The Police and Neighborhood Safety." They took their title from the observation that if one window in a building is broken and left unrepaired, others will soon be broken. They cited evidence from the experiments of psychologist Philip Zimbardo, who showed that disorder signals that no one cares, which leads to more disorder and, eventually, crime, in a "developmental sequence." This sequence could start with something small and progress inexorably: "A piece of property is abandoned, weeds grow up, a window is smashed. Adults stop scolding rowdy children; the children, emboldened, become more rowdy. Families move out, unattached adults move in. Teenagers gather in front of the corner store. The merchant asks them to move; they refuse. Fights occur."[5] And so on. Neighbors become less engaged with each other or flee; streets become less safe; the downward spiral intensifies.

Though it may not have seemed so at the time, this diagnosis was quite optimistic. It meant that policing mattered and that it could have good and substantial effects—but that such effects were more likely when police devoted considerable energy to averting or correcting the *beginning* of this cycle, and not just coping with the criminal behavior at its end. Nevertheless, it took some years before these ideas were road-tested—or, more precisely, subway-tested, when Bratton became chief of the New York Transit Police in 1990. In a nice marriage of practitioner and theoretician, he hired Kelling as his consultant and began implementing "broken windows policing."

The first "window" they fixed was turnstile-jumping. The city's many fare-beaters signaled via their success at this petty crime that the subways might be lawless and dangerous. So Bratton's transit cops didn't just write occasional citations that were easily disregarded, but swept through stations in force and booked offenders on the spot in a "Bust Bus" equipped as a mobile arrest-processing center. This made people *feel* more secure—something that should not be cavalierly dismissed if one wants to make a city livable—but also delivered real gains in safety, for it turned out that one out of seven arrestees was wanted on an outstanding warrant, and one out of twenty-one carried a concealed weapon. Then Bratton hired more transit cops and invested in better technology so they could communicate effectively and move quickly to trouble spots. As more fugitives and felons were taken out of circulation, crime rates fell, public fear diminished, ridership increased, and the addition of more law-abiding citizens to these important public spaces reinforced a virtuous safety cycle.

In 1994, Bratton took his act above ground as NYPD commissioner under newly elected mayor Rudy Giuliani. The previous mayor, David Dinkins, had ramped up the size of the police force somewhat, but Giuliani found the money to hire thousands more cops, and Bratton deployed them more efficiently than ever before. Leveraging advances in computing power and data analysis, he institutionalized his old habit of learning from crime maps via "CompStat," a database that told top brass where problems were most acute, and which they used at high-pressure biweekly "Crime Control Strategy Meetings" to hold precinct commanders accountable for addressing those problems. In effect, CompStat enabled the city's policing resources to be used in an economically efficient way, by identifying ever-changing "hot spots" where the marginal benefit of additional patrols was greatest and "cool spots" from which forces could be drawn at minimum marginal cost.

Bratton also initiated innovative programs to get guns off the streets, curb youth violence in schools, defang drug gangs, reduce domestic violence, reclaim public spaces, and reduce auto theft,[6] but his linchpin strategy was always repairing broken windows. As in the subways, citations for misdemeanors such as public urination, vandalism, and even jaywalking frequently turned into arrests on outstanding warrants, many for violent crimes. New Yorkers' sense of public order and their quality of life steadily improved. By 1996, the city's homicide rate was half what it had been the year before Bratton took over as commissioner, and he was the most celebrated cop in America. He would soon resign to write a book[7] and disseminate his ideas to other cities as a consultant, but his successors were equally committed to broken windows policing and similarly ingenious about applying it in ways that made the city's streets safer. Early on, this meant putting more bad guys behind bars: New York's prison population rose 19 percent between 1990 and 1997. Over time, though, more sophisticated methods of *deterring* criminal activity and a more pervasive sense of public order meant that crime and imprisonment rates could fall in tandem. Between 1990 and 2008, New York's homicide rate fell back to mid-1960s levels as its per-capita rate of incarceration fell 28 percent—while the national rate soared by two-thirds.[8] Clearly, broken windows policing has been a life-saver: had New York's homicide rate stayed at its 1990 peak, over thirty thousand additional lives would have been lost in the years since.

"BROKEN WINDOWS POLICING" DOES NOT EQUAL "ZERO TOLERANCE"

Despite widespread coverage of New York's progress against violent crime, the city's order-enhancing policing program is not that well understood or appreciated. A good deal of this is the result of the media's focus on, and resulting misperceptions about, the NYPD's assertive approach to apparently trivial sins. In many accounts, this is described as "aggressive policing" or "zero tolerance" for any and all transgressions—and in some as authorization to engage in racial profiling, head-cracking, and other violations of the civil rights of innocent civilians.

This is not at all what broken windows policing is about nor was it part of the plan in New York, but such practices were, indeed, on display in Los Angeles during this period. Given a huge territory to police and relatively few uniformed personnel to do it, the LAPD had long compensated for its limited capacity to apprehend bad guys by making the suspects it did catch pay a stiff price. To ensure that crime doesn't pay, after all, the police have to raise its costs somehow. Serious problems arise, however, when the population of suspects becomes excessively large or divorced from the population of actual perpetrators. That's exactly what happened in Los Angeles in the 1980s and early 1990s. To "keep the lid on" during the 1984 Olympics, Mayor Tom Bradley authorized police chief Daryl Gates to take any known or suspected gang members into custody and hold them until the games ended. It worked—at least for those two weeks—so Gates soon developed Operation Hammer. On weekend nights, as many as a thousand cops would descend on neighborhoods where gangs were active—almost always predominantly black or Latino areas—and "jack up" male teens more or less at random, making them "kiss the sidewalk" or spread-eagling them against squad cars while they checked for outstanding warrants or entered their names in databases of gang members for subsequent surveillance. Often, hundreds would be packed off to jail, only to be released on Monday morning, no charges having been filed. His rationale was simple: "This is war. . . . We're exceedingly angry. . . . We want to get the message out to the cowards out there, and that's what they are, rotten little cowards—we want the message to go out that we're going to come and get them. This is Viet Nam here."[9]

But Gates's war would end about as well as that one, for he was sending an unwholesome message to a far greater, more consequential audience than just teenage drug runners. Especially in minority neighborhoods, the LAPD was increasingly seen not as an ally in the struggle for public order but as a likely instrument of oppression. With eroding trust and limited cooperation from the law-abiding, of course, the kind of virtuous safety cycle that Bill Bratton had first seen in South Boston and would create in New York could not take hold. In 1987, Operation Hammer's first year, L.A.'s violent crime rate was 6 percent *below* New York's; a decade later it was 34 percent *higher*. And, of course, in April 1992 anger over LAPD behavior exploded following the acquittal of four cops who had beaten Rodney King after a high-speed chase a year earlier. In one of the bloodiest urban riots in U.S. history, there were fifty-three deaths, thousands of injuries, and a billion dollars of property damage over six days.[10] Hammers, clearly, do not fix windows—they break them.

True broken windows policing, in Kelling's words, involves "a negotiated sense of order in a community, in which you negotiate with residents about what is appropriate behavior in an area. If you tell your cops, 'We are going to go in and practice zero tolerance for all minor crimes,' you are inviting a mess of trouble."[11] Defining the rules that will apply in a particular neighborhood is, then, a collaboration between authorities and those with a stake in the area's viability. These rules can be subtle and vary from place to place. In walking a beat with a cop in Newark, for example, Kelling learned that "[d]runks and addicts could sit on the stoops, but could not lie down. People could drink on side streets, but not at the main intersection. Bottles had to be in paper bags. Talking to, bothering, or begging from people waiting at the bus stop was strictly forbidden. If a dispute erupted between a businessman and a customer, the businessman was assumed to be right, especially if the customer was a stranger. If a stranger loitered, [the cop] would ask him if he had any means of support and what his business was; if he gave unsatisfactory answers, he was sent on his way. Persons who broke the informal rules, especially those who bothered people waiting at bus stops, were arrested for vagrancy. Noisy teenagers were told to keep quiet."[12] Enforcing these collectively specified and somewhat elastic standards not only gave the law-abiding "regulars" in the area a greater sense of security and order but increased the odds they would cooperate with authorities about potentially more problematic behaviors.

This is an extraordinarily important process. Any neighborhood is a combination of privately and commonly owned territory. People can defend their private spaces with locks on doors or bars on windows, but if they are fearful—or just annoyed about certain repulsive behaviors such as public intoxication or urination—in the streets or parks that make up the urban commons, they may retreat behind those locked doors or flee to safer, more pleasant environs and make these areas even less secure. It is therefore crucial to the viability and appeal of cities that rights and responsibilities in public spaces are well-specified and enforced.

Ironically, during the very decades in which heroic and widely praised efforts have been made to mitigate the "Tragedy of the (Ecological) Commons,"[13] in which shared environmental assets are damaged or depleted by polluters who abuse their rights of access to such resources, similar efforts to mitigate harm to the civic order have often been portrayed unsympathetically and met with legal maneuvering aimed at preventing such mitigation. At first blush, this does not seem inconsistent. A factory owner, for example, using "our" (communally owned) air or water to dispose of industrial waste is surely worth regulating; a few teens wearing gang colors and loitering on the corner seems not. The factory owner harms many and the teens no one—and we surely do not want to infringe their freedoms of expression and assembly on speculation that they *might* do so. But some harms are imperceptible. What if elderly neighbors are simply afraid of such groups and feel imprisoned in their homes when they're present? And little things add up. We do not give the polluter of the environmental commons a pass just because he's not an evil factory owner but a lone motorist. Though the greenhouse gases *my* car emits are trivial, when many of us inflict the same small harm we create a problem that cries out for—and gets—regulation. It seems strange to argue that can't also be true when, in densely populated urban areas, lots of little incivilities or threats can add up to considerable stress or fear—and, if unchecked, might produce flight that will wreck a neighborhood and destabilize an entire city. Nevertheless, many do exactly that.

OBVIOUS COSTS, HIDDEN BENEFITS

Brooklyn resident Tyquan Brehon is the subject of a documentary that's part of the legal and public relations counteroffensive against New York's broken windows policing program.[14] Given that the epic homicide rates recorded in the 1980s and early 1990s were highly correlated with drug dealing and illegal handguns, the plan to "turn this juvenile crime thing around" (in President Clinton's words) and save lives included a highly controversial practice: if cops had a "reasonable suspicion" that someone was engaged in wrongdoing, they could *stop*, *question*, and—if their suspicions were confirmed or they judged their safety required it—*frisk* that person for drugs or weapons. In his telling, Brehon had been stopped in this way sixty times in his young life and, as far as he knew, the only reason was that he is black. The documentarians did not bother to question any of the cops involved (or put them on camera if they did), so their film isn't terribly convincing evidence that New York cops are innately racist, but it certainly records at least one useful datum: Brehon is resentful about his experiences with stop-and-frisk (the "question" part is usually left out of descriptions of the practice) and therefore distrustful of police. He's undoubtedly not alone, so we can conclude that this policy involves significant costs.

To learn that there are also benefits, we need to listen to people such as Debbie McBride.[15] When she moved to the South Bronx in 1999, her apartment building was, in her words, "like *New Jack City*. People were selling crack openly in the lobby." She worked with a local cop to put a few dealers away, and eventually took the job as her building's super and enrolled it in the NYPD's Trespass Affidavit Program (aka "Clean Halls"), which authorizes the police to patrol private buildings and stop, question, and frisk trespassers or other lawbreakers. Her opinion: "I love it! Me being a woman, I feel safe. I can get up at 4 A.M. and start working." One of her elderly, wheelchair-bound tenants seconds the sentiment and describes the problem: "As soon as [people] see that there's no police around, they ask you to let them into the lobby or to hold the door for them. 'I'm waiting on someone,' they say." Once out of view of patrol cars, the tragedy of the urban commons plays out: "You can smell their stuff in the hallway; they're cussing and urinating. Then I don't want to come in because I'm scared. I'm scared just to stick my key in the door." Once police identify and evict those who don't belong in the halls, on the other hand, "everything's A-OK. The building is safe; you can come down and get your mail and talk to decent people."

But the payoff from this tool of broken windows policing is not just an enhanced feeling of security on the part of the vulnerable but also *reduced risk to young people like Tyquan Brehon*—and the evidence that such benefits are substantial is not merely anecdotal. To date, six American and two foreign cities have conducted experiments aimed at assessing the effectiveness of policies that allocate more cops to crime hot spots and authorize them to stop, question, and frisk those acting suspiciously in order to discourage the carrying of illegal weapons. In all eight cities, researchers found that such efforts significantly reduce gun injury or death.

One of the most carefully controlled experiments took place in Pittsburgh in 1998. Two high-crime areas were selected for periodic "firearm suppression patrols" (FSPs) in which police were authorized to initiate "stop and talk" contacts with those they considered suspicious (by virtue of their actions or demeanor) and, if warranted by subsequent behavior, to pat them down or engage in more intrusive searches. Criminologists Jacqueline Cohen and Jens Ludwig compared the data on gun violence in the patrolled and "untreated" areas and concluded that the patrols reduced shots fired by 34 percent and gunshot injuries by 71 percent relative to expected levels (that is, absent FSPs). Since each gunshot injury can cost society upward of $1 million in health care and other costs, this suggests a remarkably high return for a modest increase in policing costs: "$35,000 or so in targeted antigun police patrols," Cohen and Ludwig concluded, "may yield benefits of as much as $25 million."[16] What's more, such benefits can be achieved with minimal collateral damage to personal freedom or police-community relations: the Pittsburgh experiment generated exactly zero citizen complaints.

The NYPD, on the other hand, is the frequent target of indignant news coverage and commentary, and the city spends millions annually defending the force against suits alleging that stop-and-frisk is racially biased and that such "suspicionless" searches are illegal. Have New York's finest gone too far and picked up Daryl Gates's hammer? On the surface, the statistics are troubling. In 2011, for example, the NYPD made almost 686,000 stops, 87 percent of which were of blacks or Hispanics, who make up just 53 percent of the city's population. And critics point out that stop-and-frisk's gun yield has been declining, from one illegal gun confiscated for every 266 stops in 2003, down to one gun per 879 stops in 2011.[17]

Of course, that decline is consistent with either of two possibilities: that cops have become less efficient in deciding who is dangerous, or that over time they have succeeded in deterring the routine carrying of illegal weapons. The city's continuing progress on homicide rates and the experimental evidence from Pittsburgh and elsewhere argue for the latter: when owners of illegal guns stow them away to avoid confiscation rather than keeping them close at hand, there are fewer spur-of-the-moment shootings, injuries, and deaths. Of course, it's easy to ignore these benefits because we don't know *who* would have been harmed by gun violence in the absence of stop-and-frisk—and, therefore, no one is making documentaries about these would-have-been victims or offering to represent them *pro bono* in lawsuits.

On the police bias question, two careful inquiries have found that there's a lot less to worry about here than some overheated media coverage has suggested. The problem is that the racial and ethnic distribution of the population at large does not match that of crime victims or perpetrators: a disproportionately large fraction of both is drawn from minority populations, and crime "hot spots" are also disproportionately in areas with large black and Hispanic populations. For example, blacks constitute only 23 percent of New York's population, but were 62 percent of the city's murder victims in 2011 and (according to victims' or witnesses' reports rather than allegedly racist police) committed 80 percent of all shootings. A police force seeking to save more black lives would properly deploy more officers to predominantly black neighborhoods and likely make more stops of black suspects. Accordingly, criminologist Greg Ridgeway examined over a half-million stops conducted in 2006 by almost nineteen thousand uniformed cops and compared the racial distribution of each officer's stops to a "benchmark" racial distribution that controlled for time, place, and several other salient factors. He found that only a trivially small fraction of officers—one-half of one percent of the cops most active in making stops—could plausibly be accused of bias, and only "small racial differences in the rates of frisk, search, use of force, and arrest. Nonwhites generally experienced slightly more intrusive stops, in terms of having more frequent frisks and searches, than did similarly situated white suspects." He recommended a half-dozen steps NYPD could take to address these concerns.[18]

More recently, economists Decio Coviello and Nicola Persico examined 2.6 million stops over 2003–11 and compared "hit rates"—the fraction of stops that resulted in arrests—for whites and blacks. An earlier study, using a small data sample from 1988–89, had found that blacks were less likely to be arrested after being stopped, and argued this was evidence of police bias, since cops apparently stopped and searched blacks even after these searches had hit diminishing returns, carrying a lower probability of turning up evidence of a crime than for whites.[19] With their larger, more recent data set, Coviello and Persico found exactly the opposite: after controlling for precincts, hit rates are actually lower for whites, implying they are stopped excessively relative to their probability of wrongdoing.

The authors concluded that there is "no evidence that the individual police officers who make the decision to stop this or that pedestrian are biased against blacks" and "no evidence of a significant race effect on arrest[s]."[20]

None of which means that the NYPD should cavalierly brush aside citizens' concerns about stop-and-frisk, or that it need not enhance its efforts to ensure that stops are conducted fairly and efficiently. But neither should its critics ignore the fact that the practice is, in Bill Bratton's words, "an absolutely basic tool of American policing"[21] and a key means of reclaiming the urban commons. Taking this tool away from cops in New York and elsewhere would certainly mean that some people—and, again, we don't know who or how many—would suffer injury or death. At worst, then, continuing the practice seems to involve a reasonable trade-off: residents enjoy somewhat less personal freedom in exchange for a safer, more livable city, in much the same way and for the same reason that courts have mandated we must give up the right to falsely yell "fire!" in a crowded theatre. Quite possibly, the NYPD could make this trade-off more sensitively, but the evidence is clear that it is making it successfully. And it's also worth remembering that New York's incarceration rate is actually *lower* under this form of proactive policing than it was under earlier, reactive modes. In effect, then, stop-and-frisk might well be *both* safety- and freedom-enhancing because it seems to reduce the volume of serious crimes, felony convictions, and long stretches in prison in favor of shorter-term arrests for misdemeanors. It would be a great tragedy if, in a misguided effort to ensure maximum individual freedom without regard to the cost in foregone safety, we got less of both.[22] But we've done similarly unwise things before.

THE GRATE SOCIETY

Fifty years ago, there were about 560,000 beds at public psychiatric facilities in the United States. Today there are 43,000. It would be nice to report that this precipitous decline is a happy result of spectacular improvement in the mental health of Americans or, at least, that we successfully made the transition from reliance on costly and inefficient inpatient psychiatric care to a more humane system of outpatient treatment. This was the hope in 1963, when President John F. Kennedy created federally funded Community Mental Health Centers (CMHCs) and predicted that "reliance on the cold mercy of custodial isolation will be supplanted by the open warmth of community concern and capability."[23]

Of course, neither of those things happened. The CMHCs, it turned out, were not particularly interested in treating people with severe mental disorders, focusing instead on those with lesser problems: as state mental hospitals shrank or closed, federal studies showed that less than 7 percent of their discharged patients became CMHC clients.[24] Meanwhile, the population of those with serious mental illnesses such as schizophrenia, schizoaffective disorder, or bipolar disorder has grown to 7.7 million according to the National Advisory Mental Health Council, with 3.5 million of those *getting no care* at any given time. About 10 percent of these millions do not just suffer untreated but become societal problems, accounting for a third of the homeless and a fifth of prison inmates, while committing 10 percent of the nation's homicides. The two largest psychiatric inpatient facilities in the United States today are the L.A. County Jail and New York's Rikers Island jail complex.[25] Open warmth, indeed.

This public health disaster has many causes: government failure, perverse incentives, interest-group politics, and an excessive preoccupation with the civil liberties of the mentally ill at the expense of their well-being. During the half-century before Kennedy's optimistic words and his generous funding of CMHCs, care for those suffering serious mental illness had been the responsibility of state governments, and most had been discharging it with inefficiency that bordered on depraved indifference. Press accounts described inpatient treatment at underfunded, poorly staffed state mental hospitals in Dickensian terms,[26] so it was natural to hope that outpatient care would be superior. Because the CMHCs were federally funded, however, states now had a strong incentive to discharge as many patients as possible, without much regard to whether this was clinically wise. Doing so saved them money and pleased fiscal conservatives at the same time it quelled civil libertarians' outrage over the horrific conditions in which many mentally ill had been institutionalized.

A major triumph for the libertarians was the Supreme Court's *O'Connor v. Donaldson* decision in 1975, which established that it is unconstitutional to involuntarily confine an individual who is not dangerous to himself or others and capable of surviving safely in freedom.[27] Lower-court cases held also that the mentally ill have a right to refuse treatment[28] and that any treatment must be in the least restrictive setting possible.[29] Often, of course, courts' judgments about the extent to which deinstitutionalized patients could function safely proved to be tragically in error. Accounts of the homeless mentally ill killing others or coming to harm themselves soon became staples of the mainstream press. No matter. Eventually, states' aversion to further costly litigation and damage claims meant, in the pithy summation of psychiatrist Fuller Torrey, that to be involuntarily committed a person had to be "either killing himself in front of the admitting doctor or trying to kill the admitting doctor."[30]

This means that hundreds of thousands of mentally ill might, at any point in time, be wandering city streets, camping on park benches and sidewalks, or living in homeless shelters—indeed, anyplace but where their mental and physical suffering can be treated. And given that these ill are often the last to perceive they need help, there's little that those who would like to assist them can do about it, though many have tried. One of the most notable attempts to roll back the "gains" wrought via deinstitutionalization was made by New York mayor Ed Koch in 1987. The city's huge homeless population—estimated at thirty-five thousand—was a destabilizing force in many neighborhoods, and Koch was spending more on shelters than the entire budgets of some small cities. A survey showed that one-quarter of this population had a history of serious mental illness, and a large fraction of these needed hospitalization or some form of twenty-four-hour supervision. They weren't getting this care on the streets or in shelters, so the mayor devised a bold plan. Three-member "Project Help" teams (a psychiatrist, a social worker, and a nurse) would assess whether a homeless mentally ill person was "in danger of serious harm." If so, the patient would be brought to Bellevue Hospital for further evaluation; if hospitalization was again judged necessary and the patient resisted, he or she could be held for up to two days for further observation.

Koch's program went nowhere, fast. Its first test case was that of Joyce Patricia Brown, who had spent a year camping on a hot air vent grate near a restaurant at Second Avenue and 65th Street. Neighborhood residents reported that she frequently ran into traffic, exposed herself, made threats to passersby, and occasionally urinated on money given to her or covered herself in her own excrement. Brown obtained *pro bono* representation from the New York Civil Liberties Union the same day she was picked up by Project Help staff. Hospitalized, clean, and well-dressed, she proved a sympathetic figure in court. Her attorney argued that her outlandish actions were rational adaptations to street life, and the trial judge opined that Brown's avoidance of the city's deplorable homeless shelters was evidence of her sanity. Her right to refuse medication was affirmed and she won her release within twelve weeks. After a brief residence in a single-room-occupancy hotel arranged by her attorney and some counseling from the psychiatrist who had testified on her behalf, however, she returned to panhandling and was arrested on drug charges.[31] Brown's civil liberties had been aggressively protected; her health and welfare had not. And it goes without saying that her advocates never gave much thought to the quality of life of her neighbors at Second and 65th.

Of course, if one-third of America's homeless suffer from untreated mental illness, then two-thirds do not. *But just about all need help.* The best estimates are that another third are substance abusers, though there is considerable overlap of this group with the mentally ill. Another third are broke and looking for work, but at least half of these will need considerable assistance (literacy education, job training, life counseling) in order to obtain it. Relatively few are runaways or transients who *prefer* a life-on-the-streets existence. As with the mentally ill, an overzealous defense of the rights and freedoms of these populations not only hampers efforts to get them the help they deserve but damages the rights of others to enjoy neighborhoods that are safe and pleasant.

In 1972, for example, the High Court's *Papachristou* ruling invalidated most vagrancy laws—which generally attempt to regulate loitering or "wandering . . . from place to place without any lawful purpose or object"—as unconstitutionally vague and vesting too much arbitrary power with police.[32] In addition, as noted earlier, many cities imposed more stringent zoning rules and costly building codes that have limited the availability of affordable housing to the disabled or those down on their luck. In consequence, cities have struggled mightily with their homelessness problems, at great expense and with limited success. The good news is that in recent years policy has converged toward a strategy that greatly improves the odds of bringing the homeless the care they need while simultaneously enhancing order and amenity in the urban commons.

A TIE FOR FIRST

Just as deinstitutionalization was a collaborative effort by those on both sides of the ideological spectrum, so will be the successful treatment of the homelessness problem to which that campaign contributed. In fact, progressives have already groped their way to a key element of such treatment: committing the homeless mentally ill not to hospitals or shelters but to independent living arrangements. Interestingly, in Denver—a city on the leading edge of these efforts—the impetus and funding for these efforts came initially from conservative business interests. Downtown landlords and shopkeepers, convinced that the vagrants residing in public areas were repelling customers and damaging property values, ponied up money to, somehow, relocate the most problematic and reclaim their "campgrounds" for higher-valued uses.

The result was a program that has come to be called Housing First. In contrast to triage efforts that place the homeless in shelters or "rapid rehousing" policies that sometimes condition aid on participation in substance-abuse programs, Housing First moves people directly from streets or shelters to permanent housing *without precondition*. Recipients pay 30 percent of their income (whether from wages or government transfers) as rent, and receive support services that are based on "assertive engagement" rather than coercion. This means that, quite often, recipients receive housing subsidies though they continue to resist medication for their mental illnesses or abstain from their addictions. That's life: the goal here is reducing harm rather than conforming to a utopian ideal.

Which is something those on both the Left and Right need to remember in assessing Housing First. We're not going back to pre-*O'Connor* days, and not all the seriously mentally ill are going to accept treatment or be cured if they do. We're not going to uninvent crack cocaine or find a magic sobriety pill. But lots of people need lots of help, and the evidence is that they're much more likely to get it and benefit from it if situated in a stable living environment and matched with caseworkers who can connect them with appropriate ameliorative treatments.

Just as important, this approach mitigates the *spillover harms* that arise from homelessness. A broken window is a symptom of disorder that invites worse; so does a schizophrenic threatening to assault passersby, an aggressive panhandler, or a drunk camped on a steam grate. Rotating people in and out of night-time shelters does not appreciably reduce such harms in order to make cities more orderly, safe, and pleasurable places. Only permanent housing does that. This is more expensive than shelters, of course, but when avoided spillover costs are considered, the program's return on investment may be not just positive, but quite high. Perhaps if this approach is rebranded as "Public Order First" it will be an easier sell.

Those on the Right will note that these sorts of transfers frequently produce some perverse incentives that actually harm the intended beneficiaries. This is a valid point—and one that is often underappreciated by those on the Left, who sometimes mistake resistance to entitlement spending as mean-spiritedness or mere cheapness. But the relevant question here is whether there will be *extra* disincentives arising from Housing First. Federal, state, and local governments spend colossal sums to support incomes and subsidize purchases of food, housing, medical care, and much else; these programs already damage incentives to work, invest in education, and maintain healthy lifestyles. Ideally, a national initiative to implement Housing First would be part of a comprehensive effort to better structure *all* transfer programs, reducing the extent to which current benefit formulas excessively tax work effort or other wholesome behaviors.

What's more, Housing First might *correct* some perverse incentives inherent in the status quo. For example, homeless shelters and soup kitchens are usually "free," though many of their clients receive disability payments or other income. The result is that using shelters frees up some income for added booze or drug consumption. And since some homeless feel unsafe in these shelters and choose to fend for themselves on the streets, they are less healthy and therefore empty the public purse more than they would if housed in apartments or rooming-houses. A before-and-after study of participants in Denver's Housing First program is encouraging on this score: annual costs of hospital care fell 45 percent, detox costs 84 percent, and incarceration costs 76 percent for this (unfortunately quite small) sample.[33] Total savings (including foregone shelter costs) were $31,500 per participant per year, against annual per-capita program costs of $13,800. That kind of return certainly suggests it's worth replicating the Denver experiment to see if it will work as well elsewhere.

A Housing First–like program might also correct some perverse incentives afflicting policymakers and voters. Such an entitlement would increase housing demand, and it would then be up to the market to expand supply. But many current land use, zoning, and regulatory policies—especially, as previous chapters noted, in "boutique" cities—make doing so exceedingly expensive. This approach, therefore, would make the costs of some very inequitable and inefficient policies more obvious to taxpayers, who might then become receptive to liberalization. When housing entrepreneurs point out that obsolete warehouses and factories can be cheaply converted to single-room-occupancy hotels, multi-use zoning might become more popular. When developers design rental units that are a fraction of current costs because they are smaller or have fewer baths, electrical outlets, and off-street parking spaces than current codes permit, then expect those codes to be relaxed and the supply of affordable housing to grow rapidly.

Finally, once the poor, the mentally ill, and even the addicted have a claim to a decent *private* space—combined with the assertive engagement of caregivers—then many arguments against enforcing standards of conduct in cities' *public* spaces evaporate. And when they do, one last impediment to the growth of efficient, equitable, and vibrant cities will have been removed.

CHAPTER 11

Boom Commandments

WALK THE DOWNTOWN STREETS of any American city and you're likely to find a Monument to Misguided Dreams. It is not so named, of course, and is not statuary but the residue of our post–World War II urban renewal program, the results of which range from disastrous to merely disappointing. In her classic *The Death and Life of Great American Cities*, Jane Jacobs described these places best: "Civic centers that are avoided by everyone but bums. . . . Commercial centers that are lackluster imitations of standardized suburban chain-store shopping. Promenades that go from no place to nowhere and have no promenaders. Expressways that eviscerate great cities. This is not the rebuilding of cities. This is the sacking of cities."[1]

When the ribbons were cut on these projects, of course, all were hailed as game-changers that would not just beautify blighted areas but energize urban economies, creating jobs within their borders and stimulating further growth and investment nearby. Yet from New York's Jacob Javits Convention Center to San Francisco's Western Addition district and through many equally discouraging sites in between, the promised spillover benefits rarely arrived. In successful cities and declining ones alike, these massive expenditures of public and private capital have usually failed to perceptibly improve their cities' fortunes—and often have harmed them.

Charles Center, in my hometown of Baltimore, is a typical example—and a good illustration of the chasm between rhetoric and reality in redevelopment circles. Upon its completion in the early 1960s, press coverage was adulatory and opinion leaders praised those behind the thirty-three-acre project for their good intentions, brilliant vision, bold artistic sense, and deft political touch. As the decades passed and the city spent many more taxpayer dollars in efforts to revitalize neighboring districts, Charles Center was so often referred to as a catalyst for Baltimore's renaissance that few noticed that it is, actually, a failure both within its borders and beyond them.

Many who work there consider it dull, inconvenient, unsafe, and ugly. Its sterile office towers—in which vacancy rates commonly exceed those that prevailed in the older buildings they replaced—overlook plazas that are little used during business hours and abandoned thereafter. Some of the project's acclaimed innovations, such as elevated walkways that enabled pedestrians to move between buildings without descending to street level, were eventually seen to be not just unnecessary but undesirable, and have been torn down. Its only architecturally distinctive building, a theatre in the style aptly named "brutalism," proved so unappealing that it was a chronic money-loser that has been shuttered for many years. The adjoining retail district that Charles Center was supposed to revivify continued its steep decline and remains a jumble of empty storefronts and discount shoe or wig shops. Any nearby investment of significance has been a by-product of the city's relentless renewal offensive and bought with tax breaks or other subsidies. Even in its entirety, this lavishly funded program did not reverse the city's devastating six-decade-long exodus of jobs and residents.

Why has project-based renewal underachieved? First, too often government-guided redevelopment projects are, for all the favorable spin accompanying them, poorly conceived. Many embody the mistaken planning principles that provoked Jacobs to write *Death and Life* in the first place. Their site plans are commonly guided more by utopian visions or academic dogma than human needs; their architectural elements are generally so bland that only a committee could love them; their public spaces lack appeal and, often, even a reason for being. In sum, people tend not to like them, and so they don't work. This is forgivable if, like Charles Center, everything was under construction before the works of Jacobs, and those of more contemporary critics like the New Urbanists,[2] hit print. But too many cities continue to crank out such projects. The problem is not just that too many cooks (in the form of politicians, planners, and rent-seeking developers) spoil the broth, but also that there are weak incentives to change the recipe. When bureaucracies and subsidies are the key elements of the urban redevelopment process and few of the relevant decision makers get much poorer when a project fails or richer when it succeeds, bet on the former.

The deeper reason for the lackluster performance of so many urban renewal projects—including many that are, in fact, well-designed and well-executed—is that their destinies are influenced far more by the viability of their host cities than the reverse. When planners see a district or neighborhood that is distressed and decide to remake it *without first asking whether the distress is a symptom of larger, more systemic problems*, they are setting themselves up for failure. If practitioners did this in medicine—"Nurse, I'm getting a weak pulse in this patient's wrist; prepare the ER for a vein transplant!"—it would be immediately recognized as folly; they would want to get at the heart of the matter.

In the foregoing chapters, I've tried to do exactly that: to focus on systemic rather than symptomatic measures to revive dying cities and enhance the quality of life in growing ones. One way to summarize the key principles might be to say "protect well the private property of city residents and manage efficiently that property they own in common with each other." That advice is unsatisfactorily vague, however, so in what follows I will put forth ten specific prescriptions—commandments, if you will—that aim to ensure virtuous policymaking and are the foundations of a successful and organic program of urban revitalization.

I. DON'T STEAL

Most of us see taxes as "the price we must pay for a civilized society." A few believe that "taxation is theft." Due to some peculiarities of democracy that make the political marketplace operate differently in reality than in high school civics texts, both views can sometimes be true.

American cities provide ample evidence of this fact. There are, surely, many high-tax, high-service jurisdictions that are healthy and stable, but there are many others that traveled a high-tax, low-service, high-transfer path that has had tragic long-term consequences for their viability and their citizens' welfare. The crux of the problem has generally been redistributionist policies fueled by idealism, interest-group politics, or greed. A key point to stress is that the motive matters not at all, for when income transfers are pursued aggressively at the *local* level, the effects are inevitably damaging. Donor classes will ultimately vote with their feet and exit the high-tax jurisdiction, taking their skills, income, and entrepreneurial energy with them; the capital investment that is the long-term foundation of a successful city also will flow elsewhere. We saw the same ill effects when James Michael Curley, "the Mayor of the Poor," robbed Boston's rich "Brahmins" in order to help destitute Irish immigrants as when successive corrupt mayors of Newark—the three who served from 1962 to 2006, for example, all wound up in jail—robbed that city's residents to line their own pockets.

This is not to say that those with redistributionist inclinations must change their thinking—just that these issues should be worked out at higher levels of government, and *not* where the desire to avoid (or benefit from) transfer programs can cause an unhealthy rearrangement of residents, employers, and investors within a metro area or region, with donors fleeing to lower-tax suburbs and beneficiaries arriving to replace them in core cities. A national approach to income transfers has long been the pattern in Europe, and arguably this has contributed greatly to the relative health and stability of European cities. That simply needs to be the practice here.

The good news is that when key tax rates in core cities have been made competitive with those in surrounding districts, the effects on residential location and capital investment decisions have been favorable, immediate, and dramatic. It's not necessary to fix all a city's problems or alter its political culture to turn it around; the experiences of San Francisco and Boston in the aftermath of their states' tax-cap initiatives make that clear. But it *is* necessary to secure the property rights of a city's homeowners and businesses, and to assure them that the value of their assets will not be expropriated (via tax capitalization) whenever politically convenient.

II. HOLD THE FORT

Take a spin around Detroit and you will see abundant evidence of a city on the downs: vacant office towers, long-dormant and crumbling factories, schools and shops in ruins, once-grand homes abandoned and falling down around themselves. Scattered about also are large, well-appointed buildings that stand above neighboring dwellings, signaling power and status like nobles' castles. And, to some extent, that is what they are, for Detroit's strong unionist heritage has endowed it with a string of meeting halls and social clubs that bear the insignia of cartels of labor that, starting in New Deal days, seized effective control of Motown's leading industry and therefore wielded enormous influence over the city's destiny.

This has not worked out terribly well for that industry, workers in general, or Detroit—though, as with much else that has damaged America's great cities, Big Labor's conquest of the manufacturing capital that once was concentrated there remains much celebrated in certain quarters. As with confiscatory local taxes, however, labor market regulations that facilitate the appropriation of returns due to capital both reduce local capital investment and encourage its strategic redeployment to more defensible environs.

For many years, then, most of the jobs created in the domestic auto industry (and others) have been in right-to-work states, and the unions' occupation of Detroit (and elsewhere) is very much a Pyrrhic victory. In competitive markets, the owners of labor and capital are partners in production; wage growth is enhanced most directly and reliably by added investment in physical capital and technological progress that increases labor productivity. Absent secure property rights to capital in any particular locale, that capital will move elsewhere or simply melt away, leaving laborers poorer. Accordingly, right-to-work laws and greater enforcement of laws against trespass and violence in the context of labor disputes should be seen as job- and income-creating policies.

And the damaging consequences of monopolistic or opportunistic behavior by labor cartels are not limited to the economies of deindustrialized cities and their left-behind residents. Lost benefits of agglomeration—Marshall's "advantages which people following the same skilled trade get from near neighbourhood to one another"—may hamper technological advance more broadly. Cities are and have always been centers of innovation, the benefits of which tend to spread widely. To continue to be so, they have to be places where ownership rights to capital are secure and the returns to such capital are protected from appropriation.

III. GUARD AGAINST SHORTSIGHTEDNESS

We Americans like to seize the day. On average, we save less than 5 percent of our income; even the pleasure-loving French save at three times that rate. Our present orientation is especially prominent in politics, where the election cycle almost guarantees unwholesome myopia. It is standard political practice to deliver goodies to constituents now and worry about the long-term costs if and when reelected—or, if those costs will arrive after term limits expire, not even then. So at various levels of government we see chronic deficits, extravagant promises for future entitlements (especially pensions and retirement benefits for unionized public employees), and repeated raids on capital budgets so that our public infrastructure often fails—sometimes catastrophically.

Preaching the gospel of good government and sound fiscal management will be of no avail in addressing these problems. Not that there's anything wrong with it, but many incentives to behave badly are just too deeply rooted to be countered in this way. Those incentives have to be changed. The best way to do so is to keep day-to-day decisions that require a long-term perspective out of the public sphere and in the private one.

This implies a hard-headed program of privatization of public assets. Whenever and wherever possible, franchise bidding should be employed to efficiently construct, manage, or maintain capital-intensive facilities that otherwise might become piggy-banks for shortsighted pols, whether as sources of funds to buy the support of key interest groups or as parking places for patronage employees. Private owners are not perfect, of course, but they have much stronger incentives than politicians and bureaucrats to control costs and innovate in the short run and to maintain asset quality (via responsible capital budgeting) and their wealth in the long run.

Not all the facilities that are customarily operated in the public sector may be feasibly privatized, but as the French have demonstrated with their water concessions and a few American jurisdictions have learned with respect to tollways, parking garages, and other infrastructure, privatization has enormous potential to resolve near- and far-term management and budget problems. An ancillary benefit might be a more level political playing field: fewer public assets means smaller public employee unions and less powerful interest groups pressuring elected officials to make long-term promises that will be very expensive to keep.

IV. DON'T LIE

If it is not the most sophisticated and important form of communication used by humankind, the price system is at least the oldest. Since hunters started trading with gatherers, we consumers have been telling producers what we want and how badly we want it by our willingness to pay. Their prices, in turn, provide the info we need to evaluate all of life's little trade-offs in choosing what to buy or do.

This system is breathtaking in its efficiency—*as long as the price signals sent to demanders and suppliers are truthful*. Clearly, lying prices are responsible for much of the inconvenience or waste that is typical of everyday life in city and suburb alike, from the freeways clogged with creep-and-beep traffic to the streets we cruise endlessly searching for free parking. Setting an appropriate money price for access to these facilities, rather than a price in time or fuel wasted, can instantly and effectively solve the problem. And as Stockholm showed with its congestion pricing experiment, the economic and environmental gains can be so prominent that people overcome the delusion that they can enjoy a free lunch, and actually favor honest prices instead.

More broadly, the prices of government services should not only be honest but unbundled. Arguably, chronic budget deficits signal a lying price, falsely telling voters that government costs far less than it actually does. But this is more a problem at the federal level than with states or localities, which are often subject to balanced-budget constitutional or charter requirements. Nevertheless, cities can take steps to ensure that their costs are communicated and allocated in such a way that voters can make intelligent choices about which services they want and which are too costly, as Indianapolis does with its array of fees and earmarks tied to particular jurisdictions and functions.

V. COMPETE

Everyone knows that competition is good and monopoly bad. We push ourselves a little harder, think of better ways of doing things, and waste less time and other resources doing them when a desired reward is made contingent on besting a rival or when we're a little bit worried about our job security. The problem is that outside the domain of sports, in which we clearly *enjoy* competitive dynamics, most of us seem to prefer *not* to compete: businesses commonly try to erect market-entry barriers, workers seek sinecures and tenure, and bureaucracies devise myriad rules to see that rewards are doled out by formula instead of merit.

The challenge, then, is not merely to help policymakers *see* that major benefits will arise from competitive delivery of many government services, but rather to get them to take on the interest groups devoted to insulating themselves from competitive pressures and *deliver* these benefits. Nowhere is this more clear than in public education, in which an iron alliance between teachers' unions, administrators, anti-market ideologues, and even some affluent parents (who fear that innovations such as vouchers might enable poor students to buy access to their higher-performing schools) has been very successful in fending off attempts to break up local public school monopolies.

Pro-competition advocacy groups and even some charitable organizations have done yeoman work in winning trial voucher programs in a few cities; charter schools are gaining traction in many others. These efforts are generating copious evidence of success that will inevitably lead more states and localities to consider upsetting our increasingly expensive and disappointing public education status quo. It might also be time to fight special-interest fire with fire—by, for example, forming parents' and taxpayers' unions and recruiting religious denominations as allies in the political struggle against education monopoly. In many older northern cities, for example, Catholic parish schools that enhanced the economic and social mobility of generations of immigrant families are now struggling to stay afloat as their members prospered and exited urban neighborhoods. They could serve the same function for non-Catholic residents, but it's hard to beat "free" government schools, no matter how dysfunctional those might be. It's time for such religious groups to go on the offensive and lobby for the vouchers or charters that will enable their schools to grow once again. The evidence shows that this would not only change the lives of *their* enrolled students but also improve the performance of rival (public) schools with which they'd vie for customers.

VI. GET BIG

Scale economies—through which enterprises enjoy lower unit costs as they grow larger—are one of the most important influences on the strategic behavior of firms. They often dictate production and marketing plans, mergers, spin-offs, and myriad other business decisions. Exploiting them can be the difference between enduring success and failure.

Public-sector decision makers, on the other hand, usually assume that their scale of operations is fixed and given by existing political borders. True, some cities can annex or merge with neighboring jurisdictions and "grow the business," but even when this is technically possible they often face resistance from voters suspicious that consolidation might be a scheme to pick their pockets. Fixed borders, however, need not prevent elected officials from exploiting scale economies in key government services.

For example, if costs per ton of trash collected will fall 10 percent when volume in a particular area doubles (perhaps because some overhead costs can be spread more broadly, or pickups organized more economically), then this area's jurisdictions might pool their collections and realize these savings by negotiating an appropriate contract to cover the relevant territory (using either public employees or a private concession) without adjusting their borders. That is, there can be functional consolidation without altering the political map—if officials think entrepreneurially. Absent a profit motive, bureaucrats often don't do so, of course, but elected officials have an incentive to broker these sorts of deals because they will benefit at the polls when they pass resulting savings on to their constituents in the form of a reduced tax burden, or use freed-up budget dollars to enhance other key public services.

VII. PRESERVE THE UNSEEN

The Great Migration of African-Americans from the rural South to the urban North that started during World War I and continued for almost four decades was tragically ill-timed. Prior immigrants had found more competitive (and therefore vibrant) labor markets and more secure rights to residential and business property on their arrival in America's great industrial cities than these latest migrants would find upon theirs. How this would hamper the economic and social advance of urban blacks in the last half of the twentieth century has been much written about.

Less widely appreciated is how another great pre– and post–World War II phenomenon—the extravagantly funded program to clear slums, eradicate blight, and rebuild America's aging cities—exacerbated these harms. Those implementing the era's grand renewal plans had only the best of intentions, of course, but they overlooked something very important: how invisible *social capital* affects the viability of a neighborhood and the welfare of its residents. As Harrison Salisbury elegantly summarized, "Bulldozers do not understand that a community is more than broken-down buildings and dirty storefronts. It is a tight skein of human relations. It has a life all its own. The wreckers tear this human fabric to ribbons."[3]

We Americans no longer routinely bulldoze poor neighborhoods in order to erect high-rise slums, but we still have difficulty appreciating the unseen networks that help city-dwellers of all income classes to work, play, acculturate, learn, raise children—in sum, to *live*—better. In the name of economic development, we still condemn, relocate, wreck, and rebuild altogether too cavalierly, without due regard for the intangible assets we destroy in the process. In the name of compassion and social justice, we routinely devise programs that uproot people from places about which they are knowledgeable and in which they are comfortable in favor of places where we merely *hope* they will have superior opportunities and their children better teachers and role models. We need to be far more humble in our plans for people, more respectful of their rights to enjoy the returns on social capital they've worked hard to create, and more determined to ensure that growth and opportunity flourish organically in all neighborhoods.

VIII. BE FAIR

Many of us are too busy to pay much attention to politics and become actively engaged in the policy sphere, and so we often get rolled by small and well-organized groups ("special interests") with more to gain, per individual, than the rest of us. Even when we're engaged on key issues, however, we sometimes agree to policies that are socially inefficient, inequitable, or both. Often this is because we weigh our own interests and act (or vote) accordingly. But sometimes we do this not because we're being selfish, but because we're simply unaware of a likely inequity arising from a particular policy. This can be a by-product of the fact that the people to whom we're being unfair are not at the political table (and so not informing us of their objections) when we're making a decision.

Consider growth controls, exclusionary zoning, or "greenlining" (like that imposed in Oregon), for example. There's abundant evidence that, over time, such regulations both raise housing costs for future residents and reduce vertical and horizontal equity, redistributing wealth somewhat randomly—in some cases from poor to rich, in others among similarly situated individuals. Experimental economists have also shown that *we humans don't like doing such unfair things*. We often put aside our personal interests to treat fairly those with whom we deal; some speculate that concern for fairness may be hardwired in us.

But we certainly can't avoid unfairness if we don't know it exists. It is therefore incumbent on policymakers, opinion leaders, dispassionate researchers, and voters of good will to assess carefully the equity implications of policies up for discussion and speak out about these effects. It would be naive to suggest that all voters or elected officials will always shrink from adopting policies that harm those outside their jurisdiction or those yet unborn—but perhaps enough will that some of these harms can be avoided, or alternative policies devised that can mitigate them to some degree.

IX. CUT OUT THE MIDDLEPEOPLE

In many cities, one of the unsavory leftovers from the era of Robert Moses-style urban renewal is a redevelopment bureaucracy that sits astride every deal that might bring needed capital—and fresh ideas—to urban tracts small and large. Even when a city's economic fundamentals are sound and entrepreneurs are eager to move properties from lower-valued uses to higher ones, the transaction costs associated with navigating this bureaucracy and satisfying the innumerable middlepersons with authority to modify plans or levy charges can eat up prospective gains and scotch deals. This is ironic, since these agencies often justify their existence partly by virtue of their ability to wield the power of eminent domain and reduce transaction costs by eliminating holdout problems. Often they are, instead, sand in the redevelopment gears.

Those populating the various bureaus, councils, boards, and commissions that stand between willing sellers and buyers of developable property argue that their regulatory oversight can prevent egregious errors in the design and execution of a particular project. Sometimes this is even true—just not enough. Architect Alexander Garvin, for example, *defends* these efforts by arguing that "disillusionment with planning is far from justified. Dozens of projects are triumphs of American planning."[4] Dozens! Out of thousands. All too often, then, the nettlesome process of pleasing all these intermediaries prevents things from happening at all, or raises their costs, or increases the chances that they will be unsatisfactory if and when realized.

Entrepreneurs are not infallible, of course. For every Tudor City or Rockefeller Center of enduring value, they might install a "superblock" development that works no better than, say, Charles Center. But, again, incentives matter. Individuals like Fred French or John D. Rockefeller, who put their own wealth at risk when they develop a site, have a far greater tendency to avoid architectural or planning blunders than any civil servant or committee—and to remedy any errors quickly once they become apparent. Accordingly, cities can unlock a great deal of creative energy if they will more fully and frequently trust market participants to identify what needs to be done and allow them to proceed with fewer regulatory or zoning impediments. Which does not mean that planners need to simply go away—but they need to act as facilitators of development rather than impediments to it. More of them need to go to work for (or become) developers and design creative ways to make city projects more popular and profitable rather than merely pleasing to bureaucracies.

X. DON'T BREAK THE WINDOWS

The density of cities—the fact that in them residents are closer to many other people and have readier access to facilities that they find useful and important than they might in suburbs or exurbs—is both a great virtue and a vulnerability. Density can yield troublesome externalities alongside productivity-enhancing agglomeration effects; it will attract thieves and drug-dealers along with artists and entrepreneurs.

City-dwellers must admit, therefore, that realizing the benefits of urban life involves some trade-offs. Cities are rich in their diversity, but this does not mean they can be excessively tolerant of disorder and, sometimes, mere nonconformity. In a dense environment, where people continually encounter strangers whose intentions are unknown to them, it will be *more* rather than less important to devise and enforce norms of conduct than in environments where strangers are less common. The standards of acceptable behavior can vary from neighborhood to neighborhood or even block to block, as George Kelling found when he walked the streets of Newark while he and James Q. Wilson were developing their "broken windows" theory of efficient policing, but without them cities will inevitably decline as residents defend themselves against perceived threats to their security by barricading themselves in their homes or fleeing to more defensible spaces.

This might mean, for example, that in areas where the data show that gun violence is a problem, residents might have to empower police to "stop, question, and frisk" (or, as it was practiced in Pittsburgh, to "stop-and-talk") in order to discourage the malicious or just impulsive from carrying weapons. In areas that are tempting targets for property crime, city-dwellers might have to live with technological intrusions into their privacy (for example, cameras to deter muggers). Such compromises to civil liberties will be troubling to many and intolerable to a few. But we as a society need to get past the foolish presumption that these trade-offs are never worth making, and that tiny sacrifices of liberty can never be compensated by increases in security. Clearly, we need to implement such policies sensitively as well as efficiently. Refusing to make such trade-offs, however, or to consider that maximizing our liberties may not be optimal, can do great harm to our cities and the quality of our lives.

NO CITY LEFT BEHIND

Some of the analysis and recommendations in this book may be troubling to many readers, and all of it may provoke opposition and even anger in at least a few. Those who consider themselves progressives might be especially annoyed. Commonly, to make progress requires one to *do* things, to *un*do bad things, or somehow to take an active role in transforming the world or some piece of it. Yet much of what has been discussed here has held that a great deal of progressive effort, at least as it played out in cities, has failed to move our society forward. Redistributive programs implemented at the local level have provoked flight and sprawl. Anti-competitive labor regulations have fueled urban deindustrialization and damaged economic opportunity. Attempts to eliminate slums often shredded the social fabric

woven by many poor urban residents. Bold programs to save the environment have yielded trivial ecological benefits but considerable inequity. A
presumption that crime can and should be contained solely by treating its
root causes rather than via effective policing has wrecked countless neighborhoods and cost many lives.

Future progress does not become more attainable or likely by denying
these facts or ignoring the possibility that good intentions—whether held
by progressives or conservatives or ideological neutrals—can frequently go
awry. None of the foregoing chapters should be seen as a challenge to or
dismissal of progressive thought. Rather, it simply reflects a hard-headed
commitment to figuring out what works and what does not. If there is an
underlying philosophy or ideology operating throughout this book, it is
pragmatism. If the author has a mantra, it is, "If a policy doesn't actually
work, it's not really progressive, or conservative, or anything except bad."
Just because, for example, playing Robin Hood doesn't make sense at
the local level does not mean that redistributionist policies can't or won't
make society better or fairer if implemented at higher levels of government.

If we all subject our political philosophies and urban policy prescriptions to tests of practicability or usefulness, I believe we can rescue any
city that is in decline and make those that are healthy work better. No
matter how much flight a city might have endured in recent decades or
how much decay is visible within its borders, I am confident that it can
be rescued. Every American city exists for a compelling reason and is endowed with natural, physical, and human capital that carries enormous
potential for growth; each can thrive and deliver abundant social and economic opportunities to its residents. No declining cities are truly obsolete
or should be written off as beyond hope. None of the growing ones should
be so pleased with their current status that they ignore the fundamental
determinants of viability described throughout this book and repeat the
mistakes others have made.

Most of the wisdom and energy to create the conditions for a boom
town will, of course, come from those who live there: residents, business
owners, elected officials, and others who not only have the greatest stake
in seeing their localities grow and prosper but also the best information
about how to implement the requisite strategies. But this is not to say that

those at higher levels of government can play no role. State and federal officials have been enormously generous toward urban governments over the decades—indeed, excessively so, often acting as initiators or at least enablers of demonstrably destructive policies via their support of some programs and regulatory regimes. They can nudge localities in the right direction by making some or all of their continued funding contingent on localities' adoption of sound policy fundamentals (regarding tax policy, for example). Indeed, the history of various statewide tax revolts shows that even cities unalterably opposed to policies that will help them thrive can be dragged kicking and screaming to improved health by those outside their borders.

Everyone, in sum, can have a constructive role to play in reorienting public policy as it relates to cities—and everyone should be eager to perform it. Cities are crucial to our quality of life, to national, regional, and local economic performance, and to global environmental quality. Their fate is our fate, and there's no reason every one of them can't thrive. All we need to do is start pulling in the right direction, and we can restore the urban American dream.

Acknowledgments

EVERY AUTHOR prays for a perfect editor. She must have the wisdom to see a book's Big Idea and insight about how to translate that idea, its corollaries, and supporting facts into a compelling narrative. As the writing proceeds, she must be discerning about what is working and tactful in pointing out what is not. Then she must possess formidable managerial skill in order to bring the whole endeavor to a happy conclusion. Margo Beth Fleming is that editor. I can't thank her enough for all her support and guidance throughout this project.

The book itself is the product of decades of exposure to many great minds, some of whom I have enjoyed knowing as professors and colleagues and others I have never had the pleasure of meeting but whose work I admire—even if I ultimately found myself disagreeing with some of it. I can't thank you all personally, but if you see your name in the body of this book or in a note, know that I am grateful for your diligent efforts to advance our understanding of cities and make them better places to live.

I would be remiss, however, if I failed to acknowledge my debt to illustrious thinkers such as architect Edmund Bacon; political scientist Edward Banfield; urbanologist Jane Jacobs; historian Fred Siegel; and economists Armen Alchian, Harold Demsetz, and Thomas Sowell, who fired my interest in cities and inculcated in me an appreciation for the profound effects of property rights and governing institutions on our welfare. And throughout my career, my friend and mentor Steve Hanke has inspired and encouraged me to refine the analytic tools that these intellectual forebears helped me develop and to apply them to urban problems and much else.

Many students and friends have served as sounding boards for the theories, arguments, and case studies that ultimately would find their way into this book. Louis Miserendino has been part of this process from the beginning, and has developed crucial insights about how to make some key policy recommendations workable. Jude Blanchette was also instrumental in getting this project off the ground and supplying valuable data. Sam Staley, Diana Furchtgott-Roth, and an anonymous referee were enormously helpful in suggesting improvements in the manuscript. Thanks go to them, but also to all those—especially my patient and understanding wife and kids—who listened carefully enough to my ideas to, ultimately, make them better.

Stephen J.K. Walters
July 2014

Notes

CHAPTER 1

1. Ernest H. Borden, *Detroit's Paradise Valley* (Mt. Pleasant, SC: Arcadia, 2003), p. 7.

2. Frank Hobbs and Nicole Stoops, U.S. Bureau of the Census, *Demographic Trends in the 20th Century* (Washington, DC: U.S. Government Printing Office, 2002), pp. 32–39.

3. Housing Authority of Baltimore City, *Baltimore's Housing Situation in Charts; Based on 1950 Census of Housing* (Baltimore, MD: Housing Authority of Baltimore City, 1954), p. 22.

4. U.S. Bureau of the Census, *Statistical Abstract of the United States, 1952* (Washington, DC: U.S. Government Printing Office, 1952), p. 136.

5. William Julius Wilson, *The Truly Disadvantaged*. Chicago: University of Chicago Press, 1987), p. 3.

6. Jane Jacobs, *The Death and Life of Great American Cities* (New York: Modern Library, 1993), p. 377.

7. Clarence L. Barnhart and Robert K. Barnhart (eds.), *The World Book Dictionary* (Chicago: Doubleday, 1983), vol. I, p. 1088.

8. The federal government had targeted aid to the housing market and influenced urban form (not always favorably) since the New Deal, but the effort to revive cities took off during the 1960s, when predecessor agencies were combined into the U.S. Department of Housing and Urban Development (HUD). From 1962 to 1972, HUD's budget grew 16 percent *annually*, soaring from $826 million to $3.6 billion. See Lawrence L. Thompson, "A History of HUD," available at http://mysite.verizon.net/hudhistory/.

9. George J. Stigler, *The Theory of Price* (3rd ed.) (New York: MacMillan, 1966), p. 275.

10. Matthew E. Kahn, "The Environmental Impact of Suburbanization," *Journal of Policy Analysis and Management*, vol. 19, no. 4 (Fall 2000), pp. 569–86.

11. See, for example, Richard Florida, *Cities and the Creative Class* (Oxon, UK: Routledge, 2005); Edward L. Glaeser and Albert Saiz, "The Rise of the Skilled City," *Brookings-Wharton Papers on Urban Affairs*, vol. 5 (2004), pp. 47–94.

CHAPTER 2

1. Melvin G. Holli, *The American Mayor: The Best and the Worst Big-City Leaders* (University Park, PA: The Pennsylvania State University Press, 1999).

2. Jack Beatty, *The Rascal King: The Life and Times of James Michael Curley, 1874–1958* (Reading, MA: Addison-Wesley, 1992), p. 229.

3. Francis Russell, "The Last of the Bosses," *American Heritage*, vol. 10, no. 4 (June 1959), available at http://www.americanheritage.com/content/june-1959.

4. Edward L. Glaeser and Andrei Shleifer, "The Curley Effect: The Economics of Shaping the Electorate," *Journal of Law, Economics, and Organization*, vol. 21, no. 1 (April 2005), pp. 1–19.

5. How much this discount must be depends on many factors—how long the house will last, how much inflation there is in the economy, interest rates, and so on. If we assume

the house lasts forever, there is no inflation, and the prevailing interest rate is, say, 4 percent, it might appear that the necessary discount would be as much as $60,000, because 4 percent interest on that amount is $2,400, the amount of the extra annual tax bite on the Curleyville property. But this is not quite right, because eventually the tax assessor will take note of the declining market value of Curleyville property and the Curleyville-Safe Haven tax gap will shrink. If we do the math, the Curleyville home's value will ultimately settle at $200,000 and it will carry an annual tax liability of $4,000. At that price, the $40,000 discount a buyer of Curleyville property gets would be just enough, when invested at 4 percent interest, to offset the extra $1,600 annual tax liability relative to a similar home in Safe Haven.

6. Not as much as hoped for, however. In our simple example, a 100 percent increase in the Curleyville tax rate produces only a 67 percent increase in tax receipts, thanks to the decline in property values resulting from tax capitalization.

7. Charles M. Tiebout, "A Pure Theory of Local Expenditures," *Journal of Political Economy*, vol. 64, no. 5 (October 1956), pp. 416–24.

8. Wallace E. Oates, "The Effects of Property Taxes and Local Public Spending on Property Values: An Empirical Study of Tax Capitalization and the Tiebout Hypothesis," *Journal of Political Economy*, vol. 77, no. 6 (November-December 1969), pp. 957–71.

9. The amount of the added tax liability and capital loss in Curleyville will depend on how much assessments have already fallen there. If, as in note 5, the value of the Curleyville home has fallen to $200,000 and the one in Safe Haven is still worth $240,000, then a 5 percent inflation would initially add $200 to the Curleyville owner's annual tax bill (in other words, 2 percent of the nominal increase in home value, from $200,000 to $210,000), while in Safe Haven the annual tax bill would rise only $120 (or 1 percent of the rise in value there from $240,000 to $252,000). To attract buyers to Curleyville, then, property values could rise only $8,667 rather than $10,000 to offset the higher annual tax liability there (assuming, again, the interest rate is 4 percent).

10. To $8,333 in our hypothetical example.

11. Again, this arithmetic is not quite right, because the assessed value of the facility in Curleyville would eventually fall enough—in this case to $8.33 million—to offset the added annual tax bite. Of course, rational investors will try to avoid such a $1.67 million capital loss by not building the facility there in the first place.

12. William Julius Wilson, *When Work Disappears: The World of the New Urban Poor* (New York: Alfred A. Knopf, 1996).

13. Katherine L. Bradbury, Anthony Downs, and Kenneth A. Small, "Some Dynamics of Central City-Suburban Interactions," *American Economic Review*, vol. 70, no. 2 (May 1980), pp. 410–14; David F. Bradford and Harry H. Kelejian, "An Econometric Model of the Flight to the Suburbs," *Journal of Political Economy*, vol. 81, no. 3 (May-June 1973), pp. 566–89.

14. See, for example, Fred Siegel, *The Future Once Happened Here: New York, D.C., L.A., and the Fate of America's Big Cities* (New York: The Free Press, 1997).

15. During his first term, 1914–18, Curley's opponents passed legislation preventing a mayor from serving consecutive terms, but he took back City Hall in 1922.

16. Paul F. Brissenden, "Earnings of Factory Workers, 1899 to 1927: An Analysis of Pay-Roll Statistics," Department of Commerce Census Monographs X, U.S. Government Printing Office (1929), Table 105, p. 211, and Table D, pp. 391–93.

17. For historical data on urban populations used in this and subsequent chapters, see Campbell Gibson, "Population of the 100 Largest Cities and Other Urban Places in the United States: 1790 to 1990," U.S. Bureau of the Census, June 1998, available at http://www.census

.gov/population/www/documentation/twps0027/twps0027.html#cities. For later population and demographic data on cities, see U.S. Census Bureau, *Statistical Abstract of the United States*, various issues, available at http://www.census.gov/compendia/statab/past_years.html.

18. U.S. Department of Commerce, Bureau of the Census, *16th Census of the United States, 1940*, "Internal Migration, 1935 to 1940," Table 16, pp. 164–65, and Table 24, pp. 206–12.

19. David T. Beito, *Taxpayers in Revolt: Tax Resistance During the Great Depression* (Chapel Hill, NC: University of North Carolina Press, 1989).

20. Herbert D. Simpson, *Tax Racket and Tax Reform in Chicago* (Chicago: Institute for Economic Research, 1930), as quoted in Beito, *Taxpayers in Revolt*, p. 39.

21. Beito, *Taxpayers in Revolt*, p. 81.

CHAPTER 3

1. *Time* magazine, "Nation: Maniac or Messiah?" June 19, 1978, available at www.time.com/time/magazine/article/0,9171,919744-1,00.html.

2. Robert Kuttner, *Revolt of the Haves: Tax Rebellions and Hard Times* (New York: Simon & Schuster, 1980).

3. Ibid., p. 32.

4. William A. Fischel, "Did John Serrano Vote for Proposition 13? A Reply to Stark and Zasloff's 'Tiebout and Tax Revolts: Did Serrano Really Cause Proposition 13?'" Dartmouth College Economics Department Working Paper 03-13, August 2003.

5. Statistics here and throughout the chapter are from U.S. Bureau of the Census, *Statistical Abstract of the United States*, various issues (Washington, DC: U.S. Government Printing Office, various years) and author's calculations.

6. Herb Caen, *Herb Caen's San Francisco, 1976–1991* (San Francisco: Chronicle Books, 1992), p. 69.

7. Lou Cannon, "1978: The Year the States Cut Taxes," *The Washington Post*, April 17, 1978, p. A1.

8. Lou Cannon, "California Acting to Bail Out Localities," *The Washington Post*, June 24, 1978, p. A1.

9. Office of the San Francisco Treasurer, *Annual Report*, various editions, and author's calculations.

10. *The Economist*, "California: Not-So-Golden State," November 20, 1982, p. 41.

11. *Town of Sudbury v. Commissioner of Corporations and Taxation*, 321 N.E. 2d 641 (Mass. 1974).

12. Michael Knight, "Bay State Officials Facing Fiscal Crisis," *The New York Times*, November 9, 1980, p. 34, and author's interviews with the Boston tax assessor's office.

13. Cheryl C. Sullivan, "Hub's Redevelopment Honcho Rides Rambunctious Boom," *The Christian Science Monitor*, April 11, 1985, p. B1.

14. Scott Calvert and Jamie Smith Hopkins, "Taxpayers Subsidize Pricey City Projects," *The Baltimore Sun*, August 25, 2013, pp. 1, 22.

15. I am grateful to Louis Miserendino for suggesting this strategy.

16. See, for example, Edward L. Glaeser, "Urban Public Finance," National Bureau of Economic Research Working Paper 18244, July 2012, esp. Section VI.

CHAPTER 4

1. Sidney Fine, *Sit-Down: The General Motors Strike of 1936–1937* (Ann Arbor: University of Michigan Press, 1969).

2. Statistics here and throughout the chapter are from U.S. Bureau of the Census, *Statistical Abstract of the United States*, various issues (Washington, DC: U.S. Government Printing Office, various years) and author's calculations.

3. Alfred Marshall, *Principles of Economics* (8th ed.) (London, UK: MacMillan, 1920), p. 271.

4. James M. Rubenstein, *The Changing U.S. Auto Industry* (New York: Routledge, 1992), p. 234.

5. This and following paragraph, U.S. Bureau of the Census, *Fifteenth Census of the United States, Manufactures: 1929, Vol. 3, Reports by States, Statistics for Industrial Areas, Counties, and Cities*, available at http://www2.census.gov/prod2/decennial/documents/03450419v3_TOC.pdf.

6. Richard B. Freeman and James L. Medoff, *What Do Unions Do?* (New York: Basic Books, 1984).

7. Barry T. Hirsch, "What Do Unions Do for Economic Performance?" In J. T. Bennett and B. E. Kaufman (eds.), *What Do Unions Do? A Twenty-Year Perspective* (New Brunswick, NJ: Transaction, 2007).

8. Benjamin Klein, Richard G. Crawford, and Armen A. Alchian, "Vertical Integration, Appropriable Rents, and the Competitive Contracting Process," *Journal of Law and Economics*, vol. 21, no. 2 (October 1978), pp. 297–326. For a more detailed discussion of this issue, on which much of this discussion is based, see the author's "Unions and the Decline of U.S. Cities," *Cato Journal*, vol. 30, no. 1 (Winter 2010), pp. 117–35.

9. John Barnard, *American Vanguard: The United Auto Workers During the Reuther Years, 1935–1970* (Detroit: Wayne State University Press, 2005), p. 82.

10. Fine, *Sit-Down*, p. 341.

11. J. B. Atleson, *Labor and the Wartime State: Labor Relations and the Law During World War II* (Champaign, IL: University of Illinois Press, 1998), pp. 145–47.

12. Thomas J. Sugrue, *The Origins of the Urban Crisis: Race and Inequality in Postwar Detroit* (Princeton, NJ: Princeton University Press, 1996), p. 128.

13. R. B. Freeman and J. L. Medoff, "New Estimates of Private Sector Unionism in the U.S.," *Industrial and Labor Relations Review*, vol. 32, no. 2, pp. 143–75.

14. William Julius Wilson, *When Work Disappears: The World of the New Urban Poor* (New York: Vintage Books, 1997).

15. Edward L. Glaeser, "Can Buffalo Ever Come Back?" *City Journal*, Autumn 2007, available at http://www.city-journal.org/html/17_4_buffalo_ny.html.

CHAPTER 5

1. Mark K. Metzger, "F. Kenneth Iverson of Nucor: Man of Steel," *Inc.*, April 1984, p. 85.

2. Ken Iverson with Tom Varian, *Plain Talk: Lessons from a Business Maverick* (New York: John Wiley & Sons, 1998).

3. William T. Wilson, "The Effect of Right-to-Work Laws on Economic Development," Mackinac Center for Public Policy (2002), available at http://www.mackinac.org/4290; Paul Kersey, "The Economic Effects of Right-to-Work Laws: 2007," Mackinac Center for Public Policy (2007), available at http://www.mackinac.org/8943.

4. Robert J. Newman, "Industry Migration and Growth in the South," *Review of Economics and Statistics*, vol. 65, no. 1 (February 1983), pp. 76–86.

5. William J. Moore, "The Determinants and Effects of Right-to-Work Laws: A Review of the Recent Literature," *Journal of Labor Research*, vol. 19, no. 3 (Summer 1998), pp. 445–69.

6. Thomas J. Holmes, "The Effect of State Policies on the Location of Manufacturing:

Evidence from State Borders," *Journal of Political Economy*, vol. 106, no. 4 (August 1998), pp. 667–705.

7. Stephen J. K. Walters, "Business Climate and Measured Poverty: The Evidence Across States," *Atlantic Economic Journal*, vol. 18, no. 1 (March 1990), p. 20–26.

8. Emin M. Dinlersoz and Rubén Hernández-Murillo, "Did 'Right-to-Work' Work for Idaho?" Federal Reserve Bank of St. Louis *Review*, vol. 84, no. 3 (May/June 2002), pp. 29–42.

9. Steven E. Abraham and Paula B. Voos, "Right-to-Work Laws: New Evidence from the Stock Market," *Southern Economic Journal*, vol. 67, no. 2 (October 2000), pp. 345–62.

10. U.S. Bureau of the Census, *Census 2000 Gateway*, available at https://www.census.gov/main/www/cen2000.html.

11. U.S. Bureau of the Census, *American FactFinder*, available at http://factfinder2.census.gov/faces/nav/jsf/pages/index.xhtml.

12. Edward L. Glaeser and Albert Saiz, "The Rise of the Skilled City," National Bureau of Economic Research Working Paper 10191, December 2003.

13. Peter Applebome, "Charlotte's Downtown Manages to Stay Up Late for Tournament," *The New York Times*, April 2, 1994, p. 1.1.

14. Henry Allen, "Mainstream U.S.A.: Charlotte. It's Got a Football Team and a Bright Future. All It's Missing Is Personality," *The Washington Post*, November 5, 1993, p. G1.

15. Leslie Eaton, "A Shrinking Population Shapes Buffalo's Psyche," *The New York Times*, April 9, 2000, p. 1.33.

16. Enrico Moretti, "Local Multipliers," *American Economic Review*, vol. 100, no. 2 (May 2010), pp. 373–77.

17. Kirk Shelley, "How Oklahoma Was Won: Lessons from One State's Fight for Right to Work," *Labor Watch*, Capital Research Center, April 2002.

CHAPTER 6

1. Quotes in this and the following paragraph are from Bob Marshall, "New Orleans Levee Leaks Reported to S&WB a Year Ago—Lakeview Residents' Complaints Fell Between the Cracks," *The Times-Picayune*, November 18, 2005, p. 1.

2. See, for example, R. B. Seed and others, "Preliminary Report on the Performance of the New Orleans Levee Systems in Hurricane Katrina on August 29, 2005," Report No. UCB/Citrus—05/01, November 2, 2005.

3. Gordon Russell, "Levee Inspections Only Scratch the Surface—Floodwalls Often Ignored as Officials Go to Lunch," *The Times-Picayune*, November 25, 2005, p. 1.

4. Joel Kotkin, *The City: A Global History* (New York: Modern Library, 2005).

5. Daniel B. Klein, "The Voluntary Provision of Public Goods? The Turnpike Companies of Early America," *Economic Inquiry*, vol. 28, no. 4 (October 1990), pp. 788–812.

6. Steve H. Hanke and Stephen J. K. Walters, "Privatization and Public Choice: Lessons for the LDCs," in Dennis J. Gayle and Jonathan N. Goodrich (eds.), *Privatization and Deregulation in Global Perspective* (New York: Quorum, 1990), pp. 97–108.

7. Orleans Levee District, *Mission Statement*, available at http://www.orleanslevee.com/Mission%20Statement.htm.

8. Lisa Myers and the NBC News Investigative Unit, "Is the Orleans Levee Board Doing Its Job? Critics Allege Corruption, Charge the Board with Wasteful Spending," Sept. 15, 2005, available at http://msnbc.msn.com/id/9342186/.

9. For a brief sample, see http://www.youtube.com/watch?v=fDIYmwa6vnQ. Economists refer to this phenomenon by a less memorable term, the "shortsightedness problem."

10. "The Blame Game," *The Economist*, September 5, 2005, available at www.econo mist.com/node/4366649.

11. Statistics in this paragraph are from American Society of Civil Engineers, "2013 Report Card for America's Infrastructure,," available at http://www.infrastructurereport card.org/.

12. Geraldine Lambe, "America's Crumbling Infrastructure: Can Private Capital Save It?" *The Banker*, May 4, 2011.

13. Steve H. Hanke and Stephen J. K. Walters, "Privatizing Waterworks: Learning from the French Experience," and "Reflections on Private Water Supply: Agency and Equity Issues," *Journal of Applied Corporate Finance*, vol. 23, no. 3 (Summer 2011), pp. 30–40.

14. Ioannis N. Kessides, "Reforming Infrastructure: Privatization, Regulation, and Competition," *World Bank Policy Research Report* (2004), pp. 240–57.

15. Stephen Goldsmith, *The Twenty-First Century City* (Washington, DC: Regnery, 1997).

CHAPTER 7

1. William H. Hudnut III and others, *The Hudnut Years in Indianapolis* (Bloomington: Indiana University Press, 1995), p. 58.

2. Ibid., p. 59.

3. Stephen Goldsmith, *The Twenty-First Century City* (Washington, DC: Regnery, 1997), pp. 18–22.

4. Ibid., p. 22.

5. Hudnut, *The Hudnut Years*, p. 13.

6. This phrase is associated with economist Arnold Harberger. See Prakash Loungani, "Interview with Arnold Harberger: Sound Policies Can Free Up Natural Forces of Growth," *IMF Survey*, vol. 32, no. 13 (July 14, 2003), pp. 213–16.

7. Matthew Iglesias, "The Case for Price Gouging," *Slate*, October 30, 2012, available at http://www.slate.com/articles/business/moneybox/2012/10/sandy_price_gouging_anti_goug ing_laws_make_natural_disasters_worse.html.

8. Mike Maciag, "Ranking the Nation's Worst Friday Afternoon Commutes," *Governing*, July 27, 2012, available at http://www.governing.com/blogs/by-the-numbers/worst -friday-afternoon-rush-hour-commutes-american-cities.html.

9. Anthony Downs, *Stuck in Traffic: Coping with Peak-Hour Traffic Congestion* (Washington, DC: Brookings Institution, 1992).

10. Texas A&M Transportation Institute, *2012 Urban Mobility Report*, available at http://mobility.tamu.edu/ums/.

11. Jonas Eliasson, "Lessons from the Stockholm Congestion Charging Trial," *Transport Policy*, vol. 15, no. 6 (November 2008), pp. 395–404, at p. 395.

12. Nicole Gelinas, "How to Avoid Fiscal Derailment," *City Journal* (Special Issue 2013), available at www.city-journal.org/2013/issue_special.html.

13. Donald Shoup, *The High Cost of Free Parking* (Chicago: American Planning Association Press, 2011).

14. Jeffrey M. Jones, "In U.S., Private Schools Get Top Marks for Educating Children," *Gallup Politics*, August 29, 2012, available at http://www.gallup.com/poll/156974/private -schools-top-marks-educating-children.aspx.

15. Caroline M. Hoxby, "Does Competition Among Public Schools Benefit Students and Taxpayers?" *American Economic Review*, vol. 90, no. 5 (December 2000), pp. 1209–38; Caroline M. Hoxby, "Rising Tide: New Evidence on Competition and the Public Schools," *Education Next*, vol. 1, no. 4 (Winter 2001), pp. 69–74.

16. See, for example, Paul T. Hill, Lawrence C. Pierce, and James W. Guthrie, *Reinventing Public Education: How Contracting Can Transform America's Schools* (Chicago: University of Chicago Press, 1997).

CHAPTER 8

1. Jeff Benedict, *Little Pink House: A True Story of Defiance and Courage* (New York: Grand Central Publishing, 2009), p. 27.

2. *Kelo v. City of New London*, 545 U.S. 469 (2005).

3. *Berman v. Parker*, 348 U.S. 26 (1954).

4. Jacob A. Riis, *How the Other Half Lives: Studies Among the Tenements of New York* (2nd ed.), edited with an introduction by David Leviatin (New York: Bedford/St. Martin's, 2011), p. 149.

5. *The Economist*, "Why the Pruitt-Igoe Housing Project Failed," October 15, 2011, available at http://www.economist.com/node/21533149.

6. *Post-War Planning: Hearings Before the United States House Committee on Public Buildings and Grounds, Seventy-Eighth Congress*. Washington, DC: U.S. Government Printing Office (1944), pp. 508–10.

7. Daniel Thursz, "Where Are They Now?" pp. 28–33, as quoted in Alexander Garvin, *The American City* (2nd ed.) (New York: McGraw-Hill, 2002), p. 271.

8. Chester Hartman, "The Housing of Relocated Families," in James Q. Wilson (ed.), *Urban Renewal: The Record and the Controversy* (Cambridge, MA: MIT Press, 1966), pp. 293–335.

9. Marc A. Weiss, "The Origins and Legacy of Urban Renewal," in J. Paul Mitchell (ed.), *Federal Housing Policies and Programs: Past and Present* (New Brunswick, NJ: Rutgers University Press, 1985), pp. 253–54.

10. "Urban Redevelopment," *Dictionary of American History* (2003), available at http://www.encyclopedia.com/topic/Urban_renewal.aspx.

11. Marc Fried, "Grieving for a Lost Home: Psychological Costs of Relocation," in Wilson, *Urban Renewal*, at pp. 359–79.

12. Robert D. Putnam, *Bowling Alone: The Collapse and Revival of American Community* (New York: Simon & Schuster, 2000), p. 319.

13. Ibid., esp. chapters 16–20.

14. "Tudor City Historic District Designation Report," City of New York, Landmarks Preservation Commission, 1988, typedraft.

15. Ibid., p. 25.

16. Dennis Coates and Brad R. Humphreys, "Professional Sports Facilities, Franchises and Urban Economic Development," *Public Finance and Management*, vol. 3, no. 3 (2003), pp. 335–57.

CHAPTER 9

1. Jane Jacobs, *The Death and Life of Great American Cities* (New York: Modern Library, 1993), p. 379.

2. Molly Moore, "Old Money, New Money Flee France and Its Wealth Tax," *The Washington Post*, July 16, 2006, available at www.washingtonpost.com/wp-dyn/content/article/2006/07/15/AR2006071501010.html.

3. William A. Fischel, *Regulatory Takings: Law, Economics, and Politics* (Cambridge, MA: Harvard University Press, 1995), at pp. 226–27.

4. Rolf Pendall, Jonathan Martin, and William Fulton, "Holding the Line: Urban Con-

tainment in the United States," The Brookings Institution Center on Urban and Metropolitan Policy, discussion paper, August 2002.

5. Randal O'Toole, "A Portlander's View of Smart Growth," *The Review of Austrian Economics*, vol. 17, no. 2/3 (2004), pp. 203–12, at p. 208.

6. Wendell Cox, "Property Values 11 Times Higher Across Portland's Urban Growth Boundary," *New Geography*, October 12, 2010, available at http://www.newgeography.com/content/001808-property-values-11-times-higher-across-portlands-urban-growth-boundary.

7. Cyrus A. Grout, William K. Jaeger, and Andrew J. Plantinga, "Land-Use Regulations and Property Values in Portland: A Regression Discontinuity Design Approach," *Regional Science and Urban Economics*, vol. 41, no. 2 (March 2011), pp. 98–107.

8. Case-Shiller home price data are maintained by S&P Dow Jones Co., and are available for download at http://us.spindices.com/index-family/real-estate/sp-case-shiller.

9. Edward L. Glaeser, Joseph Gyourko, and Raven Saks, "Why Is Manhattan So Expensive? Regulation and the Rise in Housing Prices," *Journal of Law and Economics*, vol. 48, no. 2 (October 2005), pp. 331–69.

10. Joseph Gyourko, Christopher Mayer, and Todd Sinai, "Superstar Cities," National Bureau of Economic Research Working Paper 12355, 2006, at pp. 4–5.

11. Joel Kotkin, "Urban Legend," *Democracy: A Journal of Ideas*, no. 2 (Fall 2006), available at http://www.democracyjournal.org/pdf/2/DAJOI2_20-33_Kotkin.pdf.

12. Texas A&M Transportation Institute, *Annual Urban Mobility Report 2012*, available at http://mobility.tamu.edu/ums/national-congestion-tables/.

13. Matthew J. Holian and Matthew E. Kahn, "The Rise of the Low Carbon Commuter City," National Bureau of Economic Research Working Paper 18735, January 2013.

14. O'Toole, "A Portlander's View," at p. 207.

15. Jan K. Brueckner and Robert W. Helsley, "Sprawl and Blight," *Journal of Urban Economics*, vol. 69, no. 2 (March 2011), pp. 205–13.

16. Alex Anas and Hyok-Joo Rhee, "Curbing Excess Sprawl with Congestion Tolls and Urban Boundaries," *Regional Science & Urban Economics*, vol. 36 (2006), pp. 510–41, at p. 537.

17. B. Bolitzer and N. R. Netusil, "The Impact of Open Spaces on Property Values in Portland," *Journal of Environmental Management*, vol. 59, no. 3 (2000), pp. 185–93; Soren T. Anderson and Sarah E. West, "Open Space, Residential Property Values, and Spatial Context," *Regional Science and Urban Economics*, vol. 36 (2006), pp. 773–89.

18. In one survey of IZ's impact in the San Francisco Bay area, the median subsidy per IZ unit was about $350,000, and in a quarter of jurisdictions subsidies exceeded $500,000 per unit. See Benjamin Powell and Edward Stringham, "Housing Supply and Affordability: Do Affordable Housing Mandates Work?" Reason Public Policy Institute, Policy Study 318, April 1, 2004.

19. Powell and Stringham, "Housing Supply and Affordability," p. 8.

20. Ibid., p. 21; Benjamin Powell and Edward Stringham, "Do Affordable Housing Mandates Work? Evidence from Los Angeles County and Orange County," Reason Public Policy Institute, Policy Study 318, June 1, 2004, p. 16.

21. Jenny Schuetz, Rachel Meltzer, and Vicki Been, "Silver Bullet or Trojan Horse? The Effects of Inclusionary Zoning on Local Housing Markets in the United States," *Urban Studies*, vol. 48, no. 2 (February 2011), pp. 297–329, at p. 321.

22. Bernard H. Siegan, "Non-Zoning in Houston," *Journal of Law & Economics*, vol. 13, no. 1 (April 1970), pp. 71–147.

23. See Joel Kotkin, "Opportunity Urbanism: An Emerging Paradigm for the 21st Century," Greater Houston Partnership, 2007.

24. See Samuel R. Staley, "Reforming the Zoning Laws," in Jane S. Shaw and Ronald D. Utt (eds.), *A Guide to Smart Growth* (Washington, DC: The Heritage Foundation, 2000), pp. 61–75.

CHAPTER 10

1. Steven Levitt, "Understanding Why Crime Fell in the 1990s: Four Factors that Explain the Decline and Six That Do Not," *Journal of Economic Perspectives*, vol. 18, no. 1 (Winter 2004), pp. 163–90, at p. 168.

2. Ibid., at pp. 169–70.

3. Michael R. Gottfredson and Travis Hirschi, *A General Theory of Crime* (Stanford, CA: Stanford University Press, 1990), p. 270.

4. Nathan Glazer, "On Subway Graffiti in New York," *National Affairs*, no. 54 (Winter 1979), pp. 3–11.

5. George Kelling and James Q. Wilson, "Broken Windows: The Police and Neighborhood Safety," *The Atlantic Monthly*, March 1982, available at http://www.theatlantic.com/magazine/archive/1982/03/broken-windows/304465/.

6. Rudolph W. Giuliani and William J. Bratton, *Police Strategy Nos. 1–6* (New York: City of New York Police Department, 1994).

7. William Bratton with Peter Knobler, *Turnaround: How America's Top Cop Reversed the Crime Epidemic* (New York: Random House, 1998).

8. Heather MacDonald, "It's the Cops, Stupid!" *The New Republic*, February 2, 2012, available at http://www.newrepublic.com/book/review/franklin-zimring-new-york-urban-crime-control-city-safe?page=0,1.

9. Mike Davis, *City of Quartz: Excavating the Future in Los Angeles* (New York: Verso, 1990), esp. Chapter 5, "The Hammer and the Rock," pp. 265–322.

10. Dave Zirin, "Want to Understand the 1992 LA Riots? Start with the 1984 LA Olympics," *The Nation*, April 30, 2012, available at http://www.thenation.com/blog/167630/want-understand-1992-la-riots-start-1984-la-olympics#.

11. John Buntin, "The LAPD Remade," *City Journal*, vol. 23, no. 1 (Winter 2013), available at http://www.city-journal.org/2013/23_1_william-bratton.html.

12. Kelling and Wilson, "Broken Windows."

13. Garrett Hardin, "The Tragedy of the Commons," *Science*, vol. 162, no. 3859 (December 13, 1968), pp. 1243–48.

14. Julie Dressner and Edwin Martinez, "The Scars of Stop-and-Frisk," *The New York Times*, June 12, 2012, available at http://www.nytimes.com/2012/06/12/opinion/the-scars-of-stop-and-frisk.html.

15. Heather MacDonald, "Courts v. Cops," *City Journal*, Winter 2013, available at http://www.city-journal.org/2013/23_1_war-on-crime.html.

16. Jacqueline Cohen and Jens Ludwig, "Policing Crime Guns," in Jens Ludwig and Phillip J. Cook (eds.), *Evaluating Gun Policy: Effects on Crime and Violence* (Washington, DC: Brookings Institution Press, 2003), pp. 217–50, at p. 239.

17. Al Baker and Joseph Goldstein, "2 Opinions on Stop-and-Frisk Report," *The New York Times*, May 9, 2012, p. A27, available at http://www.nytimes.com/2012/05/10/nyregion/police-stop-and-frisk-tactic-had-lower-gun-recovery-rate-in-2011.html?_r=0. Annual data on stops are available for download at http://www.nyc.gov/html/nypd/html/analysis_and_planning/stop_question_and_frisk_report.shtml.

18. Greg Ridgeway, *Analysis of Racial Disparities in the New York Police Department's Stop, Question, and Frisk Practices* (Santa Monica, CA: RAND, 2007).

19. Andrew Gelman, Jeffrey Fagan, and Alex Kiss, "An Analysis of the New York City

Police Department's 'Stop-and-Frisk' Policy in the Context of Claims of Racial Bias," *Journal of the American Statistical Association*, vol. 102, no. 479 (2007), pp. 813–23.

20. Decio Coviello and Nicola Persico, "An Economic Analysis of Black-White Disparities in NYPD's Stop and Frisk Program," National Bureau of Economic Research Working Paper 18803, February 2013, pp. 11–12.

21. David Feith, "William Bratton: The Real Cures for Gun Violence," *The Wall Street Journal*, January 19, 2013, p. A11.

22. New York's stop-and-frisk policy was ruled unconstitutional in 2013 by a U.S. district court judge; former Mayor Michael Bloomberg appealed this ruling, but his successor Bill DiBlasio dropped that appeal. For updates, see http://topics.nytimes.com/top/reference/timestopics/subjects/s/stop_and_frisk/index.html.

23. John F. Kennedy, "Special Message to the Congress on Mental Illness and Mental Retardation" (February 5, 1963), available at http://www.presidency.ucsb.edu/ws/?pid=9546.

24. E. Fuller Torrey, *Nowhere to Go: The Tragic Odyssey of the Homeless Mentally Ill* (New York: Harper & Row, 1988).

25. Sally Satel, "Out of the Asylum, into the Cell," *The New York Times*, Nov. 1, 2003, p. A15; E. Fuller Torrey and Doris A. Fuller, "The Potential Killers We Let Loose," *The Wall Street Journal*, December 18, 2012, p. A19; E. Fuller Torrey, "Fifty Years of Failing America's Mentally Ill," *The Wall Street Journal*, Feb. 5, 2013, p. A15.

26. Albert Q. Maisel, "Bedlam 1946: Most U.S. Mental Hospitals Are a Shame and a Disgrace," *Life* magazine, May 6, 1946, pp. 102–18.

27. *O'Connor v. Donaldson*, 422 U.S. 563 (1975).

28. *Rogers v. Okin*, 478 F.Supp.1342 (1979).

29. *Dixon v. Weinberger*, 405 F.Supp.974 (1975).

30. Torrey, *Nowhere to Go*, note 22, p. 212; see also pp. 10–21.

31. David A. Rochefort, *From Poorhouses to Homelessness: Policy Analysis and Mental Health Care* (Westport, CT: Auburn House, 1993), pp. 149–66.

32. *Papachristou v. Jacksonville*, 405 U.S. 156 (1972).

33. Jennifer Perlman and John Parvensky, "Denver Housing First Collaborative: Cost Benefit Analysis and Program Outcomes Report," December 11, 2006, available at http://documents.csh.org/documents/ResourceCenter/SysChgToolkit/CredibleData/DenverCostStudy.pdf.

CHAPTER 11

1. Jane Jacobs, *The Death and Life of Great American Cities* (New York: Modern Library, 1993), p. 6.

2. See, for example, the Congress of the New Urbanism's charter, available at http://www.cnu.org/charter.

3. Harrison Salisbury, "The Shook-Up Generation," in Jewel Bellush and Murray Hausknecht (eds.), *Urban Renewal: People, Politics and Planning* (Garden City, NY: Anchor, 1967), p. 429.

4. Alexander Garvin, *The American City: What Works, What Doesn't* (2nd ed.) (New York: McGraw-Hill, 2002), p. 1.

Index